FAMOUS
MOZART OPERAS

FAMOUS
MOZART OPERAS

*An analytical guide for the opera-goer
and armchair listener*

by

SPIKE HUGHES

WITH 343 MUSICAL ILLUSTRATIONS

SECOND REVISED EDITION

DOVER PUBLICATIONS, INC., NEW YORK

Published in Canada by General Publishing Company, Ltd., 30 Lesmill Road, Don Mills, Toronto, Ontario.
Published in the United Kingdom by Constable and Company, Ltd.

This Dover edition, first published in 1972, is a revised republication of the work originally published by Robert Hale Limited in London in 1957.

International Standard Book Number: 0-486-22858-4
Library of Congress Catalog Card Number: 70-166535

Manufactured in the United States of America
Dover Publications, Inc.
180 Varick Street
New York, N.Y. 10014

To

AUDRIE

in the confident belief that her sons will
grow up to share her love of her
favourite composer, this study is
affectionately dedicated by their uncle

CONTENTS

PREFACE

In recent years the whole nature of the gramophone record repertoire, the appearance of the very catalogues themselves, have changed beyond recognition. Works have been recorded which, so far from never having been recorded in the entire history of the gramophone, were barely known to any but the most erudite concert, opera or radio audiences. This has particularly been the case with opera. One has only to look through the growing list of L.P. recordings of complete operas to see that the gramophone now has a repertoire of works unapproached even by the vast repertoires of the opera houses of Vienna and Munich. Indeed, the discriminating buyer of gramophone records can gain a wider knowledge of opera nowadays than the most regular opera-goer.

It is to this public that this book on Mozart's most famous operas is largely directed. To them, but also—and particularly—to those for whom the experience of Mozart opera is new and tentative, I hope this study, which is not intended as a critical essay addressed to experts, will serve as a supplement to those programmes found in most opera houses or to the analytical notes on the picturesque "sleeves" of L.P. records which tell the story in more or less intelligible terms but do not always explain in detail why the tenor should suddenly want to burst into song, nor what he is singing about when he does.

I have also designed this book with the student in mind: the student of orchestration. Because Mozart's orchestration has been taken for granted for so many years the student may look in vain for any detailed analysis, or indeed for as much as a respectable passing reference to it in even the most exhaustive studies of his operas. I would even go so far as to say that the average student's education barely touches on the subject of Mozart's genius for orchestration at all in the ordinary way, and that many years pass before one learns to find in the full scores of Mozart an opera composer with as peculiar and personal an *orchestral* language with which to express his comedy and drama as Wagner, Verdi or Puccini. Because I still feel that not nearly enough attention is paid to the sound of Mozart's operatic voice, as distinct from the words he uses and the thoughts he utters, I have made a point in this study of drawing attention to some of the more remarkable instrumental ingenuities to be found in the operas.

While many of these may seem pretty obvious instances of Mozart's orchestration, it is precisely because they *are* obvious that I propose to draw attention to them, for the obvious is far too seldom pointed out to the student. In his anxiety to "get on" and express himself he very rarely stops to consider that he may learn more about the orchestra if he can score a chord of C major like Mozart than if he tries to do it like Richard Strauss.

To the reader who is not a student, I feel I ought to apologize if, in the course of this book, he encounters one or two passages which he feels do not concern him; on the other hand, I may be acting a little pessimistically and overcautiously in this in view of my own experience as a broadcaster, when the lay listener has shown a most encouraging and enlightened interest in a subject which—as in the case of orchestration—one might fear tended to be professional musicians' "shop". But in the way that opera itself is becoming better and more widely understood as every year passes, so the understanding of the medium has come to include an intelligent appreciation of the orchestra as an indispensable component of all great opera. For the convenience of the student I have made an index of Mozart's orchestration on p. 245.

The Author Wishes to Thank

The Columbia Graphophone Co., the Decca Record Co., the Gramophone Company (HMV), the Heliodor Record Co. (Deutsche Grammophon Gesellschaft), Nixa Record Co., and Philips Electrical Ltd., whose practical assistance and co-operation were invaluable in the preparation of this book;

Mr J. H. Davies, for allowing me access to the Mozart scores in the BBC Music Library of which he is Librarian, and his staff whose unfailing courtesy and helpfulness in being able to put an instant finger on a pertinent reference has made my work many hours easier.

WOLFGANG AMADEUS MOZART

BORN: Salzburg, January 27, 1756
DIED: Vienna, December 5, 1791

MOZART AND THE OPERA

The public, which is often more discriminating and intelligent than it is given credit for, has on the whole decided that for all practical purposes Opera begins with Mozart.

It does not deny, of course, that there were important composers of opera before Mozart; but though it is willing to listen to Gluck's *Orpheus* or *Alceste* once in a while, it inclines to regard the experience as a duty which, since it is a public of self-confessed "opera-lovers", it feels bound to fulfil from time to time in order to show awareness of its heritage. It is impressed by Gluck and his reforms, but since the average member of this opera-going public is extremely hazy about the exact nature of these "reforms" and even less interested in what was wrong with opera before Gluck that it needed reforming at all, he is content to be impressed and leave it at that. And—to be honest—the average opera-goer really gets no less out of Gluck than the serious student of opera—at least from the point of view of the sensuous enjoyment of the music. For while the student may be impressed by technical details which are over the head or no concern of the average opera-goer, neither student nor amateur will ever truthfully be more than *impressed* by Gluck.

Nobody, professional or layman, can surely ever feel much affection for Gluck's operas, in the sense that they can feel affection for the operas of Rossini or Donizetti, Verdi or Puccini. Or—particularly—for the operas of Mozart.

In a curious way this quality of lovableness is one of the most important characteristics of opera. It is something peculiar to an art which is essentially theatrical, and the theatre, as one knows, has a magic and fascination unique among the many forms of culture and entertainment evolved by mankind. So it is that the Jupiter Symphony, even to the most devoted of Mozart enthusiasts, will never have quite the attraction and—I can think of no other word—*reality* of *Figaro* nor its ability to inspire affection, as distinct from admiration or astonishment.

This sensation of reality is not easy to define, nor is it easy to decide what it is that causes it in the first place. It is certainly not a matter of the category of the composer. Handel, for instance, may be considered a greater figure as a composer than Puccini; but while his other music lives gloriously in the hearts of the public not one of Handel's 40-odd operas holds the stage at all today. Scarcely a day passes, on the other hand, when at least one of Puccini's four or five most popular operas is not performed in one hemisphere or another.

The answer lies perhaps in the nature of opera as it has developed since Handel's day. Opera, "music drama", or whatever one may choose to call it, is essentially an art concerned with the emotions and behaviour of human beings, and the more alive and convincing those human beings can be made to appear to us by purely musical means the greater the impact of opera on the listener and the stronger the feeling of reality.

With Mozart opera at last came fully alive in this way, and the characters on the stage began to have definite musical personality. As a result of this Mozart not only seems to speak the same operatic language as ourselves, to give us what we expect from opera, but has virtually invalidated everything that went before. In consequence it seems to us that at their best Mozart's predecessors did little more with their music than underline dramatic situations (which, since the same librettos were set by one composer after another, were already familiar to the audience) and create the right kind of atmosphere to fit in nicely with the sort of emotions a character ought to be expressing at a particular moment in particular circumstances. It was a frequent occurrence, too, in these earlier works to encounter a number taken from an entirely different opera and interpolated because it happened to suit the situation invented —or newly employed—by the librettist.

Mozart's conception of opera, however, rendered this practice virtually impossible: you can no sooner switch the music about in a Mozart opera from one character to another, than you can hand round the speeches in a Shakespeare play to one and all as though they were canapés.

Mozart, in short, was the first composer to perceive clearly the vast possibilities of the operatic form as a means of creating characters, great and small, who moved, thought and breathed musically like human beings. In contradistinction to his operatic predecessors Mozart introduced what may be called the "opera of movement". In earlier works for the stage, especially in those by Gluck, there had been movement of a kind; but it had not been essentially dramatic movement. It had been achieved by the introduction of ballets as a diversion between the long static periods when the singers stood around and held up what little action there was by singing lengthy formal arias. In Mozart's operas the singers discarded the masks of Greek drama, as it were, and appeared as individuals with a recognizable personality; they took an active part instead of looking on and commenting. (Comparison with the discarding of the masks of Greek drama is not altogether fanciful, of course, for it was in fact the idea of the Attic theatre which those 16th-century Florentine composers aimed to revive when they first developed the idea of the melodramma or dramma per musica which grew to be what we today call Opera.)

Mozart wrote nineteen stage works of one kind and another—the first of them, Die Schuldigkeit des ersten Gebotes, as a boy of 11, the last, The Magic Flute, three months before his death in 1791. Of these operas five had German texts, one was in Latin and the rest in Italian. To anyone unfamiliar with the history and development of opera it may appear a little puzzling that an Austrian composer should have used Italian librettos so often, but it must be remembered that in the 18th century not only was the universal language of music Italian: opera itself was generally regarded as an almost exclusively Italian form of entertainment. In the same way that today—rightly or wrongly—when we think of The Cinema we think of films coming primarily from Hollywood. The French, the Russians, the Italians and even the English make films too, of course, but the majority of films we see and care about are made in America.

So it was with opera in Mozart's day; it was predominantly Italian because that was the nationality of the most popular singers, the librettists, the impresarios, the designers, a great many of the architects who built the theatres and of the rest of the people concerned with the production of opera. That was the way Courts and people liked it, and that was why composers like Gluck (who was Bavarian), Handel (who was Anglo-German), Martin y Soler (who was Spanish), Mysliveczek (who was Bohemian), Marcos Antonio Portugal (who was Portuguese), Isouard (who was Maltese), and Bortniansky (who was Russian), all wrote operas to Italian texts.

In the circumstances it is hardly surprising that Mozart, whose musical upbringing was wholly Italian and whose temperament was characteristic of that 18th-century cosmopolitanism which made Italian the *lingua franca* of cultured musical society, should have taken instinctively to the form of Italian opera. That the first and last operas discussed in this volume should both have been composed to German texts, with spoken German dialogue taking the place of the rapid recitative of Italian opera, is of no great relevance; for while it was through Italian opera that Mozart came to express and develop his genius for the theatre and for the creation of human musical characters, in the end it is the music by which he achieved his ends that matters—music which in its depth and variety, its colour and wit, gives its composer a universality and peculiar sublimity unique in the whole history of music.

NOTE

I have included as an Appendix what I can only describe as an "Index of Contexts". Its purpose is to enable the reader who is listening to an excerpt from a Mozart opera, either as an item in a concert or as part of a "recital" on L.P. records, to refer quickly to the dramatic situation in the opera from which it comes. Thus, if the item concerned is "Là ci darem la mano" the reader need do no more than look it up in the Appendix under *Don Giovanni* to learn at once that its context is to be found on page 93.

Finally, a word about the musical examples. These will be seen to have numbers attached to them—e.g. Ex 3 in *The Marriage of Figaro* is marked "No 1". These numberings of individual items date from Mozart's original scores and have been universally retained to this day, so that the reader who finds himself with a vocal score of *Don Giovanni* translated into English or some other language in which he cannot recognize the lyric of "Là ci darem la mano", need only look through its pages until he encounters it under its number—No 7.

DIE ENTFÜHRUNG AUS DEM SERAIL

Opera in three acts. Libretto by Gottlieb Stephanie. First performed at the Burgtheater, Vienna, on 16th July, 1782, conducted by the composer. First performance in England: Covent Garden, 24th November, 1827 (in English as *The Seraglio*). First performance in the United States: by the Brooklyn Operatic Circle, 16th February, 1860, in German (?) as *Il Seraglio*.

F O R the purpose of this study the earliest of Mozart's five most famous operas will be referred to by its German title—as a matter of convenience to myself who have always known it by this name, and also because it was as *Die Entführung aus dem Serail* that it was first performed and is now best known. This does not mean, of course, that either composer or librettist had always referred to their opera as *Die Entführung*. Far from it. Mozart's first reference, in a letter to his father in August 1781, is to the composition of a libretto he has been given called "Bellmont und Konstanze, oder Die Verführung aus dem Serail." His confusion of "Verführung" (seduction—or at best, enticement) with "Entführung" (abduction) is charming and, one presumes, an intriguing slip of the pen which should delight all Freudians as a fine example of sub-conscious expression, for at this time Mozart was much occupied with the question of marrying Constanze Weber and with assuring his disapproving father of her strong moral qualities.

The misspelling of the hero's name as "Bellmont" has also intrigued some commentators enough to add the hasty disclaimant "sic" when they quote the letter. While Mozart was an erratic and wayward speller at any time (he signed his letters indiscriminately as "Amadeus", "Amadé", "Amdè" and even "Adam"), there was a general reluctance altogether among those concerned to settle on a permanent form of describing the hero. In the first edition of the full score, which was engraved at least from a copy of Mozart's manuscript, the name is spelt variously and unconcernedly as "Bellmont", "Bellemont", "Belmont" and "Belmonte", while "Constanze" alternates with "Constance", and "Blonde" changes her sex altogether in one aria and becomes "Blondo".

"Belmont and Constanze", whatever the spelling, however, is important for being the title of a libretto by Christoph Friedrich Bretzner which had been set to music by Johann André and performed in Berlin in 1781. This libretto, considerably but by no means unrecognizably altered, reached Mozart's hands from Gottlieb Stephanie, an actor who graduated to playwright and eventually to *Inspizient* or inspector of the Imperial Opera in Vienna. It was in this last official capacity that he was able to approach Mozart with the commission to compose an opera for the Court Theatre, choosing as a subject Bretzner's libretto "adapted" by himself.* It

* Bretzner later gained immortality for himself by publicly protesting that his libretto had been set to music by "a certain person by the name of Mozart" who had had the impertinence to "misuse" his drama, *Belmont and Constanze*, for an opera text.

should be explained that until 1776 it had been the custom for the Imperial Theatre in Vienna to be leased to an impresario who was responsible for providing entertainment there during his tenancy. The Emperor Joseph II, however, in a moment of patriotic zeal decided that his theatre should become a National Theatre in the fullest sense. It was taken over by the Court for the purpose of encouraging "German Opera". Though there was remarkably little "German Opera" to encourage and the repertoire consisted largely of translations of French and Italian comic operas, the theatre became known officially as the "National-Singspiel". Italian opera (or opera in Italian, which was not necessarily the same thing) was banned and its place taken by German musical plays which were "operas" only in the Gilbert-and-Sullivan sense. Indeed, one of the most influential models of this so-called German "opera" had been the very opera which began the English tradition followed by Gilbert and Sullivan: *The Beggar's Opera*, which first appeared in 1728.

It was as a composer of music for the undeveloped and naïve medium of the Singspiel (literally, sing-play—i.e., play with songs) that Mozart wrote his first stage work for Vienna. *Die Entführung* is a pure Singspiel with action which takes place mostly in the course of the spoken dialogue, where the characters burst into song to air their feelings, and music is used to underline rather than to create situations though it does occasionally move the story along. Mozart's own instinct was towards action in music and because that instinct had automatically to be controlled, if not entirely suppressed, in *Die Entführung*, there has always been a slight tendency to compare this opera unfavourably with those operas which followed, like *Figaro* and *Don Giovanni*, in which Mozart was able to give full rein to his genius for dramatic music.

All this really amounts to, however, is a disappointment that *Die Entführung* should not be something entirely different from what its composer and librettist intended it to be. Nobody has ever complained that *Die Entführung* was not a *better* Singspiel; only that it should have been a Singspiel at all.

Until comparatively recently it has been difficult to refute many of the charges made by critics against *Die Entführung*. It is far from being an easy opera to sing; in fact, it is extremely difficult; and in consequence it is not performed so often that we can get to know it as intimately as it deserves or encounter sufficient opportunities to remind ourselves, once having heard it, how really good it is. The vocal score of *Die Entführung* makes very little sense except to the experienced student of Mozart and even he cannot imagine what it really sounds like until he has had a look at the full orchestral score. For, as in all Mozart's operas, the orchestral character and quality of *Die Entführung* are a peculiar and inseparable part of the whole.

Today, however, as a result of the development of the long-playing record, even if we cannot get a "live" performance of *Die Entführung*, we have a readily available means of recalling that the work is as entrancing as anything Mozart ever wrote, that its greatest virtues are those qualities which custom and convention would sometimes have us believe are its greatest faults, and that a great deal of pretentious criticism has been levelled at one of the least pretentious masterpieces in the history of opera. For nowhere in Mozart's entire output for the stage is there to be found quite the same charm, high spirits and spontaneous good humour that characterizes *Die Entführung aus dem Serail.*

CHARACTERS IN ORDER OF APPEARANCE:

BELMONTE, *a young Spanish nobleman* . .	*Tenor*
OSMIN, *head of Pasha Selim's household* . .	*Bass*
PEDRILLO, *Belmonte's servant* . . .	*Tenor*
PASHA SELIM	*Speaking part*
CONSTANZE, *a Spanish lady* . . .	*Soprano*
BLONDE, *her English maid* . . .	*Soprano*

Scene: Turkey   Time: The 18th century

ACT I

Scene: The terrace of Pasha Selim's country palace, overlooking the sea.

Mozart's "Turkish" overture to *Die Entführung* is still very much in the form of the old Italian "sinfonia"—two fast movements linked by an Andante. Whether intentionally or not Mozart has summed up what may be called the Conflicting Powers—or at least the Principal Ingredients, of the plot in the contrasting sections of the overture: the opening and closing Presto is "Turkish", while the little Andante interlude can be associated with the love of hero and heroine.

While we are well enough accustomed to 19th- and 20th-century composers telling us unceasingly what their music "means" and how we should listen to it, it is rare to find an 18th-century composer—and least of all a composer as indifferent to "theories" as Mozart—with the time to tell us something about his music. With a great deal of the composition of *Die Entführung*, however, Mozart was unusually communicative about his musical intentions and the form they finally took.

He wrote to his father in September 1781: "I have sent you only fourteen bars of the overture which is very short, with alternate *fortes* and *pianos*, and the Turkish music always coming in at the fortes."

The "fourteen bars" are the opening phrase of the overture:

As Mozart indicates, the "Turkish" music is "always coming in at the fortes", which means that the orchestra is reinforced at these moments by a piccolo (displacing the flute altogether in the two fast sections of the overture), cymbals, triangle and bass drum and the result is satisfactorily exotic according to 18th-century standards.* Less obvious than the instrumentation of Mozart's "Turkish" passages, however, is the metrics of his "Turkish" phrases and it is this aspect of the music of *Die Entführung* which I must confess has begun to strike me only in the course of making this study.

---

* Mozart apologized, when sending the score to his father for copying, that the parts for trumpets, drums, flutes and clarinets and the Turkish music were missing "because I could not get any music paper with so many staves. Those parts were written out on extra sheets which the copyist has probably lost, for he was unable to find them. The first act, when I was sending it somewhere or other—I forget where, unfortunately fell in the mud, which explains why it is so dirty."

The opening 14-bar phrase of the overture is so familiar that one scarcely gives it a single analytical thought any longer. But isn't it—when we consider it—a slightly eccentric, unbalanced phrase? Three phrases of 4 bars, then instead of a fourth 4-bar phrase to round it off the tune is cut off in its prime, with two bars to go, and we return to the 4-bar phrases once more. I would not mention this at all if this odd melodic asymmetry did not crop up again on a couple of occasions later in the score of *Die Entführung* when, in moments of "Turkish" music, Mozart comes out with phrases entirely on the "wrong foot", as it were,—passages founded on tunes seven and (to give the whole thing a thoroughly mystic air) eleven bars long.

It is the unexpected oddness of these passages which leads me to wonder whether Mozart's "Turkish" music was not, after all more than just a matter of banging triangles and cymbals; whether, in fact, he was not translating the metric unevenness of oriental melody (as heard by occidental ears) into the everyday language of European music in such a way that while the modern ear, accustomed to the din and dissonance of the past half-century, would not notice it, to Mozart's contemporaries the effect was strikingly novel and exotic, and that it was these melodic quirks as much as the orchestral decoration that Mozart regarded as typical of what he described to his father as "the style of Turkish music".

The Turkish music in the overture is developed into a vigorous sequence which the older among us will immediately associate with the accompaniment of dramatic scenes in the days of the silent cinema (at least, anybody whose film education—like mine—was received in Vienna will remember it serving for films with Emil Jannings as happily as for those with Douglas Fairbanks, Charles Ray and William S. Hart):

"The overture", as Mozart says, "modulates through different keys"—adding with considerable truth, "and I doubt whether anyone, even if his previous night has been a sleepless one, could go to sleep over it"—and eventually the Turkish liveliness is succeeded by a plaintive little Andante in 3/8 time:

This little tune, although one cannot know it on a first hearing, is a version in the minor of Belmonte's first aria heard on the rise of the curtain, and it is introduced into the overture with great effect as a contrast to the bustling alternation of "fortes and pianos" which has gone before. The opening Presto movement is recapitulated and this time, ignoring the subtle entries provided for it when the overture first began, the triangle instead of merely "coming in at the fortes" now plays without ceasing through *f* and *p* until the overture comes to an inconclusive conclusion and the curtain rises.*

The last bars of the overture lead directly to the introduction to Belmonte, alone on the stage, singing in the major the Andante tune which formed the middle section of the overture: "Hier soll ich dich denn sehen, Constanze" ("This is where I shall find you. . . ."):

One of the more familiar generalizations made about *Die Entführung* is that for the most part the characters are "types" rather than individuals. Perhaps, compared with the vivid flesh-and-blood creatures of Mozart's later operas this is so, but to anybody hearing *Die Entführung* as their first Mozart opera it is a technical quibble which will probably seem very much beside the point. This is particularly the case with Belmonte, for from a purely musical point of view the part is an intensely sympathetic one. Few tenors in opera make such a good impression on the audience at their first appearance, are so manifestly in love and so immediately likable for it.

It was only thanks to Mozart's unerring and impatient instinct for the theatre that Belmonte had an aria to start with at all. In the original —that is, the unlucky Bretzner's, libretto, the scene opened with a spoken monologue and Stephanie, in "adapting" it, kept it as it was. Mozart, on the other hand, insisted that Belmonte should be introduced with an arietta and in doing so automatically gave his hero personality, which the spoken word (at least, as supplied by Bretzner and Stephanie between them) would never have done.

Belmonte has come to Turkey in search of his bride, Constanze, a Spanish lady who has been captured by pirates and whom he believes to be held prisoner in the harem of Pasha Selim. As a stranger in these parts Belmonte is relieved to encounter Osmin, head of the Pasha's household. Osmin, however, is very much preoccupied with his own thoughts about love and is apparently deaf to all Belmonte's questions and attempts to get into conversation. Osmin's preoccupation takes the form of a surprisingly gentle and wistful air—surprising for it reveals a side of his character which we do not encounter again: Osmin in love. Or perhaps it would be better to say that Osmin in love does not appear in such a sympathetic and lyrical mood again as the story goes on: for while he

---

* Ironically, the "concert" ending which rounds off the overture for performance outside the opera house, was made by Johann Anton André, son of the composer of that same *Belmont and Constanze* whose librettist, Christoph Bretzner, protested so indignantly against "a certain Mozart" who "misused" his drama.

remains in love the constant damping of his hopes and shattering of his
dreams scarcely brings out the best in him.

Osmin's air is a simple ditty of three verses, beginning with: "Wer ein
Liebchen hat gefunden" ("When a maiden takes your fancy . . ."):

and ending with the cadence:

which Mozart harmonizes differently each time with wonderfully telling
effect.

Belmonte speaks to Osmin after the first and again after the second
verse, but the Turk takes no notice and continues his singing. After the
third verse Belmonte breaks into song with an impatient echo of Osmin's
cadence:

Belmonte's singing has the desired effect. Osmin takes notice and
answers.

The long duet which follows was also Mozart's idea, for in the original
libretto there was nothing but dialogue after Osmin's short song. In a
letter to his father Mozart gives some indication of how and why the
figure of Osmin, which was an insignificant part in Bretzner's libretto,
was developed into the magnificently-conceived character of *Die
Entführung*: "As we have given the part of Osmin to Herr Fischer who
certainly has a superb bass voice . . . we must take advantage of it,
particularly as the entire Viennese public is on his side. But in the original
libretto Osmin has only this one short song to sing and nothing else,
except in the trio and the finale; he has therefore been given an aria in
Act I and will have another in Act II."*

So long as the questions Belmonte asks Osmin are straightforwardly
tourist and in innocuous phrase-book style—such as "Is this the Pasha
Selim's house?" and "Are you in the Pasha's service?"—Osmin is polite
if rather anxious not to have his time wasted by too many questions.
When, however, Belmonte asks him if he could speak to a young fellow
called Pedrillo, who was also captured and sold into the Pasha's service,

---

* He did get another but not until Act III.

Osmin explodes with fury. Pedrillo, Belmonte's former servant, has not only insinuated himself into the Pasha's favours and has been appointed his head gardener, but is a more successful rival to Osmin for the love of Constanze's English maid, Blonde; he is a gallows-bird, he should be hanged, disembowelled, filleted, roasted on a spit, and his head cut off and impaled. Belmonte suggests, with praiseworthy reasonableness, that Osmin cannot know Pedrillo very well if that's what he thinks of him. Osmin thereupon turns on Belmonte, threatening him with the bastinado in a passage of quite remarkable wrong-footedness, consisting as it does of a seven-bar phrase played in canon, with a cadence which brings it to the odd and eccentric total of 11 bars, when the theme is repeated in canon in A major before returning to the original D:

The effect of this passage, played so fast that the strings are virtually playing *tremolando*, is not so much exotic as downright sinister on a first hearing; after a repetition of the opening phrase in D, however, the duet settles down to a brilliant but more conventional Presto finish and Osmin hustles Belmonte off the scene.

Pedrillo now arrives, young, cocksure and impertinent, teasing and goading what Mozart described as the "stupid, surly, malicious Osmin" into another outburst of rage. When Pedrillo asks why Osmin should want to throttle him, Osmin replies that in addition to Pedrillo spying on him and stealing his women from him, he just can't bear him anyway— "Solche hergelauf'ne Laffen" ("All these up-start puppies . . ."):

Osmin's fury rises to a climax as he swears vengeance by the beard of the Prophet. The music stops for a moment to allow Pedrillo to protest that Osmin really is being a shade unreasonable and unkind, particularly as he isn't doing him any harm. "You have the face of a gallows-bird," replies Osmin, "and that's enough", and continues his blood-curdling threats.

Mozart's own description of this whole aria is detailed and explicit: "Osmin's rage is made comical by the accompaniment of the Turkish music. [Piccolo, cymbals and bass drum.] In working out the aria I have given full opportunity now and again to Fischer's beautiful deep notes. . . . The passage 'Drum beim Barte des Propheten' ['By the beard of the Prophet'] is certainly in the same tempo, but with quick notes; but as

Osmin's rage gradually increases, there comes (just when the aria seems about to end) the Allegro assai, which is in a totally different time and in a different key; this is sure to be very effective. For just as a man in a tremendous rage oversteps all the bounds of order, moderation and decency and completely forgets himself, so the music too must forget itself. But as passions, whether violent or not, must never be expressed in such a way as to inspire disgust, and as music, even in the most terrible situations, must never offend the ear, but must please the hearer, or in other words must never cease to be *music*, I have gone from F (the key of the aria), not into a remote key, but into a related one, not, however, into its nearest relative D minor, but into the more remote A minor."

The "more remote A minor", in which cymbals and drums at full tilt add colour to Osmin's threat to spit, roast, draw and finally flay Pedrillo, ends with a whirl of horror-music worthy of a Beethoven scherzo:

Osmin stamps off, fuming and raging, a superb example of Mozart's genius for characterization—in this case of a monumental figure of grotesque frustration and ineffectual fury and indignation.

Pedrillo and Belmonte now meet and Belmonte learns all the news—how Pedrillo, Constanze and Blonde were sold into the Pasha's service, which has proved fortunate for all of them, Pedrillo having turned his knowledge of gardening to good account while Constanze is the Pasha's favourite. Belmonte shows understandable signs of concern at this last item of news, but Pedrillo assures him there is nothing to worry about.

Belmonte explains that he has a ship anchored outside the harbour and all that is needed now is for everybody to board it and escape. Pedrillo points out that things are not so simple as that, and as a preliminary step he will play on the Pasha's passion for building and gardening by introducing Belmonte as a famous architect. This, as Pedrillo explains, will have the initial result of enabling Belmonte to see Constanze; after that, things will have to be planned carefully.

Belmonte, left alone, reflects on the prospect of seeing his Constanze again. Four subdued bars of expressive recitative (with orchestra) lead into his aria: "O wie ängstlich, o wie feurig klopft mein liebevolles Herz" ("How anxiously and ardently my heart beats . . .").

Once again Mozart has provided programme notes in a letter to his father and writes: "Would you like to know how I have expressed it—

and even indicated his throbbing heart? By the two violins playing in octaves. This is the favourite aria of all who have heard it, and it is mine too. I wrote it expressly to suit Adamberger's voice. One feels the trembling, the faltering, how his throbbing breast begins to swell; this I have expressed by a crescendo. One hears the whispering and sighing—which I have indicated by the first violins, muted, and a flute playing in unison." (It is interesting to note that Mozart's indication "muted" appears in the first edition of the orchestral score as "sotto voce" instead of the more usual "con sordine.")

"O wie ängstlich", which one is not surprised to learn was Mozart's own favourite aria in the opera, is filled with passages of unanalysable charm and warmth—unanalysable because inspiration, technique and craftsmanship are so indissolubly bound up together; and nowhere is his genius for saying the right thing at the right moment more apparent than in the little epilogue to the aria, with its enchanting passage for flute, oboe and bassoon in octaves:

Those bars look so insignificant on paper, so unremarkable even in the full score, that I would hesitate to draw attention to them were they not typical of Mozart's remarkable feeling for detail, rounding off Belmonte's aria in a way which cannot be described, only experienced. My purpose in referring to them is to nudge the listener and make sure that when he hears them he listens to them, and does not let them pass by as he may the codas of other opera composers.

Mozart's codas are worthy of separate study, anyway, for they are little masterpieces of theatrical timing, always to the point and never leaving the audience in any doubt of the emotional mood of the music it rounds off. The three bars of indignant puffing and blowing which end Osmin's list of threats to Pedrillo (Ex 10, p. 28) are admirably timed to allow the orchestra to take its final burst to the tape in its natural stride; while the earlier duet between Belmonte and Osmin is given a long, eight-bar coda to allow Belmonte time to leave the stage and so not "kill" his exit by making him leave *after* the music has finished.

The aria and its lovely little coda at an end, Pedrillo rushes on to tell Belmonte that Pasha Selim and Constanze have just landed from what is described in some English synopses as a "water excursion", though "pleasure cruise" would be a more literal translation of the original German. At any rate, the Pasha and Constanze have been out together in a boat and on their return (Pedrillo having removed Belmonte from the scene until a more opportune moment arises to introduce the famous "architect") they are greeted by a chorus of janissaries singing the Pasha's praises.

"The Janissaries' chorus" (wrote Mozart to his father) "is all that can be desired—short and lively, and just what pleases the Viennese." It is also highly "Turkish" in style, and not only because the bass drum and piccolo are added to the score (cymbals and triangle are unaccountably absent from this item). The tune the chorus sings is quite exceptionally eccentric and wrong-footed, consisting of an opening passage made up of a phrase of 7 bars and a second of 4 bars (which add up to the mystic 11), followed by another phrase of seven and 9 (which add up to a more conventionally symmetrical 16).

It was this passage which more than any in *Die Entführung* prompted me to consider the possibility of Mozart's melodic "Turkishness":

We now meet Pasha Selim for the first time. Selim's is a speaking part, a circumstance which in itself upsets a number of people who consider that it would be more satisfactory altogether if he were allowed to sing; while others think that by *not* singing Selim's part is endowed with a peculiar distinction of its own. Personally I find it a controversy that leaves me unmoved, for I do not at all care for opera with spoken dialogue, and the fact that Mozart, Bizet, Weber and Beethoven all wrote masterpieces in this form does not alter my feelings at all, but merely shows that a composer of genius can overcome my prejudices to such an extent that they do not spoil my enjoyment of *Die Entführung*, *The Magic Flute*, *Carmen*, *Der Freischütz* or *Fidelio*.

However, the question of Pasha Selim and whether he should sing or not is largely a matter of personal preference, and in any case what he has to say is always short and to the point, and if not the cause of music in himself, at least the cause of music in others.

Selim, either way, is nevertheless a dignified and courteous figure, and in the comparatively few lines he has to speak reveals a sympathetic personality. Although, as master of his own harem, Selim could treat Constanze as a slave he prefers to treat her like a lady, and his taking her on "water excursions" is all part of his plan to win her love in a gentle manner. Constanze recognizes and is grateful for his devotion and consideration; the relationship between them is civilized and calm. When, for what is clearly the twentieth time, Selim asks the reason for her sadness and tears and her continued rejection of his suit, Constanze tells him—with a delicate regard for his feelings—that her heart belongs to the man she has left behind her in her own country—"Ach, ich liebte" ("I loved and was happy, never knowing the pain of love . . ."):

This Adagio introduction leads to a coloratura aria which, while it is brilliant and exciting, never for a moment ceases to be an expression of Constanze's steadfastness and resolution to remain faithful to the memory of her lover (she does not yet know, of course, that Belmonte has arrived in Turkey). Mozart's ability to satisfy the demands of both vocal convention and dramatic situation at the same time was not the least of his unique gifts as an opera composer. He admitted having "sacrificed Constanze's aria a little to the flexible throat of Mlle Cavalieri [the original Constanze]" and to have "tried to express her feelings, as far as an Italian bravura aria will allow it."

The Italian bravura aria allowed it well enough. It was the German words of the Allegro which disconcerted Mozart more than anything:

"Doch wie schnell schwand meine Freude" ("Yet how soon my joy faded . . .") was originally "Doch wie hui schwand meine Freude"— "hui" being an interjection comparable for poetic imagination with such lyrical strip-cartoon gems as "Zing!" or "Swoosh!" or "Wham!" Mozart substituted the more usual "schnell" to mean "quickly" and commented: "I really don't know what our German poets are thinking of. Even if they do not understand the theatre, or at any rate opera, at least they should not make their characters speak as if they were addressing a lot of pigs."

In the middle of the aria Constanze repeats the words of the opening Adagio. She also repeats, with slight variations, the music of the introductory stanzas as well, so that the tune of Ex 14 becomes

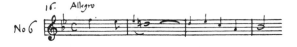

and the cadence leading to the reprise of the Allegro theme is also an extension of its first Adagio statement.

This transplanting of the Adagio into the Allegro section is of no great aesthetic significance, of course, but it shows plainly Mozart's genius for exploiting a musical form to its utmost limits. He wanted to repeat the sentiments of the introduction, but having embarked on a bravura aria could not logically interrupt the line of the music, so he extended the original phrases to fit the tempo of the main sequence, thereby giving (*a*) an irrefutable indication to conductors that the Allegro is just twice as fast as the Adagio, and demonstrating (*b*) that underlying the Adagio-Allegro form of aria or overture used by so many 18th-century composers there is a fundamental "pulse" which acts as a metronomic common denominator.

Constanze finishes her aria and Selim gazes after her as she leaves. "Her sorrow, her tears, her fidelity," he says, "have won my heart for ever. No, Constanze, no—Selim has a heart too, and Selim knows what it is to love."

Pedrillo breaks in on Selim's little reverie, bringing with him Belmonte whom he introduces as a young architect come to offer his services. Selim, in a thoroughly generous and expansive mood, engages him and leaves Pedrillo and Belmonte rejoicing that the first step, at least, has been taken successfully.

Belmonte, however, is still impatient to see Constanze; Pedrillo replies that while the question has been constantly uppermost on his mind, there is still great need of care, patience and discretion. Pedrillo and Belmonte are about to go into the palace garden when their way is barred by the ample form of the irascible Osmin.

Pedrillo explains that Belmonte is the new architect, just that moment engaged by the Pasha. Osmin retorts that he couldn't care less if he was a prison governor; as far as he is concerned, Pedrillo and his friend are both foreigners—highly undesirable aliens, in fact, and therefore clearly bent on outwitting him in some way (Osmin is not only a xenophobe but suffers from persecution mania as well). The Pasha (continues Osmin) may be as soft as butter, letting foreigners infiltrate into his service in this way, but he, Osmin, is made of sterner stuff. The scene ends with a trio begun by Osmin ordering Pedrillo and Belmonte to be off:

Mozart's own description of this gay and exhilarating trio is given in the same informative letter which has supplied us with most of the composer's own programme notes on *Die Entführung*: "Now for the trio at the end of Act I. Pedrillo has passed off his master as an architect—to give him an opportunity of meeting his Constanze in the garden. Bassa Selim has taken him into his service, Osmin, the steward, knows nothing of this, and being a rude fellow and an enemy of all strangers, is impertinent and refuses to let them into the garden. It opens quite abruptly—and because the words lend themselves to it, I have made it a fairly decent piece of real three-part writing. Then the major key begins at once pianissimo,* it must go very quickly, and finish up with a great deal of noise, which is always appropriate at the end of an act. The more noise the better, and the shorter the better, so the audience do not have time to cool down with their applause."

And with practical demonstration of Mozart's instinct for timing, the curtain falls as Pedrillo and Belmonte push their way past Osmin.

* Only one p survives in the score today.

ACT II

Scene: The garden of Pasha Selim's palace, with Osmin's house at one side of it.

Blonde, who is known to Pedrillo and sometimes on the cast-sheets of *Die Entführung* as "Blondchen", is discovered at the rise of the curtain keeping Osmin very much in his place. In Europe, she says firmly, people would never dream of treating girls in the rough, unmannerly way he expects to be able to treat her. And in a charming little aria (richly scored for strings only with the violas often playing the tune an octave lower than the first violins, which produces a wonderfully warm sound), she proceeds to tell him how a maiden's heart may be won—by tenderness and flattery, courtesy and gentle fun—"Durch Zärtlichkeit und Schmeicheln . . .":

Osmin listens to Blonde's aria and is unimpressed—largely because he has no idea what she is talking about. He is a Turk and there is only one way of treating a woman in Turkey: rough. What may do for the fine ladies and gentlemen of Europe cuts no ice in Turkey; she is his slave and must obey him.

Blonde retorts that she doesn't give a fig for Turkey or the Turks; she is not a chattel; she is an Englishwoman, born to freedom and one of a nation that never, never, never, etc. The argument is continued in a duet in which Blonde tells Osmin bluntly to get out of her sight as she can't bear him and the sooner the better:

Osmin threatens that he will not move a step until she obeys, and does so in a phrase to give scope to the famous Herr Fischer's deep bass notes:

Blonde answers back with the assurance that she wouldn't dream of obeying him, not even if he were the Grand Mogul himself, and she mocks him by plumbing the depths of her own high soprano:

Poor Osmin, defeated by the unconventional weapons of his adversary, lapses into a slow and melancholy little tune in the minor, in which he bemoans the idiocy of the English in allowing their women freedom to plague them and do as they please. Blonde repeats her earlier sentiments on the subject of liberty and slavery, and a charming little duet develops ending, in the famous 1950 Decca–London recording, with a remarkable low C for Osmin.* This is not written in the score but it is hardly out of character, since the range of Osmin's part in any case is:

and if the C below the D was not provided for Herr Fischer then it is perhaps because he did not have the note, whereas the modern Herr Koréh did have it, used it and no structural damage was done to the music.

The gentle C minor Andante gives way to a final section (Allegro assai) and the unfortunate Osmin (one is beginning to feel a little sorry for him in the face of the unequal struggle) is driven away by Blonde's threat of physical violence.

Matters between Blonde and Osmin being temporarily settled, if not altogether to the satisfaction of both parties, a serious note returns to the action of *Die Entführung*. Constanze enters and in a recitative accompanied by the orchestra soliloquizes on her unhappiness and the unending sadness of being parted from her lover. As so often with Mozart, the orchestrally-accompanied recitative can be as revealing of character as any aria and the Adagio introduction, accompanied by strings only, which leads into Constanze's aria, lifts the whole action high above the level of mere Singspiel. In this outpouring of grief there is no longer any suggestion of Constanze being a "type"; she is highly individual and human in her expression of sorrow, which Mozart punctuates with a plaintive and moving figure:

Mozart's ability to be "serious" is a quality which often surprises those who have been brought up to regard him as the composer of all that is

* Great Britain: Decca LXT 2536/7/8; USA: London XLLA-3.

most scintillating, gay and brilliant in music. He is just that too, of course; but while most clowns might have enough technique to give a tolerable performance of Hamlet, Mozart's "seriousness" is not just a tour de force to cause one to remark—perhaps a little patronizingly—that he is revealing "hidden depths" or the like. There are no hidden depths in Mozart; it is all there as clear as daylight, if you will only open your musical eyes to see it, as it were. And one of the most striking aspects of his genius is not just that he can be "serious", but that nobody in the history of opera, not even Verdi, has ever expressed grief so convincingly and affectingly in music as Mozart. There are sometimes sighs and perhaps tears with this grief—as Constanze suffers it, for instance—but in the main it is music which expresses, as only music can, that sorrow which lies too deep for tears.

The aria which follows Constanze's recitative is in the key of G minor, Mozart's elegiac key of the great String Quintet (which cheers up enough to have a finale in the major), the G minor Symphony (which does not), and Pamina's heartrending aria, "Ach, ich fühl's", in *The Magic Flute**. Constanze's lament begins "Traurigkeit ward mir zum Loose" ("Sorrow has been my lot. . . .")—

In the course of this aria, for which a pair of basset-horns (or tenor clarinets) are introduced to darken the orchestral colour, Mozart demonstrates a gift shared only by Verdi—that of being able to make the same kind of phrase mean two entirely different things. Superficially there is little difference between

and

and yet the first expresses Belmonte's excited and loving heart-beats, while the second is a clear expression of Constanze's tears and sighs. One other feature common to both arias is a moving little coda—charming and optimistic in Belmonte's aria, sad and inconsolable in Constanze's.

In practice this aria is sometimes shortened, for the purely practical reason of sparing the prima donna an over-strenuous curtain-raiser to her main aria of the evening, which follows after the briefest possible respite provided by a couple of lines of dialogue spoken by Selim. The Pasha comes

* See p. 225.

on at the end of her lament and adopts an entirely new method of approach to Constanze. Where before he was reasonable and gentle, his patience is now exhausted and he threatens her, not with death, but with tortures of all kinds—"Martern aller Arten".

These words provide the inspiration for "Martern aller Arten", Constanze's long, six-minute aria which follows, and though she has to wait through a lengthy instrumental introduction before she actually sings the words her scornful reaction to the Pasha's threats is expressed immediately by the entry of the orchestra on the cue:

This aria is fashionably described as a movement from a concerto for coloratura soprano, four solo instruments (flute, oboe, violin and violoncello) and orchestra, and indeed it might well be so. But even though it is a complicated and lengthy form in which to construct a dramatic aria (especially, of course, in a simple little business like a Singspiel), Mozart does not lose sight of the first purpose of the scene: the courageous, angry defiance by Constanze of the Pasha's threats. There may be an introduction of some 60 bars for the orchestra and four *concertante* instruments before she sings, but the impact of Constanze's first, scornful "Martern aller Arten" is still powerful and in character and, given satisfactory performance, thrilling as well. And if it still sounds like a concerto to you, then there is nothing for it but to point out that there are many far less comfortable and romantic surroundings in which to hear a Mozart concerto than an opera house where they happen to be doing *Die Entführung* that night.

Constanze ends her aria with a final defiant declaration, daring Selim to do his worst; she has no fear of him or of death, which she will hail as a welcome release from his tortures and cruelties. And she strides out with one of the most effective exits in all opera—a stormy unison passage of 30 bars which she and the orchestra share between them.

It is small wonder that Selim is left rather breathless and a little puzzled by what he has just heard. He is astonished by Constanze's courage and audacity in defying him, but since neither gentle pleading nor violent threats seem to have any effect, he decides to try cunning—though exactly what form this cunning is to take is never disclosed either at this or at any later stage of the opera.

Pedrillo and Blonde now meet in view of the audience for the first time and the English girl learns that Belmonte has arrived and is planning great plans for their escape. Blonde grows even more excited when Pedrillo tells her that the escape is planned for that very night at midnight, and she turns to rush off and tell Constanze all about it. Pedrillo tells her not to be in such a hurry; he hasn't told her what is going to happen yet. At midnight, he says, Belmonte will be at Constanze's window with a ladder, and Pedrillo will have one at Blonde's. With that Pedrillo hurries away leaving Blonde to express her excitement and impatience in a charming and gay little aria—"Welche Wonne, welche Lust" ("Oh, what pleasure; Oh, what joy . . .") :

This aria of Blonde's is another admirable example of Mozart's gift for characterization—the witty, resourceful and engagingly human soubrette, elated and scarcely able to wait to dash into the palace and give her mistress the news.*

Pedrillo returns to wait for Belmonte, carrying with him two flasks of wine, one large, one small—the "props" he needs to fulfil the first part of the escape plan which is to get Osmin speechlessly drunk, adding a sleeping draught to his wine for good safe measure. Pedrillo, however, seems to have lost some of his initial enthusiasm for the scheme when it comes to the point of putting it into practice; but he pulls himself together and reflecting that faint heart never won fair lady's freedom he sings a battle song to keep his courage up—"Frisch zum Kampfe!" ("Haste to battle! Only cowards are afraid . . .") :

There now follows what can be one of the most richly comic scenes in opera—Pedrillo getting Osmin drunk against all the Mussulman's religious principles. It is no easy business, as Pedrillo discovers, for Osmin's battle with his conscience is fierce and ding-dong. It is only in the course of a duet, in which he is tempted by Pedrillo's stanza in praise of Bacchus —"Vivat Bacchus!"—that Osmin, after a moment or two's hesitation and conscience-searching, finally throws all restraint to the winds and takes up the song with enthusiasm himself, drinking down the contents of the

---

* I still insist that this is successful characterization even though I know the tune is lifted bodily from the final Rondo of Mozart's Flute Concerto in D major (K.314), written four years earlier. The real test is, does the music to Blonde's aria suit her character or not? Obviously it does, otherwise one would hear of audiences protesting that it sounded more like a flute concerto. It should not be forgotten that clothes taken "off the peg" can be just as expressive of "personality" as those made to measure.

larger (doped) flask of Cyprus wine.

This drunken duet, Mozart wrote to his father, was specially designed to the taste of "i signori viennesi", and consists "entirely of my Turkish tattoo"; which means that full use is made of "Turkish" orchestration—cymbals, piccolo, triangle and bass drum. Only the horns are omitted for some reason from a score which otherwise employs double wood-wind, trumpets and strings.

By the end of the duet Osmin is what is sometimes known to the Irish as "parlatic", and Pedrillo, with an unexpected display of physical strength, manages to carry him bodily into his house and leave him to sleep it off—which will not, he imagines, be until well after midnight when the plan to escape is to be put into operation.

With Osmin disposed of, Pedrillo returns to keep an appointment with Belmonte who arrives followed almost immediately by Constanze and Blonde. Belmonte greets Constanze with an aria of quite remarkable and moving restraint, in which he recalls the tears and sorrow they have suffered during their separation from each other—"Wenn der Freude Thränen fliessen" ("When tears of joy are shed . . ."):

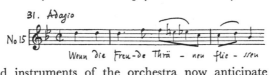

The wind instruments of the orchestra now anticipate Belmonte's change of mood from the Adagio of the first part of the aria to the 3/4 Allegretto of the second, in which he looks forward to an untroubled life with Constanze:

It should be pointed out that very often in performance this aria of Belmonte's is omitted at this point in the action (as it is in most recordings) and transposed to the beginning of Act III in place of the aria which is found there in the score. This operation brings us more quickly to the quartet which ends Act II and enables Constanze and Belmonte to embrace each other musically more or less as soon as they meet.

The orchestral introduction

becomes the main tune of a fully-fledged quartet passage as Blonde and Pedrillo join in after contributing their own expressions of excitement.

Suddenly, though, the music gets unexpectedly serious. The key changes to G minor and the tempo to a 3/8 Andante. Belmonte unwisely gives voice to doubts about Constanze's virtue—"Doch ach! bei aller Lust" ("But, alas, joy is tempered with cares . . ."):

Belmonte takes an unconscionable time to get to the point (which is to suggest that Constanze has been the Pasha's mistress), and while he is dithering Pedrillo emulates him and starts suggesting to Blonde that perhaps she isn't really worth all the trouble of ladders at midnight either. Constanze begs Belmonte to tell her what's on his mind, while Blonde plainly accuses Pedrillo of being drunk. At last master and servant manage to blurt out their questions. Constanze bursts into tears and Blonde, with that typical Englishwoman's indignation which always accompanies any suggestion that she would ever "dream of such a thing" as sex, gives Pedrillo a smart box on the ear.

The men immediately grovel in their contrition, though clearly relieved to find their worst fears unfounded. Constanze for her part, is terribly hurt that Belmonte should ever have suspected her of being unfaithful, while Blonde is downright indignant and particularly piqued by Pedrillo's insinuation that she is so lacking in taste as to consider the fat and un-attractive Osmin as a lover anyway.

The quartet develops through another 15 serious bars as the characters express their particular viewpoints in their individual musical way and combine to present an ingenious display of Mozart's genius for character-drawing. Their differences are buried and the quartet ends the act happily with some sly little musical jokes by the composer. As Constanze forgives Belmonte, Blonde's forgiveness of Pedrillo follows in canon:

while the same process of imitation is extended when Constanze's praise of true love is followed first by Blonde, then by Belmonte, whose phrases in turn are followed at a respectful distance by his servant, thus suggesting that while lovers may think the same things their social position doesn't always allow them to say so at the same time.

ACT III

Scene 1: Open space before the Pasha's palace. The palace is on one side of it, Osmin's house on the other; at the back there is a view of the sea.

The last act begins at midnight with a great deal of comic business performed by Pedrillo with ladders—a long ladder that is placed against the wall of the palace for Constanze to come down, a short ladder against Osmin's house for Blonde. So that nobody should be suspicious of any change in the nightly routine Pedrillo gets Belmonte to sing, for it seems that Pedrillo sings a serenade to Blonde every night and the entire neighbourhood would miss it if midnight ever arrived in silence. Belmonte accordingly obliges with a song while Pedrillo goes about the business of preparing for the escape.

Where his aria, "Wenn der Freude Thränen fliessen" (see p. 39) does not replace it, Belmonte is intended to sing another reflective number at this point, very much more difficult than the first one (which may account for its frequent omission) and entitled "Ich baue ganz auf deine Stärke" (I place all my trust in Love . . ."):

This ode to the omnipotence of Love develops into something of a coloratura piece, not so much in its range (it does not rise above a normally attainable B flat and there are only six of them all told in a substantially long aria) as in its use of decoration, of figures and scales which have so far not been prominent in Belmonte's part. In addition to Mlle Cavalieri, Mlle Teiber (Blonde), and Herr Fischer, it seems that Herr Adamberger, the tenor, also brought considerable vocal distinction to the original cast of *Die Entführung* to stimulate Mozart to vocal writing demanding an unusually and consistently high technical standard of performance.

Having lulled everybody into a state of complaisant and careless unwatchfulness with Belmonte's song, Pedrillo now sings himself and so provides the cue for the escape operations to begin. Fortunately Constanze, whose turn it is to come to her window first, is a little slow in appearing. The delay worries Belmonte, but not us who sit in the audience for it enables Pedrillo to sing two verses of one of the most immediately enchanting serenades ever written—"In Mohrenland gefangen war" ("A maiden was captive in Moorish lands . . ."):

37. [Andante]

As nothing happens after two verses of this song, which tells so topically of the rescue of a captive maid at midnight, Pedrillo sings two more to the same magically effective 12-bar phrase, and the hushed pizzicato accompaniment leaves off in mid-air.

An attentive neighbourhood, one believes, would have been suspicious of something irregular happening from the very first verse of Pedrillo's serenade. If he is singing to Blonde as usual, why does he refer to the *black* hair of the captive maiden? Or—since his song is concerned with rescue and escape from infidel hands—is that deliberately done to put people off the scent?

Constanze appears at the window at last, Belmonte climbs up the ladder, disappears into her room, and a few moments later the two of them come out through the door of the palace on the ground floor. The purpose of the ladder, in this case, is a little obscure, for if the palace door can be opened from the inside then surely Constanze could have let herself out without Belmonte having to climb up and risk drawing attention to the whole escapade with such a conspicuous accessory as a ladder. However, it may well be that Constanze needs help with her luggage, in which case, of course, she had to have her lover to carry it for her.

When Belmonte and Constanze have left the scene Pedrillo sets about rescuing Blonde; he climbs up the ladder and disappears through the window into her room. Meanwhile a black mute, woken by all the singing, rouses Osmin who is still befuddled but sober enough to see that something is wrong. There is considerable comedy in the scene that follows. Osmin gets involved with the ladder and there is much dashing up and down it by Pedrillo, who eventually escapes with Blonde through the ground floor door. It is hardly a moment, however, before Pedrillo and Blonde, together with Belmonte and Constanze, are brought back on to the scene as prisoners; the guard has been roused and the four fugitives recaptured.

Pedrillo tries to blackmail Osmin by reminding him of his un-Mussulman-like enthusiasm for the bottle the night before, but Osmin is not to be intimidated. The Prophet, he is sure, will forgive him his sins, and even if he doesn't everything will be more than compensated for by the pleasure of bringing Pedrillo and his companion to justice. And Osmin sails exuberantly into his last and finest aria which ends the scene—"Ha! wie will ich triumphieren!" ("Ha! to think how I shall triumph! . . ."):

38. Allegro vivace

This aria, accompanied by a much-featured piccolo, is a tremendous show-piece for the bass, with great sweeping intervals of an octave and more and fine opportunities to show off the low notes of the singer's register, including a low D sustained for 8 bars.

While reminiscence hunting is an over-rated and meaningless pastime in music, it is nevertheless intriguing to note the obvious devotion Mozart showed to two phrases in this aria. The first is the orchestral variant which accompanies Osmin's first phrase:

The other is a prominent orchestral passage between two of Osmin's outbursts:

Now, the opus number of *Die Entführung* is K.384; the work Mozart wrote immediately after it (K.385) was the "Haffner" Symphony in D major. The finale of the "Haffner" begins:

which is not far removed from Ex 39; while the first movement of the same symphony opens with:

which, in turn, is little more than a D major version of the F major theme of Ex 40. All this is mentioned, not to suggest that Mozart made a habit of repeating himself, but to show how in one work he could develop on a symphonic scale ideas which were scarcely more than fragments in another context altogether.

Scene 2: The hall of the Palace. Later.

This is often, and rightly, regarded as an unnecessary change of scene, interrupting the flow of the action and contributing little that cannot be as well done in the same stage set as the rest of the act.

By keeping the same scene it means that instead of sending somebody
out to see what the disturbance is all about outside and having the
offenders brought in, the Pasha goes out to see for himself. Either way
Osmin, still a little drowsy from his sleeping-draught, is called on to
explain what has happened and reports that he has caught the four
Europeans redhanded trying to escape. Belmonte and Constanze are
brought on under guard; Selim reproaches Constanze with treachery,
but she pleads that what she has done has been for the man she has loved
so faithfully, and she asks the Pasha to spare Belmonte's life.

"Are you shameless enough to plead for him?" asks Selim.

"More than that," Constanze replies, "I will die for him."

Belmonte now intervenes and kneels to plead before the Pasha, saying
that he is the son of a Spanish family who will give all they possess to
ransom him. His name, he says, is Lostados (in some editions of the opera
it is given as "Latades").

This turns out to be a most unfortunate revelation, for Selim learns
that Belmonte is the son of his bitterest enemy, the Commandant Lostados,
who deprived Selim of all he held most dear—his betrothed, his honour,
his happiness and his homeland. The lucky coincidence of now having the
"barbarian" Lostados' son in his power is one which delights Selim and
he goes off with Osmin to discuss the details of the torture he intends to
inflict on the two lovers.

Belmonte and Constanze, left in the charge of the guards, resign themselves to their fate in a long and serious duet which begins, after a moving
recitative, with Belmonte blaming himself bitterly as the cause of Constanze's fate:

Constanze assures her lover that it is not his fault, but hers, and that
she is willing to die with him. The duet changes to a note of exaltation
as the lovers determine to be united in death:

Belmonte and Constanze are joined by Pedrillo and Blonde, who are
also willing and happy to face death together calmly. Pasha Selim now
returns and to everybody's surprise sets Belmonte and Constanze free.
He despises Belmonte's father too much, he says, ever to want to follow his
example in anything.

"Take your freedom and your Constanze," he says to Belmonte, "and
tell your father that though I had you in my power I chose to set you
free."

Pedrillo, hoping to benefit by this unexpected display of magnanimity, pipes up on behalf of Blonde and himself. Osmin objects vociferously—Pedrillo deserves death and Blonde is his slave, but his objection is overruled by the Pasha who says slyly to Osmin: "I'm looking after you better than you realize." And then, speaking for himself as well, he adds: "Those whom you cannot win by kindness it's better not to try and keep by force."

Belmonte starts a song of praise of Pasha Selim, a charming little vaudeville—"Nie werd' ich deine Huld" ("Your princely kindness will never be forgotten . . .")—which begins with this phrase:

and ends with

which is then echoed by the five singing principals. The routine is repeated as first Constanze, then Pedrillo and then Blonde sing what one might consider a "verse" each. Only Blonde's contribution is not followed by the refrain. She teases Osmin beyond endurance and goads him into such a fury that though he starts out singing a paraphrase of the refrain he becomes so increasingly agitated that he finally rages with his famous "raging sequence" in Act I* and storms off.

Quiet returns and after a final verse and refrain from Constanze, the lovers move towards the harbour; the tempo changes to Allegro vivace and the Janissaries sing a vigorous chorus of praise to the just and merciful Pasha. Mozart gives this finale the full "Turkish" treatment with piccolo, cymbals and the rest, and brings down the curtain to a tune which reminds me irresistibly of a later classic called "Hitchy-Koo". Its obvious ancestor was the Janissaries'

Perhaps the finale is a little slight, but it is not entirely out of character; for it serves to remind us that in spite of the magnificence of much of the music we have heard in *Die Entführung aus dem Serail* it is, after all, only a Singspiel.

* See Ex 10, p. 28.

THE MARRIAGE OF FIGARO*
(Le nozze di Figaro)

Comedy for music in four acts by Lorenzo da Ponte, based on Beaumarchais' comedy *La Folle Journée, ou le Mariage de Figaro* (1784). First performed at the Burgtheater, Vienna, on 1st May, 1786, conducted by the composer. First performance in England: 18th June, 1812, Haymarket Theatre, London. First performance in the United States: 10th May, 1824, New York (in English).

It might be appropriate on encountering his name for the first time in this book to say something briefly about the character and career of the librettist of *Figaro*, Lorenzo da Ponte. As his name suggests, he was an Italian (he was born at Ceneda, near Conegliano in Venetia in 1749), but it was a name adopted only after his father, a Jewish leather merchant called Geremia Conegliano, had been received into the Catholic church on marrying, in 1763, a second wife who was a Gentile. Geremia and his three sons, Emanuele, Baruch and Anania, received instruction and in due course were baptized respectively Gasparo, Lorenzo, Girolamo and Luigi.

The surname Da Ponte was assumed by the converts in place of the original Conegliano in accordance with the custom of the time of taking the surname of the dignitary by whom they were baptized: Monsignor Lorenzo da Ponte, Bishop of Ceneda.

The young (or new) Lorenzo da Ponte developed into a colourful figure. He was educated, with his two brothers, by the Bishop† and became a priest. As Abbé da Ponte he then set out to combine the writing of poetry with a life of picaresque, almost Beaumarchaisian dissolution, spending a year in Venice in pursuit of sacred, profane and just ordinarily amorous intrigue. He was expelled from Venice not, as might be supposed, as a result of any glaringly unclerical adventures, but for expressing unorthodox opinions and general dislike of the authorities in libellously satirical pamphlets.

In due course Da Ponte arrived in Vienna. Here in 1783, he was appointed theatre-poet to the Court Opera which, although it was still officially described as the "National-Singspiel", had now reverted to the production of Italian comic opera. The Emperor Joseph II had lost his first enthusiasm for the idea of "German Opera" and had revived the kind of music he understood best.

Mozart met Da Ponte soon after the poet's arrival in Vienna and was promised a libretto by him, a promise which came to nothing, however, until a couple of years later Mozart himself approached Da Ponte with

---

* Mozart's opera has fortunately become so familiar that the English title may be accepted as common usage in English-speaking countries. In practice, however, it is almost universally known simply as *Figaro*.

† This patronage doubtlessly proved most welcome, for the newly-converted head of the family proceeded to have no fewer than another ten children by his new wife.

the idea of making an opera out of Beaumarchais' *La Folle Journée, ou le Mariage de Figaro*.

Beaumarchais' play, the second of what may be called the Almaviva Trilogy, had been written shortly after the first, *The Barber of Seville* (1775)*—at least, the author said so, although French critics consider that the social ideas in the second play are too far advanced for such an early date, even allowing for the speed at which ideas moved in the years preceding that Revolution which, the French have said, "had no more terrible harbingers than the laughter and genius of Beaumarchais."

Whether Beaumarchais was exaggerating or the critics were unwilling to credit him with ideas ahead of his time, there was no question that by the time *La Folle Journée* was first performed in 1784 it was already at least three years old, for that is the length of time the Comédie-Française spent persuading the authorities to permit its production. When it was finally allowed on the Paris stage it was a tremendous success; but while a German translation of the play was published in Vienna its performance was completely prohibited in the Austrian capital.

Mozart nevertheless went ahead with his plan to make an opera out of it, reasoning perhaps that while the authorities might refuse to allow the performance of a play called in German *Figaros Hochzeit*, it would really be too uncharacteristically logical for them to object to an Italian opera called *Le nozze di Figaro*.

Although Mozart's father considered Beaumarchais' to be "a tiresome play" the composer himself was content to have Da Ponte follow the original closely enough. Italian comic opera was such a universally acceptable dramatic form in the 18th century that Beaumarchais originally wrote *The Barber of Seville* as an opera libretto. It was rejected by the Opéra-Comique but the author quickly adapted it as a prose comedy, introducing one or two familiar popular airs, some French, some Spanish, and in this form it was accepted by the Comédie-Française.

His second comedy, *Le Mariage de Figaro*, although it was written slightly less in the style of a comic opera libretto than its predecessor, still made provision for the inclusion of *ariettes* or "numbers" and a conventional everybody-on-the-stage musical finale.

The traditional Italian finale was something which clearly drove Da Ponte frantic when he first encountered it. It was a dogma of theatrical theology, he said, that in a finale all the singers should appear on the stage —even if there were three hundred of them—"by ones, by twos, by threes, by sixes, by sixties, to sing solos, duets, trios, sextets and sessantets." And if the plot of the play didn't allow it, he continued, then the poet must find some way of making the plot allow it.

It was just such a finale on which Beaumarchais based his curtain in *Le Mariage de Figaro*, when no fewer than ten verses of a vaudeville are sung by the eight principals before a merciful *ballet général* finally brings the pl᷉v to an end.

---

* The third play in the trilogy is *L'autre Tartuffe, ou la Mère coupable* ("The Guilty Mother"), written in 1792 and the last play written by Beaumarchais before his death in 1799, aged 67.

In Mozart's opera Da Ponte, as we shall see, solves the problems posed by operatic convention most successfully. Although the bill announcing the first night of *Figaro* at the National-Singspiel describes the work in German as an "Italian Singspiel in Four Acts", Da Ponte and Mozart in fact described the opera not as an "opera buffa", which might have been expected, but significantly as a "commedia per musica"; and when, in his preface to the libretto, Da Ponte wrote that it was the intention of composer and poet to offer "a new type of spectacle" he was not merely expressing the usual mock-modest apology or "pious hope" of the conventional preface. The word he used was "intention", and it was an intention that was clearly fulfilled by the great skill of the poet and the genius of the composer.

The Emperor, who had viewed the project of this Beaumarchais opera with considerable distaste, was eventually won over, it is said, by Mozart playing large parts of the score to him, and it was by command of Joseph II that *Figaro* was produced at the Burgtheater in May 1786. In spite of Leopold Mozart's belief, expressed in a letter to his daughter, that it would be surprising if *Figaro* was a success—"for I know that very powerful cabals have been ranged against your brother"—the opera was not a failure by any means at its first performance.

But it did not hold the public. It was repeated another eight times in the season and then dropped from the repertoire until a year later *Don Giovanni* raised a furore and public interest was aroused in *Figaro* once more.

CHARACTERS IN ORDER OF APPEARANCE:

FIGARO, *valet to Count Almaviva* . . . *Baritone*

SUSANNA, *personal maid to Countess Almaviva* . *Soprano*

DOCTOR BARTOLO, *a physician* . . *Bass*

MARCELLINA, *a duenna* . . . . *Soprano*

CHERUBINO, *a page* . . . . . *Soprano*

COUNT ALMAVIVA . . . . *Baritone*

DON BASILIO, *a music master* . . . *Tenor*

COUNTESS ALMAVIVA . . . . *Soprano*

ANTONIO, *a gardener* . . . . *Bass*

DON CURZIO, *counsellor-at law* . . . *Tenor*

BARBARINA, *Antonio's daughter* . . . *Soprano*

Scene: The Count's château at Agua-Fescas, outside Seville.

Time: 17th century*

* Present-day convention dresses *Figaro* in the costume of Mozart's time. Beaumarchais'
play, like *The Barber of Seville* before it, was a satire on contemporary French manners,
but for the sake of peace and quiet he laid the scene in Spain a century earlier.

ACT I

Scene: A sparsely furnished room, containing a dressing table at one side and a large armchair in the centre of the room.

The curtain rises on *The Marriage of Figaro* after an overture I have seen described in my time as "romping". This is wildly off the mark and, I fear, a typically English misunderstanding—or misrepresentation—of the entire nature of the opera. Mozart always set the atmosphere of his operas in the first few bars of his overtures, and the overture to *Figaro* begins with a whispered suggestion of the intrigue, blackmail and deplorable aristocratic skulduggery which were the objects of Beaumarchais' satire. Whatever else it may do, this overture does not "romp". It insinuates, it flutters and it intrigues; its story is told with the ease of the expert story-teller who understates and times his climax perfectly.

It begins with the unison Presto:

and stays Presto through loud and soft, gay and grotesque passages, an overture surely unmatched in the whole of opera for the feeling of expectancy in which it leaves the audience. It is self-contained inasmuch as it does not quote any music from the opera which follows—which is what happens in the case of *Die Entführung, Don Giovanni, Così fan tutte* and *The Magic Flute*, all of which give the audience a pre-view, or at least a trailer, of what is to come.

The overture to *Figaro* on the other hand, is complete in itself; and if it does not suggest the idea behind Mozart's opera within the first ten seconds or so, then it is not Mozart's fault.

While generations of opera-goers must have heard and enjoyed Mozart's *Marriage of Figaro* without knowing anything of either the first of the Beaumarchais comedies—*The Barber of Seville*—or even the Rossini opera on that subject, it may add to the listener's understanding of *Figaro* to be reminded briefly of what occurred in *The Barber of Seville*.

The earlier episode tells how Count Almaviva marries Rosina under the nose of her guardian, Dr Bartolo, who had hoped to marry her himself. The brains behind the intrigue were those of Figaro, a barber whose profession enabled him to know exactly what was going on in every house in Seville. Among the hangers-on of Dr Bartolo's household were the duenna, Marcellina (formerly Dr Bartolo's mistress), and a thoroughly disreputable priest-cum-music-master called Don Basilio who plays the organ at a convent and is willing to take part in any shady scheme as long as he is paid for it.

By the time the first act of *The Marriage of Figaro* begins the Count and Countess have been married for some time. The barber Figaro has been taken on as personal valet by the Count, as a reward for his services during the course of the plot of *The Barber of Seville*. The Countess, for her part, has acquired a maid called Susanna, and Mozart's opera concerns the marriage of Figaro to Susanna.

In the first scene we discover Figaro and Susanna in the room which is to be their married quarters. It is only half furnished, and in Mahler's great Vienna production of *Figaro* before the First German War, the room was presented as a kind of junk room, a free-for-all right of way in the Count's château where unwanted pieces of furniture were dumped, and the panels of once beautiful damask hung in tattered strips. The curtain should rise, in short, on the dirt and squalor of the 18th century—the servants' quarters of an elegant household in which the Seigneur still has the traditional right to spend the first night with any newly married bride who happens to be in his employ.

It is the wedding day of Figaro and Susanna. Figaro is discovered measuring the floor of the room while Susanna, in front of the mirror, is busy trying on the wreath of orange blossom (known as *le chapeau de mariage*) which she is to wear at her wedding. Figaro is measuring the floor to see if the bed—a present from the Count—will fit or not. He does his counting in a preoccupied tone of voice against an orchestral figure:

Susanna, sitting at the dressing table, is delighted by the success of her headgear which she says is so perfect that it might have been made for her:

Figaro continues his measuring to the accompaniment of his rigid little orchestral figure while Susanna tries in vain to get him to take an interest in her hat. In the end she grows petulant, Figaro puts his ruler away, and like any man in any age, rather absent-mindedly says he likes Susanna's hat. The duet continues happily with Susanna's tune predominating and we discover that, as we suspected all along, the confection that might have been made for her *was* in fact made for her—by herself.

Susanna, we learn, is not in favour of having the room she and Figaro have been given, and in a duet which follows almost immediately they both discuss the question with this figure as accompaniment:

While Figaro points out that the room will be very handy for her when the Countess rings, Susanna suggests—echoing Figaro's onomatopoeic "din-din",—that the room will be equally handy for the Count, who will ring for Figaro—send him off on a distant errand—and—

Figaro now learns from Susanna that the Count has tired of looking for amusement away from home; he is beginning to look a little nearer home for his amorous adventures and his latest quarry is Susanna herself. He proposes, Susanna has heard from Don Basilio, to renew the *droit de seigneur*—a right which he had recently foregone. In the 18th century this right could also include comparatively material and harmless things like demanding the first calf, a share of farm produce off the estate and so on. For Beaumarchais' purpose, however, the *droit de seigneur* meant only one thing. Figaro interprets the *droit de seigneur* that way too, and when Susanna leaves to answer the Countess's bell he rubs his hands and says in effect: "This has gone far enough! The Count wants to be ambassador in London, for instance; and I'm to be his courier to be sent off in all directions while Susanna, I suppose, will be a secret ambassadress. Oh no —take it from Figaro—NO!"

Figaro, alone on the stage, sings the famous aria which so admirably sums up the underlying conflict of the opera, "cunning *versus* force"— "Se vuol ballare, signor contino . . ." ("If you want to dance, my dear respected Count, then you shall—but to *my* music!"):

Though Susanna is perfectly aware of the Count's intentions and is quite able to look after herself to see that he makes no headway with them, Figaro tends to be a little jealous. After all, he knows the Count—and his habits—intimately from *The Barber of Seville*.

We are now introduced to Dr Bartolo and Marcellina. The old duenna has lent Figaro some money and she is encouraged by the Doctor to insist on her rights according to an agreement signed by Figaro: that if Figaro does not repay the money then he must marry Marcellina. This suits Dr Bartolo down to the ground; it would enable him to get his own back on Figaro, who had aided and abetted the Count to marry Rosina in the first place, and it would also mean that Dr Bartolo would be rid of Marcellina, an extremely unattractive figure who so far forgot herself many years before as to bear Dr Bartolo an illegitimate son.

Bartolo swears in a vigorous aria to be revenged—a busy, indignant scene in which the old man gets increasingly excited in the grand *buffo* tradition:

The Doctor storms off, obviously highly delighted by the opportunity now arising to gratify his antagonistic feelings towards Figaro.

Susanna returns, carrying her bridal dress over her arm, and in the duet which she sings with Marcellina we encounter one of the clearest examples of Mozart's great gift of characterization. In the Susanna-Marcellina duet we have the old duenna behaving with sarcastically exaggerated politeness towards Susanna, referring to her bitterly as "the Count's beautiful Susanna." Susanna, being a perfect lady herself (she is, after all, maid to the greatest lady on the operatic stage, as we shall see), behaves with great dignity, but permits herself the sly and apparently irrelevant observation that her dress is so old—a remark which (as intended) is misunderstood by Marcellina to refer to herself.

This duet is almost a "throw-away" sequence in *Figaro*, but it is full of delicious and witty touches. There is a neatly suggested air of insincere and over-formal politeness in the violin figure which runs through the scene:

and in the way in which the two women make their reverences and insist (in canon) that they are well-bred and know how to behave:

(That tune is one which Mozart first used in the slow movement of the Serenade in D—K.203—written in 1773 and the Andante grazioso of a work otherwise full of rather obvious allusions suitable to the wedding festivities for which it was composed. Again we have Mozart's perplexing ability to make the same thing have two different meanings.)

The character of Susanna, whom we have now heard in three duets, will be seen to dominate *Figaro* from the very first moment she sings, and for all that she may seem to some to be no more than a charming soubrette, she is in fact the one person who keeps her head and succeeds in sorting out everybody else's troubles as well as her own.

The next of Susanna's troubles is Cherubino, the Countess's page. Cherubino has been described as having a genius for being found in the wrong place. He is a wild boy—young enough to be sung by a soprano—who is suffering from Love's Awakening; he falls in love with everybody in sight and it is always with the wrong woman. The wrong woman, on Cherubino's first entry, seems to be Barbarina, the gardener's daughter, with whom he had been discovered by the Count on the previous evening. As a result the Count has given the page notice.

In a short scene with Susanna, Cherubino reveals that he is also in love with the Countess and how envious he is of Susanna (whom he adores shamelessly) that she should be allowed to undress the Countess at night. He grabs a hair ribbon which belongs to the Countess from Susanna's hand; he refuses to give it back, but in exchange makes her a present of a *canzonetta* he has composed.

"What am I supposed to do with it?" asks Susanna.

"Read it to the Countess," replies Cherubino, "to Barbarina—to Marcellina—to every woman in the palace——"

The poor boy doesn't honestly know whether he's on his head or his heels and in a most revealing aria—"Non so più cosa son, cosa faccio" ("I don't know what I am, nor what I'm doing . . .")—he confesses that every woman he meets makes him dizzy, confused and speechless:

The room belonging, we are told, to Figaro and Susanna, is now invaded by the Count (we have already had Dr Bartolo, Marcellina and Cherubino dropping in to pass the time of day), and on the Count's approach Cherubino hides himself behind a chair—the only article of furniture, apart from the mirror, specifically mentioned in the stage directions for this "partly furnished" room.

The Count brings up the question of his ambassadorship in London, and is trying to persuade Susanna what an admirable thing it would be for their relationship if she came with him when there are more footsteps outside. The Count makes a move towards the door. Cherubino takes advantage of this to leave his position behind the chair and sit *in* the chair, where Susanna covers him with her bridal dress. The Count decides not to leave the room, but hides instead behind the chair in exactly the same place as Cherubino has just left.

The newcomer is Don Basilio, the corrupt and gossiping music master, who arrives with a number of insinuating details about Cherubino's behaviour towards Susanna and the Countess. The Count overhears this and emerges from behind the chair. In the course of an admirable trio in which he is joined by Susanna, who is appalled by the turn things are taking, and by Basilio, who is delighted, the Count relates the shocking incident of Cherubino and Barbarina, how he had gone to Barbarina's room and (to his obvious fury at being forestalled) had found Cherubino hidden there, under the table.

There is one intriguing musical phrase which recurs from time to time
in various forms during this trio:

It is heard most effectively as the Count, picking up the dress from
Susanna's chair by way of demonstration, says: "I drew aside the table
cloth, and there—was the page." For the second time in a couple of days
the Count has discovered Cherubino in a compromising situation, and
Mozart illustrates the reaction of the three onlookers with a wonderfully
subdued and unexpected inversion of the phrase I have just quoted—
with the Count extremely surprised, Susanna horrified, and Don Basilio
curled up with malicious laughter:

The Count now naturally thinks the worst of everybody. He is convinced that Susanna is having an affair with the page; he is furious with
the page not only for being more successful with Susanna than he is himself, but also because Cherubino, who swears he tried to overhear as
little as possible, must have overheard him making love to Susanna.
Don Basilio slaps his thighs at all this, as it has turned out far better than
he ever imagined in his own most lurid dreams.

As the trio gets under way again the careful listener may discern Don
Basilio's first remark (on the Count's suspicion of Susanna) that "all
beautiful women behave like that—it's as old as the hills"—words which
in the original Italian are significantly prophetic of a subsequent Mozart-
Da Ponte masterpiece: "Così fan tutte le belle. . . ."

The Count, one way and another, is in an awkward position when
Figaro arrives with a chorus of the Count's staff who strew flowers, sing a
tribute to the Count's magnanimity in abolishing the *droit de seigneur*, and
bring Susanna's wedding veil which the Count is asked to place on her
head as a symbol of the bride's innocence. The hint of irony in Figaro's
voice as he explains the significance of the veil doesn't pass unnoticed by
the Count and he decides to postpone the wedding ceremony until
another time. The chorus which praises, among other things, the Count's
noble defence of virtue and the white purity of his soul, repeats its little
laudatory hymn and departs.

The question of Cherubino is opened again, and the Count, pointedly
observing on Susanna's intercession, that the page isn't nearly such a child
as she thinks, forgives him. More than that: he gives him a commission
in his own regiment to be taken up that very day. The Count leaves with
Don Basilio, his *entrepreneur* in extra-marital matters, remarking out of the
side of his mouth that *that* was something nobody expected.

The scene ends with Figaro's famous aria "Non più andrai"—a military song used nowadays by the Coldstream Guards as a regimental march—in which Figaro warns Cherubino that his days of philandering are over. Figaro dilates on the glories and advantages of a military career, and he does so with extra relish, for the departure of Cherubino means the departure of an ever-present menace to his own happiness. We, in the audience, know Susanna far better than Figaro does; but on the stage—perhaps rightly—nobody trusts anybody else an inch.

And so Act I comes to a close with this tune:

There is one production touch to be noted which I remember was introduced by Bruno Walter in Berlin in the late 1920's. On the general exit, Susanna pushes Figaro through the door ahead of her and stays behind for a moment to kiss Cherubino. So perhaps we don't know Susanna as well as we thought.

ACT II

Scene: The Countess's room, luxuriously furnished and containing an alcove. To the right, a door; to the left, a dressing room; at the back, another door leading through to the servants' quarters. There is a window with a balcony at one side of the stage.

The curtain rises at once to introduce the Countess, who is alone with her thoughts—a situation, one imagines, to which she has been no stranger since her marriage to the Count. Her thoughts take shape in an aria, "Porgi amor", in which she beseeches the god of Love to bring relief to her pain and sighs, and, if not to return her love to her, at least to allow her to die in peace.

There is a quality of dignity about this aria which it seems only Mozart was ever able to translate into music without becoming either pompous, sanctimonious or tedious. It is a quality, indeed, so peculiar to the composer that it explains, I believe, why the Italians seem unable either to perform Mozart properly or to understand him. The Italians are by nature incapable of portraying on the operatic stage the elusive characteristics of what we understand by a Lady, and this is never more noticeable than when an Italian soprano attempts either of the Countess's two arias in *Figaro*. She may be the finest Violetta, Desdemona, Aïda, Mimi or Butterfly of her time, but the moment she tackles Mozart's Countess she is out of her class. It is not a question of sounding "aristocratic", of having the right voice even; it is just a matter of being that indefinable, inimitable thing which has nothing to do with "class"—a Lady. And in the Italian opera tradition no provision is made for the woman who has the instinctive good manners and natural breeding necessary to qualify. There is nothing, indeed, between the enchanting but hardly aristocratic perkiness of Rossini's Rosina (who could ever imagine her developing into the superbly poised figure of *The Barber*'s operatic sequel?) and the high tragedy of Amneris and Aïda.

Nobody will imagine, of course, that the Countess being a lady prevents her from showing her real feelings—at least, when she is alone—and we are not altogether surprised to hear a phrase of such genuine pathos as this:

A short, moving two-bar coda is shared by the clarinet and that least likely of instruments, the bassoon, from which Mozart seemed uniquely able to draw the most touching and unexpected lyrical sounds.

Susanna enters, closely followed by Figaro, and between the three of them a plot is hatched to make the Count jealous: an anonymous letter is to be sent to him telling him that his wife has made a rendezvous with another man. It is also arranged that Cherubino (who has not yet left the castle) shall be dressed up in Susanna's clothes and sent to meet the Count in the garden in an assignation which Susanna is to make with her master.

Figaro leaves, singing a few threatening bars of his song, "Se vuol ballare, signor contino." The plot is obviously a good one.

Cherubino now appears and is persuaded by Susanna to sing the song he has written for the Countess—"Voi che sapete" ("You who know what love is, tell me if that is what I have in my heart"):

This aria (ostensibly sung to Susanna's guitar accompaniment, but in fact to the chamber-music combination of flute, oboe, clarinet, bassoon, a pair of horns and pizzicato strings) does not throw any new or unusual light on Cherubino's character, though it shows him to be an abnormally promising young composer and lyric-writer. But "Voi che sapete" is no more than a song in its own right, introduced to entertain the Countess and to allow the page to hold her attention. The real Cherubino is heard in "Non so più cosa son, cosa faccio", for there he is being himself and not performing a deliberate party-piece, which in any case had always been part of the action of Le Mariage de Figaro before Da Ponte started transforming a comedy with music into a comedy for music. In Beaumarchais' original comedy the "romance" sung at this point was written to fit the tune of the old French folk-song "Marlbroug s'en va-t-en guerre," which is better known in Anglo-Saxon countries as "For he's a jolly good fellow" and "We won't go home till morning."

Cherubino, having finished his little recital, is noticed by the Countess to be carrying his commission patent in his belt; she notices too that the seal is missing.

Susanna now starts to dress Cherubino in women's clothes, and she does so in her first solo number—an aria which gives us yet another insight into her character; we are shown her sense of fun, and her firmness with the page who will not pay attention but keeps turning round to look at the Countess. The scene takes place to "Venite, inginocchiatevi" ("Come here and kneel down"):

While Susanna is dressing Cherubino the Countess notices that the page has one of her ribbons bound round his arm—to tie up a small cut, the boy explains. The Countess asks for the ribbon back and tells Susanna to get some "English taffeta" to use as a bandage in its place. She likes the colour of the ribbon and doesn't want to part with it. Cherubino reluctantly returns the ribbon.

Cherubino is now fully disguised, when the Count is heard knocking at the Countess's door. The page flees into the dressing-room, Susanna hides behind a curtain and the Countess opens the door. The Count, who has come to see about the anonymous letter he has just received, is immediately suspicious of his wife's obvious embarrassment. She doesn't usually lock her door, he points out, and his suspicions grow stronger when he tries the door into the dressing room and finds it locked. The Countess explains lamely that Susanna is inside.

"Susanna?" asks the Count. "Are you so perturbed because of *Susanna*?"

The Countess raises her eyebrows: "I? Susanna?"

"Well, you're excited, anyway," retorts the Count; to which his wife replies slyly: "If anybody's getting excited over Susanna, it's you, not me——"

The Count angrily orders the Countess to open the locked door and shouts to Susanna (whom he supposes to be inside) to come out. The Countess does her best to stall, and a duologue is transformed into a trio by the return of Susanna who hides in the alcove, invisible to the other two, and contributes her own comments in a scene which begins with the angry orchestral phrase:

The Count goes off to fetch the necessary tools to open the door, taking his wife with him and locking the main door to her room.

Susanna comes out of her hiding place, calls Cherubino from the dressing room, and at the end of a breathless duet, accompanied by strings only and marked Allegro assai,

the page boy escapes by the window into the garden. Susanna now locks herself in the dressing room.

The Count and Countess return, and though she refuses to give her husband the key, she confesses that it is only Cherubino in the inner room anyway. This information makes the Count angrier than ever, and he starts to break down the door, crying, "Esci ormai, garzon malnato" ("Come out at once, miserable boy!"). This inaugurates the Finale of Act II, an episode of some 150 pages of score without parallel in opera as a scene of monumental invention and design.

For some time the musical action is confined to a somewhat acrimonious duet between the Count and Countess—the husband intolerably aggressive, the wife trying to reason with him and convince him of her innocence and Cherubino's, but making things worse by saying that the page in the closet is only half dressed. The Countess is so flustered, indeed, that she scarcely knows what she is saying, and the argument sways backwards and forwards with variants of this theme predominating:

The Count breaks down the door and, sword in hand, he is confronted by Susanna. Both Count and Countess utter only one word: "Susanna!" —he with a slightly disappointed air of surprise, she with amazed, inexpressible relief at having got out of a dilemma which had seemed insoluble. Susanna stands at the door, the picture of wide-eyed innocence and the most delightful anti-climax in the musical theatre; and assuming an air of surprise which both matches and mocks that of the Count and Countess Mozart reproduces this mass-astonishment with this wonderfully understated phrase in the orchestra:

Susanna, mistress of nearly every situation in which she finds herself, permits herself the little ironical comment: "What is this excitement? The drawn sword? To kill the page? And it's only me after all!" The Count, so far from being humiliated by being made a fool of, refuses to believe that Susanna was alone in the dressing room and goes inside to search it. While he is out of the room the tempo of the music changes and Susanna is able to tell her mistress not to worry as Cherubino has escaped. This change of mood introduces a new figure,

which is developed through a variety of keys and ingenious transformations while the Count, his suspicions finally proved unfounded, tells the Countess that he loves her and asks her forgiveness. The Countess ironically retorts that as the guilty, unfaithful wife *she* is the one who should ask forgiveness. The Count then turns to Susanna and asks for her help; he gets an ironic answer from her too, but she turns to the Countess and asks her to forgive her husband.

The Count goes down on his knees before his wife and addresses her, for the first time in our hearing, as Rosina. The Countess turns on her husband with a sudden angry bitterness—"Crudele! più quella non sono!" ("No, not Rosina any more . . .")

and then sadly suggests that all she is now is the unhappy victim of his neglect and indifference.

Those three bars can have an astonishing effect in the theatre, with the pause to let their significance sink in before the easy course of the Allegro is resumed with the return of the theme in Ex 22. It is only a tiny incident in the finale, but a tremendously telling one, a point which Mozart makes with all his unerring sense of timing and dramatic emphasis.

The Count is still puzzled by the way the Countess behaved—by her story that the page was in the dressing room, by her obvious embarrassment; but she laughs it off by saying it was all done to provoke and tease him. But the anonymous letter? Susanna and the Countess answer together that it was only a joke of Figaro's. The Count asks the Countess's forgiveness again and this time is granted it.

Figaro now appears, full of his usual busy brashness, with a phrase which is admirably contrasted with the trio that has just ended:

This is a tune for which Mozart seems to have had a particular affection, for it is taken over all but bodily from a symphony he had written 21 years before, when as a child of nine at The Hague he had used the theme in his Symphony in B flat (K.22):

Figaro, on his entrance, tells the Count enthusiastically that everything is ready for the wedding celebrations—trumpets, pipers, singers and dancers. The Count quietens him down, to the consternation of the Countess and Susanna, who fear the worst.

"Tell me, Figaro," says the Count, showing him the anonymous letter, "do you know anything about this?"

Figaro, who has learned the art of craftiness and mendacity in the best houses of Seville, denies all knowledge of the affair and ignores all the efforts of the Countess and Susanna to prompt him and get him to admit that he wrote it. They beseech him to the strains of a wonderful warmly-scored tune which could hardly fail to persuade the most obstinate:

(This is another passage where the student of orchestration should study Mozart's writing for the viola; this time instead of playing in octaves with the first violins—a favourite and effective habit—the violas play in unison with violoncellos.)

In the final stages of this little quartet the Count, who has not yet given his consent to the marriage of Figaro and Susanna, prays out loud for the arrival of Marcellina, whose claim on Figaro can alone justify the Count's delay in giving his consent.

It looks as if everything is going to turn out all right for Figaro and Susanna when the tempo and key change once again and to the accompaniment of this figure:

Antonio, the drunken gardener, appears complaining that somebody has jumped out of a window on to his flower bed and broken a flower pot.

Figaro quickly asserts that he was the culprit and, what is more, hurt his leg in the process. The tempo suddenly slows to an ominous kind of Andante and to a four-bar figure which Mozart keeps going as the background to the ingenious scene which follows:

On Figaro's admission of responsibility for the broken flower pot Antonio says, "Ah, then you must have dropped this paper"; and he takes from his pocket Cherubino's commission patent. The Count grabs the paper and turning to Figaro asks exactly what kind of document it would be. The Countess recognizes it, tells Susanna, who passes on the information in a whisper to Figaro, who gives the correct answer.

The Count now asks why the paper should have been in Figaro's possession. There is an awkward silence, some clever stalling by Figaro while the Countess prompts him *via* Susanna, and Figaro, with great confidence, is able to announce that Cherubino gave him the paper because the seal is missing.

This explanation is just about to satisfy the Count and a happy ending is dawning when Marcellina appears, accompanied by Dr Bartolo and Don Basilio. They address the Count as one, demanding justice and a hearing of Marcellina's case against Figaro. This long-hoped-for coup delights the Count; he still hopes to prevent Susanna marrying Figaro, and he consents to hear the case. Or rather—to try and listen to the case. The uproar caused by all the interested parties becomes so clamorous that the Count frequently, but rather unsuccessfully, has to call for silence with what sounds to be a commanding phrase, but its effectiveness never lasts long; the contestants resume their arguments after scarcely more than a moment's *silenzio*:

The upshot of this general debate is that the Count postpones Figaro's wedding, and the act ends with an ensemble of seven characters which had begun its musical life with the Count on his own asking for the key of the inner room.

This finale to the second act of *Figaro* is one of the most remarkable pieces of music ever conceived for the opera house. Though no fewer than eight characters are introduced in the course of it, and there are as many changes of tempo—from the understated Andante that greets Susanna's appearance from the dressing room to the furious, drunken outburst which introduces Antonio—the whole scene (which plays the best part of twenty minutes) builds up steadily with never a false climax nor an inconsistent or artificial stroke.

Perhaps, on paper, the principle of this finale is not so far removed from that of the typical Italian finale which Da Ponte described so amusingly*, but in practice it differs in one important respect: while there had been hundreds of librettos providing surprise after surprise in the action, there had hitherto been no Mozart to provide them in the music.

* See p. 48.

ACT III

Scene: A large room in the Count's palace, decorated for the wedding feast of Susanna and Figaro.

The Count enters alone and reflects, in recitative, on the state of the plot so far: an anonymous letter, a serving maid in the dressing room, one man jumps out of the window and another says *he* did it—it makes very little sense. While he is soliloquizing the Countess and Susanna appear in the background—Susanna reluctant to proceed with the plot to lead the Count, literally, up the garden path, and the Countess egging her on, her peace of mind (she reminds Susanna) depending upon it.

The Countess leaves and Susanna approaches the Count, asking him for a bottle of smelling salts she needs for her mistress who has the vapours. She thanks him and promises to return it. "Oh no," says the Count, "keep it for yourself."

Susanne replies that a girl of her class can't enjoy the luxury of the vapours. The Count suggests that for a girl who is losing her fiancé on her wedding day—. But Susanna retorts that she is proposing to pay off Marcellina with the dowry the Count promised her.

"That *I* promised?" asks the Count. "When?"

"Well," says Susanna, "that's what I understood."

"If only," the Count sighs, "you would ever understand me"—and there follows one of the most ravishing and subtle duets ever written.

It begins with an eager, anxious phrase from the Count—"Crudel! perchè finora farmi languir così?" ("Why do you torment me so cruelly?")

31. Andante

Cru-del! per-chè fi-no-ra far- -mi languir co-si?

With consummate coolness Susanna switches the key from a restless A minor to the calm C major with: "Signor, la donna ognora tempo ha di dir così" ("There is always time for a woman to change her mind"):

32. Andante

Si-gnor, la don-na o-gno-ra tem-po ha di dir co- si.

The Count suggests a rendezvous later in the garden; Susanna agrees to it but from time to time says "yes" when she means "no"—"You'll come to the garden?—Yes—You won't forget?—Yes—Yes?—No . . ."

In this duet we have our first glimpse of the Count as a seducer; at least, we cannot doubt that he is sincere in his designs on Susanna when he sings:

Susanna, musically and physically, keeps him at arm's length, but promises him the rendezvous.

As Susanna leaves she meets Figaro for a moment in the background and tells him that the case against Marcellina is all over bar the shouting.

The Count overhears this and sings his only solo aria in the opera. It is a surprising song; a bitter, vindictive outburst against Figaro which leaves us with the impression that the Count is as full of blind revenge as Dr Bartolo. This unexpected side of the Count's character is emphasized not only by the vigorous and angry orchestrally-accompanied recitative in which his first reactions are expressed, but also by the violent introduction to the aria itself.*

The Count's opening words of the aria—"Vedrò, mentr'io sospiro" ("And is my servant to enjoy the pleasures that I am denied?")—are transformed from a rough declamatory phrase into a firm, determined tune,

and the aria ends on an almost sinister note as the Count, with increasing anger, cries that no servant of his was born to torment him and laugh at his misfortune.

The student of orchestration will find several subtle touches in this aria, notably the wonderfully effective writing for the timpani which, together with trumpets, are introduced to add fierceness to the music, as they were in Bartolo's first-act "Vendetta" aria. Otherwise trumpets and drums occur only in the finales, choruses and more military moments of *Figaro.*

* The bass part of this seems to be yet another variant of the opening of the "Haffner" Symphony (see p. 43).

The scene is now invaded by the breach-of-promise brigade—Marcellina, Bartolo and their stuttering lawyer, Don Curzio. A trial has been held off-stage (in Beaumarchais' play it is held in front of the audience) and Figaro is condemned to marry Marcellina. This, however, Figaro tells us he cannot do without the consent of his parents and he doesn't know who or where his parents are, though he hopes to find them some day. He has a mark on his arm, he says, which may help to identify him. Figaro shows his birthmark and his identity is established at once: he is Marcellina's son and Dr Bartolo is his father.

The subsequent quintet of recognition (the Count plays an independent and surly part in it, for he—like Don Curzio—has nothing to rejoice over) is turned into a sextet by Susanna as eavesdropper. Susanna has the money which the Countess has given her, to pay off Marcellina's claim, but seeing Figaro kissing the old harridan affectionately immediately thinks the worst. This, like everything else in the opera, is successfully explained away, Figaro indicating first his mother and then his father—"Who will tell you themselves":

35. Andante

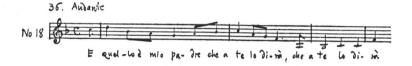

No 18

E quel-lo è mio pa- dre che a te lo di-rà, che a te lo di- rà

Susanna embraces her future parents-in-law (for they have decided to get married at the same time as Susanna and Figaro) and a general exit leaves the stage empty once more.

A short scene in recitative follows between Cherubino and Barbarina, the gardener's daughter. Cherubino has still not left for the Count's regiment and is only too willing to be persuaded to dress up as a peasant girl and stay for the wedding festivities.

The Countess now enters, expecting to find Susanna. In a short recitative she laments that she should be brought to such low tricks as planning to change clothes with Susanna in order to regain her husband. (The original plan to disguise Cherubino as Susanna has been dropped.) This recitative—one of the few in *Figaro* accompanied by the orchestra—reveals Mozart at his greatest as a delineator of character. In the ordinary way, of course, recitative is a convenient way of performing dialogue between the set numbers of an opera; it should be sung at the speed of spoken dialogue and written to fit the cadences of the language in which the libretto is written. (One reason why the recitative in Italian operas so often sounds ludicrous in English or German is that nobody has remembered to rewrite the vocal line to fit the natural speech cadences of the performers.)

In this solo scene, however, Mozart's recitative allows the Countess to express her thoughts as deeply and clearly as she does in the aria which follows, for while the words of the aria are poetic, the words of her recitative are direct and personal. It is the dialogue, in fact, of a woman whose heart is near breaking.

In the aria itself we have a complete portrait of the Countess, whose disappointments have never allowed her to become embittered, who— though her husband has obviously deceived her from her wedding day— bears no malice, and who, above all things, remembers that good manners are the foundation of society.

"Dove sono," sings the Countess, "i bei momenti di dolcezza e di piacer?" ("Where are they, those lovely moments of sweetness and pleasure, and the promises of those lying lips?"):

Once more, in this aria, there are those little touches of detail in the orchestral writing which make the study of Mozart's scores so fascinating. In this case it is the use of the oboe, sometimes solo, sometimes with the bassoon in octaves, as a means of adding a plaintive, between-the-lines comment of a movingly sad and wistful nature. A final Allegro section brings the aria to a close with the Countess praying for the fulfilment of what is now her only hope: that somehow her constancy will change her husband's ungrateful heart.

Susanna now appears and the Countess begins to dictate a letter to confirm Susanna's assignation—"under the pines when the gentle zephyrs blow."

In this scene Mozart shows what must have been a wonderful and revolutionary sense of stage timing. The Countess dictates her letter and Susanna repeats it, but like any stenographer, misunderstands words and phrases from time to time and has to be told again. When the letter is finished mistress and servant read it out together and we hear a reprise of the opening tune:

The letter, when written, is addressed to the Count. He is to meet Susanna in the garden—only it will not be Susanna, but the Countess dressed in Susanna's clothes. As there is no means of sealing the letter a brooch is used to close it, and a request written on the back of the envelope that the brooch be returned to the sender.

The quiet atmosphere of the duet is now disturbed by the arrival of a chorus of peasant girls strewing flowers before the Countess:

In addition to the chorus there comes Figaro, Cherubino (dressed as a peasant girl), Barbarina, Marcellina, Dr Bartolo, and the Count. Antonio, the gardener, follows not far behind carrying Cherubino's hat, which he ostentatiously claps on the page's head (nothing, it seems, ever gets past Antonio). Barbarina comes to Cherubino's rescue by publicly reminding the Count that when he kissed her he promised to grant anything she wished: and she wants Cherubino as a husband—an unexpected development which really makes the Count begin to wonder whether it is man, devil or angel that is upsetting all his plans.

The wedding ceremony now begins, and a procession approaches to a march whose basis is

The Count and Countess mount a dais and take their seats with the Count muttering vengeance ("Let us be seated and meditate on revenge" are his words).

The principal part of the ceremony now follows. Susanna is taken by Dr Bartolo and presented to the Count, Marcellina by Figaro who presents her to the Countess. The two brides kneel and receive their bridal wreaths, veils and gloves. As an accompaniment to the ceremony two girls sing a little song in praise of the wise *seigneur* who, by so generously foregoing the ancient *droit*, enables the brides to begin married life in a state of virginal innocence:

It may be because nobody listens to or cares what small-part singers are singing about that, in my experience, the full flavour of the delightful irony of this little duet is rarely recognized or appreciated; but if ever there was an inappropriate song to sing in such inappropriate circumstances, this is it—with Marcellina being made an honest woman of while the Count is entirely preoccupied with the prospect of seducing her soon-to-be-legitimized son's bride without benefit of seignorial rights, renounced or otherwise.

A few bars of choral praise end the scene and the music switches to a dance rhythm—a fandango—which is Mozart's only suggestion of local

Spanish colour during the whole course of an opera which, after all, is supposed to be set on the outskirts of Seville. The fandango

42. Andante

No 22

was already familiar as a popular dance tune to the audience hearing *Figaro* for the first time, for it had been interpolated in very much the same form in Gluck's ballet of *Don Juan* (1761).

Dramatically the fandango is the background music of some important stage action. While dancing is going on Susanna kneels before the Count, tugs at his coat and shows the letter she has in her hand. She raises her hand to straighten the wreath on her head and as she does so the Count helps her to adjust it and takes the letter. He hides it quickly, Susanna rises to her feet, curtsies and is escorted to the dance by Figaro. Marcellina, in turn, curtsies to the Countess and joins the general company with Bartolo.

The Count finds an opportunity to read the letter but in opening it pricks his finger on the pin of the brooch which has been used to fasten it. "How like women," he complains, "always pins everywhere!" Then he understands its purpose.

Figaro, who has been watching all this, makes both comment and running-commentary to Susanna on the actions of the Count (whom he refers to as "il Narcisso") remarking that it was clearly a love-letter, that the Count had pricked himself with the pin and, having thrown it away, is apparently looking for it again. The Count retrieves the pin and rising to his feet invites the company to take part in the wedding banquet, dancing and fireworks to be held that night.

The act ends with a fully choral version of the song first sung by the two girls and which might be paraphrased as

> *O happy bride, give praise to him*
> *Who for your sake, 'tis said,*
> *Has nobly sacrificed his right*
> *To share your bridal bed.*

Or words—very roughly—to that effect.

ACT IV

*Scene: The garden of the Count's castle, with a pavilion on either side of the stage.
It is night.*

Barbarina enters carrying a paper lantern; she has lost the brooch
which the Count has given her to take to Susanna with a message. As she
searches hopelessly Barbarina sings her only solo in the opera—a short,
charming little lament for the lost brooch which starts off in the deliberately inappropriate and serious key of F minor,

and ends in a half-finished way with:

If this tiny scene is not omitted altogether from the opera (which it
sometimes is) it sometimes takes place, not in the garden, but in a dark
corridor. There is no good reason either for omitting the music or changing
the scene (which is a trick peculiar to German "production" and some
German vocal scores, for some reason—it is not in Da Ponte's original),
for Barbarina's cavatina is a delightful, if slightly exaggerated, portrait
in miniature of a simple and bewildered girl. Barbarina's simplicity,
indeed, leads to her giving away the whole story of the Count and his
rendezvous with Susanna when Figaro arrives to ask her what she's
looking for.

She tells him, and when Marcellina arrives on the scene Figaro takes
a pin from his mother's dress and hands it to Barbarina, telling her to
give that to Susanna.

Figaro goes off in a burning rage, leaving Marcellina to sing an aria in
which she expresses her belief that all women should unite to deal with
the fickle and quarrelsome race of men: "Il capro e la capretta" ("The
goat and his mate, the ram and his ewe—they can all live in peace . . ."):

This minuet leads into a final and florid Allegro:

Marcellina leaves and Barbarina returns, carrying a basket of food for Cherubino whom she has planned to meet in one of the pavilions. She disappears inside it as Figaro comes back followed by Dr Bartolo and Don Basilio. Figaro bids them reflect on what he tells them: that if they will hang around unobserved for a little while they will see the Count keeping an appointment to revive the archaic but interesting custom of the *droit de seigneur*.

Once more Figaro leaves, saying that when he whistles they must hurry to him at once. Dr Bartolo is rather puzzled by the whole situation, but Don Basilio, whom none will trust with a secret but from whom equally it is impossible to keep one, knows all about everything already and explains something of his method: "In quegli anni" ("Through all these years I have pretended to be a fool . . ."):

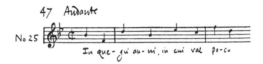

Like Marcellina's, Basilio's aria opens in one tempo and ends in another—Basilio, for some reason, before coming to his final Allegro, breaking into a longish interlude in the form of a minuet:

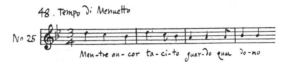

These arias for Marcellina and Basilio are often omitted, and with far more justification than Barbarina's little cavatina, for they tell us nothing about these characters that we did not know already. The music in each case sounds—as it probably was—something of an afterthought by Mozart as though he had suddenly and all too obviously remembered that these smaller characters ought to do something to justify their engagement.

I have nevertheless referred to these two numbers in a little detail, however, because although one rarely hears them in the theatre, they are included in most complete gramophone recordings of the opera.

The first important musical contribution in Act IV comes from Figaro in an aria inspired by the information he has received from Barbarina. Figaro has had two arias before, both of them good-humoured; this third one, however, which is introduced significantly with an orchestrally-accompanied recitative, shows him playing the part of the deceived husband in a fury as he admonishes all men to open their eyes a little and look at what women really are—"Aprite un po' quegli'occhi. . ."

The aria ends with an admirable musical pun. Figaro's anger at being deceived, as he thinks, receives loud orchestral comment from the horns, traditional symbols of the cuckold:

Meanwhile, Marcellina has warned Susanna to watch out for trouble from Figaro, so when Susanna arrives with the Countess (each wearing the other's clothes) she asks if she may rest alone for a while among the pine trees. Figaro, who has hidden himself and overheard this, knows that the rendezvous with the Count was to be at just this spot, and Susanna knows that he knows it too. What Figaro doesn't know is that he, not the Count, is the subject of Susanna's reflections when she sings "Deh vieni, non tardar . . ." ("Ah come, do not delay, dear joy!").

Again, as in the case of the Countess' great aria, "Dove sono", Mozart introduces Susanna's scene with a recitative which belongs completely to her character. We have learned that Susanna is level-headed, that she has a sense of fun; we know too, from the conversations she has had with the Countess, that she is much more than a mere personal maid. It is not until this moment that we really suspect Susanna of any great depth of feeling. But just as the Countess, in her two great arias, movingly expresses resignation, so Susanna movingly anticipates the happy ending to which she believes her married life with Figaro, will lead. Knowing what an incorrigible cynic Beaumarchais was, it may be too much to believe that this would really happen. But while Susanna sings her lovely, subdued aria—perhaps the most sensual and perfect that Mozart ever wrote—we believe and pray wholeheartedly that a love-affair which leads to such music as this can only end in sublime happiness:

The miraculous atmosphere of this aria is achieved by the simplest possible means—an accompaniment of strings and three solo wood-wind instruments framing the incomparable line of an incomparable tune.

From now on we have the finale—some fifteen minutes of it—which is devoted to the ravelling and unravelling of typical comic opera complications and mistaken identities. First to arrive is Cherubino, dressed as an officer (the first time we have seen him in male costume for quite a while), who starts making love to the Countess, thinking—from the clothes she wears—that she is Susanna. The Count turns up in the middle of a flirtation which is obviously more than the Countess can cope with, and receives the full force of the page's kiss; whereon the Count is angry, not because Cherubino was trying to kiss the Countess, but because he was—apparently—trying to kiss Susanna. The confusion continues when Figaro steps out of the background and the Count boxes his ears in mistake for the page's. Figaro and Cherubino vanish and the Count is left making love to the supposed Susanna, giving her a ring in token of his intentions and arranging to meet her later.

Next Figaro, wandering and peering around the garden to the momentary breather provided by this Larghetto,

finds the real Susanna and, assuming from her disguise that she is the Countess, suggests that she should go with him and catch the Count with Susanna.

As in the finale of the second act the development and ingenious exploitation of little themes plays a great part in the construction of this finale. This scene between Susanna and Figaro is based on the simple string phrase:

and on one which, forgetting for a moment to disguise her voice, Susanna sings and so gives herself away:

Figaro pretends not to notice but starts to make love to the supposed Countess to annoy Susanna. The trick does annoy Susanna, and she boxes Figaro's ears soundly—a reaction which greatly pleases Figaro and leads to the differences of at least two of the characters being cleared up. Figaro celebrates the outbreak of peace with a gay little tune to which he

explains (to her delight) that he recognized Susanna by the voice he loves
so much:

But things are still pretty chaotic among the rest of the characters.
The Count, fooled by Susanna's costume, turns up during this same 6/8
movement to find Figaro making love to her and accuses him of trying to
seduce the Countess.

The Count, true to character, leaves the "Countess" in the highest
possible dudgeon and immediately makes his way to one of the pavilions
to keep his assignation with Susanna; he opens the door to meet Cherubino coming out, who has been inside with Barbarina.

The whole confusion is cleared up by the sudden appearance of the
Countess, dressed in her own clothes, while the rest of the assembled
company is asking the Count to forgive what he believes is his wife's
infidelity with Figaro. The Count—as if he were in any moral position
to forgive anybody anything—is busily shouting "No," when the Countess
enters to a graceful phrase which immediately puts everybody in their
place. To the words "Perhaps at least I may intercede for them . . .?" the
Countess sings:

Once more, in the space of four bars, Mozart sums up the character
of the Countess, her dignity, her good manners and her belief that it is
high time everybody grew up and stopped playing the fool. While
Susanna may be said to have dominated the opera until now, it is the
Countess who finally stands out as the great and wholly enchanting figure
that she is.*

A complete change of mood and tempo accompanies the Count's own
change of heart—or at least, of attitude—and he asks the Countess's
forgiveness with this somewhat uncharacteristic phrase:

* I was surprised and not a little shocked to see that in recent productions of *Figaro*
the Vienna State Opera—of all people—allow the Countess to reappear in this final
scene wearing *Susanna's* clothes. In Bruno Walter's superb Berlin production in 1928 the
Countess's clothes matched the dazzling breath-taking effect of those four bars in the
music. It was such a tremendous moment, indeed, that I had the impression that the
conductor allowed a suggestion of *espansione* of the tempo at that point, but reverted
a tempo immediately afterwards—a hint of rubato to allow us all to recover our breath
before going on with the rest of the story.

It is an uncharacteristic phrase because Mozart has told us too much about his whole personality for us to believe in the Count's sincerity, even at this stage of the opera. By some curious, indefinable twist of genius, Mozart suggests that the future of the Almaviva household, while it promises to be temporarily peaceful, is not likely to remain so. Many years before I knew that Beaumarchais had ever written a sequel to *Le Mariage de Figaro* in which the Countess has a child by Cherubino, I had always been struck by the uneasy question-mark which seems to hang ominously over the three bars linking the quiet Andante started by the Count as he asks his wife's forgiveness, and the final Allegro assai:

If Mozart anticipated a sequel then it can only have been the purest intuition and an almost psychic understanding of Beaumarchais' characters, for Mozart died a year before the final part of Beaumarchais' trilogy appeared in 1792.

To all intents and purposes, however, the opera ends happily and Beaumarchais' "Crazy Day" ends in the key of D major—the key of the overture. Mozart had an unusual sense of unity and his operas always end in the key in which their overtures were written. In *Figaro* this unity is maintained by no haphazard modulation; he builds his finale steadily and symphonically from the entrance of Cherubino, through all the emotional and dramatic complications in which the characters find themselves—Cherubino, the Countess, the Count, Figaro, Susanna, Don Curzio, Don Basilio, Dr Bartolo, Barbarina, Marcellina, old drunken Antonio, and finally the Countess again—all are sketched unerringly and completely in a finale which is a fitting end to a masterpiece of comic opera which has never been equalled.

DON GIOVANNI

Originally *Il dissoluto punito, ossia il Don Giovanni.* "Dramma giocoso" in two acts by Lorenzo da Ponte. First performed at the Nationaltheater, Prague, on 29th May, 1787, conducted by the composer. First performance in England: His Majesty's Theatre, London, 12th April, 1817. First performance in the United States: Park Theatre, New York, 23rd May, 1826.

IF there is one subject which is rapidly becoming more popular and absorbing than the figure of Don Juan himself it is the controversy surrounding the exact status of Mozart's opera *Don Giovanni.*

For nearly 170 years great minds on both sides of the footlights have been exercised by the question whether Mozart's opera is high tragedy, romantic melodrama or sheer harmless fooling. So, at least, it appears to the innocent onlooker like myself who in the end is inclined to leave the last word to Mozart and enjoy everything the composer offers for all it is worth. I find myself indeed regarding the whole problem rather as the American lady behind me at the Opéra-Comique regarded the question of the Mona Lisa's "enigmatic" smile. "What does it mean?" she echoed her companion's question. "If you ask me it don't mean a damn' thing!"

The supporters of the high tragedy school of thought have it constantly pointed out to them that author and composer described their work as a "dramma giocoso", while those who regard it (as Mozart himself described it in making a catalogue of his works) as *opera buffa* are immediately asked what is so *buffa* about a murderer being devoured by the flames and devils of Hell.

The voice of the romantic school, of course, is not heard so much to-day as a century ago, when in 1830 for instance the opera was staged at the Adelphi Theatre, London, as a "Grand Romantick Comick Opera"; but there is no certainty that there will not one day be a great romantic revival and we shall find *Don Giovanni* being taken with that desperate teutonic seriousness which over the past fifteen decades has done untold harm to the enjoyment of the arts and of music in particular.

While ignoring all consideration of the claims of the romantic school (romanticism, after all, is more often in the eye of the beholder than in the mind of the creator of a work of art) we can safely concede that the status of *Don Giovanni* as an opera lies roughly between tragedy and comedy. Mozart himself was never a composer to keep his music in rigid compartments. He was as likely to include a bravura aria in a Mass as a grief-stricken outpouring like Constanze's "Traurigkeit" in a Singspiel or the Countess's "Porgi amor" in a *commedia per musica.*

The whole question, however, is one better left until the end of this chapter on *Don Giovanni,* for there is little point in discussing it until we have a clear and detailed picture of the opera itself and the reader has before him the facts without which opinion is worthless.

The commission to compose *Don Giovanni* was a direct result of the popularity in Prague of *Figaro*, which was performed in the Bohemian capital for the first time in December 1786—some seven months after the Vienna première. It is difficult for us in the 20th century to imagine what an operatic success could mean even in the 19th century—let alone the 18th—for we have no comparable standards of taste to enable us to understand the extent of the public excitement and enthusiasm caused, for instance, by Verdi's *Nabucco* or Rossini's *Tancredi*. In the case of *Figaro* in Prague, however, it is clear that the effect of the music on the public was exceptionally unusual, and we find Mozart himself writing from Prague in January 1787 and describing a ball at which "people flew about in sheer delight to the music of *Figaro*, arranged for quadrilles and waltzes. For here they talk about nothing but *Figaro*. Nothing is played, sung or whistled but *Figaro*. No opera is drawing like *Figaro*. Nothing, nothing but *Figaro*."

When he travelled to Prague with his wife to enjoy the success and publicity of *Figaro* Mozart arrived there to be welcomed by an appreciative and enthusiastic public and a grateful impresario. The impresario was Pasquale Bondini, the Italian manager of the new Prague National Theatre which had been built in 1783, and though the local aristocracy of what was, after all, still only a provincial city, were able to support an opera scheme its finances were not always bursting with health. In the winter of 1786, however, the almost uninterrupted run of *Figaro* at Bondini's theatre not only improved the financial situation but encouraged the impresario to take advantage of Mozart's visit and great personal popularity and commission the composer and librettist of *Figaro* to write a new work for Prague for the following winter season.

Mozart, who was liking Prague as much as Prague was liking him, accepted the offer with enthusiasm and returned to Vienna to consult with Da Ponte. The poet, at that time busy on two other librettos, suggested the subject of Don Juan and, as far as we know, Mozart fell in with the idea at once. This must have been something of a relief to Da Ponte who was able to make considerable use of the libretto of an opera on the subject newly produced in Venice (in February 1787) with music by Giuseppe Gazzaniga and words by Giovanni Bertati. (The idea of copyright and the sanctity of an author's property had no place in 18th century literary morality and it would have been uncharacteristic of the times if Da Ponte had had any compunction in lifting bodily or only faintly disguising such parts of Bertati's work as suited him.)

That Mozart should have found the subject as Da Ponte presented it an attractive one is hardly surprising, for the Italian poet's treatment of a fascinating and age-old theme was in every way theatrical and effective, offering a dramatic composer an endless variety of situation, mood and atmosphere. It is, indeed, the immense opportunity for purely musical variety which one suspects was more than anything what attracted

Mozart to the subject of *Don Giovanni*. As we shall see, there is scarcely a side of human experience which is not touched on—love, hatred, grief, laughter, courage, devotion, humiliation, vengeance, pain, jealousy, hypocrisy, cruelty, pride, desire, vacillation, anger, death—everything except childbirth and habitual drunkenness are all expressed in music in the course of a drama which provided the composer with an unprecedented opportunity for musical character-drawing, an opportunity which in its vastness never presented itself to the composer again.

As it happened the character-drawing in *Don Giovanni* did not prove of such a consistently high standard as that in *Figaro*, which is convincing throughout; but if, in *Don Giovanni*, there are occasionally instances of a comparatively stereotyped operatic approach to stereotyped operatic figures the range of emotion involved is still so wide that the score must be considered the most extensive and ambitious of all Mozart's operas in this respect.

CHARACTERS IN ORDER OF APPEARANCE:

LEPORELLO, *Don Giovanni's servant* . . *Bass*

DONNA ANNA, *daughter of the Commendatore* . *Soprano*

DON GIOVANNI, *an extremely licentious young nobleman* . . . . . . *Baritone**

THE COMMENDATORE . . . . *Bass*

DON OTTAVIO, *Donna Anna's betrothed* . *Tenor*

DONNA ELVIRA, *a noble lady from Burgos, abandoned by Don Giovanni* . . . *Soprano*

ZERLINA, *a peasant* . . . . . *Soprano*

MASETTO, *her lover* . . . . . *Bass*

Peasants, musicians, servants.

Scene: A city in Spain.   Time: Middle of the 17th Century.

* The part is frequently sung by a bass for its range is not by any means a wide one, and indeed its highest note is E—the same note which is expected of those who sing such uncompromisingly bass roles as Leporello and the Commendatore. Two of the finest Don Giovannis of recent times have, in fact, both been basses—Ezio Pinza and Cesare Siepi. It is, however, not a practice to be encouraged as it tends to upset the vocal balance of the ensembles.

ACT I

For all that we are told to expect a *dramma giocoso* the overture to *Don Giovanni* begins in a highly dramatic fashion in a very unjocose key— D minor—and gives the listener a pre-audition of music to be heard later in the opera:

1. Andante

The Andante opening to the overture is recalled towards the end of the work when the Stone Guest (the statue of the Commendatore) arrives in acceptance of Don Giovanni's invitation to dinner. It must surely have been due to this impressively solemn and dramatic introduction that the 19th century came to regard the opera as "tragic", for we find that the Mozart of this mood was looked upon as a "forerunner" of Beethoven and—as such—more readily acceptable to 19th-century audiences who grew increasingly unimpressed by "the classics". The sombre D minor of this introduction is not a key which Mozart used extensively, and it is significant that those same audiences who became so fanatically attached to the idea of *Don Giovanni* as a "tragedy" should also have admired Mozart's D minor Piano Concerto (K.466) to the almost total exclusion of his other works in the same form, considering it to be highly charged with the Storm and Stress of the romantic movement which they were convinced it anticipated. There was obviously something about the key of D minor which affected the romantics in a peculiar way.

The initial impact of the first bars of the overture to *Don Giovanni* is in all conscience a misleading introduction to a comic opera, and its effect on a susceptible, romantically-minded 19th-century audience is understandable enough for one not to be surprised that it coloured their outlook on the whole of the rest of the opera which followed. Nor, to be honest, does drama end with the Andante introduction. The Molto Allegro in D major which succeeds it is festive and brilliant:

2. Molto Allegro

but the development of the second subject,

especially of the first five notes of the phrase, is extremely dramatic in
a fully symphonic treatment, and the tension is not lessened by the inconclusive ending to the overture where the composer takes us right away
from the original D major and modulates to the F major on which the
curtain rises without a moment's break in musical continuity.

*Scene 1: The garden of the Commendatore's Palace. Night.**

Leoprello is discovered walking restlessly up and down outside the
building which his master, wearing a mask, has entered in an attempt to
abduct Donna Anna.

The servant (Da Ponte specifically states that he wears a cloak) is in a
thoroughly disgruntled and impatient mood which the composer suggests
with this striding-backwards-and-forwards movement:

He complains sarcastically of the conditions of employment by a libertine master like Don Giovanni—the irregular meals, the lack of sleep,
the constant waiting around in wind and rain. "What a *nice* gentleman!"
Leporello reflects bitterly. "There you are, indoors with a beautiful
woman, while I hang about outside like a watchdog. Who'd be a servant!
Well, *I'm* not going to be one, for a start!"

Leporello's rebellious indignation is interrupted by the sound of
people approaching. He hides away in the shadows and the whole mood,
if not the tempo, of the music changes as Don Giovanni and Donna Anna
come out of the house, Anna hanging on to his arm and trying desperately
to unmask him. A running fight ensues with Donna Anna and Don
Giovanni struggling and threatening each other, while Leporello contributes a grotesque commentary on the "tumulto", the screams, and his
master's genius for getting into trouble. Donna Anna cries for help and
abuses her assailant with a recurring phrase:

* I have deliberately kept to the original descriptions of the scenes as they appear in
Da Ponte's libretto and also to his stage directions, for they are direct and to the point.

She repeats this cry five times until it is eventually answered by her father, the Commendatore, who arrives sword in hand to defend his daughter. When she hears her father Donna Anna releases Don Giovanni and runs into the house.

The Commendatore challenges Don Giovanni to fight. The younger man refuses and is accused of cowardice. The Commendatore persists in his challenge and provocation, until after a dramatic silent bar, Don Giovanni draws his sword and fights. The music leading to the actual duel (we are back in the fatal D minor again) is an intensely dramatic sequence in which Mozart characterizes the old man's persistent and foolhardy challenge, Don Giovanni's reluctance to be drawn into a serious and mortal quarrel, and Leporello's terrified cowering in a corner in anticipation of the disaster he knows is going to happen. Leporello's busy chattering that accompanied the struggle with Donna Anna (which, after all, was scarcely something out of the ordinary for a servant in his position to witness) gives way to a serious and obviously genuine terror of the probable consequences of the duel, with the orchestra accompanying in unison Leporello's fervent wish that he were anywhere in the world rather than where he is:

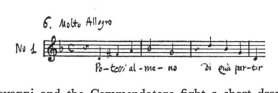

Don Giovanni and the Commendatore fight a short dramatic bout which ends as the older man falls mortally wounded. There now follows a strange and impressive Andante passage which accompanies the death of the Commendatore. Leporello is horrified by what has happened, for it is clear that murder, or at least homicide, however or by whomsoever provoked, is the last thing he or his master ever intend. Leporello, indeed, goes so far as to refer to the "crime" and the "eccesso" he has witnessed, while Don Giovanni himself, *mezza voce*, is plainly not unmoved by what has happened; and as the Commendatore lies dying he surveys the scene, echoing in a minor version, Donna Anna's cry (Ex 5):

I doubt if this echo of the earlier phrase has any particular thematic significance, for Mozart's mind did not work along those lines; it is far more likely, I feel, to be a purely subconscious association of musical ideas (there is another even more striking instance of this later in *Don Giovanni*) which it is fun to notice and point out and to which it is probably purposeless to attach any great importance.

The scene of the Commendatore's death ends with a subdued and moving little orchestral epilogue, less than five bars long,—a characteristic instance of Mozart's effective use of a falling chromatic phrase.

And so the first incident—called by composer and librettist the "Introduzione"—of our *dramma giocoso* comes to an end: with a corpse on the ground. But the gloom cast over the proceedings doesn't last long; without the formality of a full close the orchestral epilogue dissolves into recitative and Don Giovanni and Leporello, having found each other in the darkness, quickly take us into the realm of *opera buffa*. Leporello, with mock anxiety and the stupidity expected of the operatic comic servant, asks which of them is dead—Don Giovanni or the old man—and on being reassured congratulates his master on having so successfully concluded two pieces of business: the seduction of the daughter and the elimination of the father. Don Giovanni points out that the Commendatore "wanted it that way" ("l'ha voluto, suo danno"). And Donna Anna? What did she want? Don Giovanni tells Leporello to shut up if he doesn't want a box on the ears. Leporello shuts up and they leave the scene together.

If I should appear in the course of this study of *Don Giovanni* to be noticing in unusual detail what is said in the recitative of the opera it is because Da Ponte's dialogue is well worth consideration in its own right. It is witty and to the point and is not just a mechanical means of getting on with the plot. Indeed, even casual study of the recitative will discover remarkable little touches of character-drawing in a medium which can be said to bear the same relation to the rest of the music as the prose dialogue bears to the verse of Shakespeare's plays. But while nobody would ever dream of omitting or not listening carefully to the prose dialogue of Falstaff, Toby Belch or Bottom the average opera-goer pays remarkably little attention to the recitative in a Mozart opera unless it is accompanied by the orchestra, when he considers he is at last getting his operatic money's worth and will then give it more careful consideration. By being inattentive to the recitative, however, he is missing a great deal of fun, even if the musical reward to be derived from it is negligible.

As Don Giovanni and Leporello leave, Donna Anna returns ("con risolutezza") with Don Ottavio and servants carrying torches to help the Commendatore, Don Ottavio, with equal *risolutezza*, draws his sword, but the garden is deserted. Four sudden discordant bars from the orchestra lead dramatically to Donna Anna's discovery of her father's body:

In the orchestrally-accompanied recitative which follows, Donna Anna is horrified by her father's death and describes his appearance and "deadness" in detail; but most of all she decides to avenge him and makes Don

Ottavio promise to bring the unknown murderer to justice. The Commendatore's body is carried from the scene and Donna Anna bids it farewell—"Fuggi, crudele, fuggi! lascia che mora anch'io" ("Go, cruel sight, and let me also die . . ."):

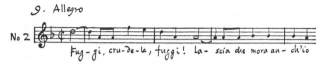

Don Ottavio tries to comfort Donna Anna in her distraction and takes the music into a gentle kindly F major from the inconsolable D minor it starts in—"Forget the bitter memories, for you have both a lover and father in me":

This passage occurs twice in the duet. I have quoted it as it occurs the second time (when it is spread out for an extra two bars) to show the use Mozart makes in both orchestra and its echo in the voice part of the interval of a falling seventh. This interval, used here to give a lyrical grace to Don Ottavio's promises, later became part of the overworked stock-in-trade of the 19th-century romantic composers, who seemed incapable of writing about Love without resort to it. Wagner did most to debase it as musical currency, but (devaluation or not) it persisted as legal musical tender until Puccini's *Girl of the Golden West*, if not later.

I will not claim that its use in this sentimental context first occurred in *Don Giovanni*, but I will cover myself by suggesting that this is one of the first instances of it in the operatic repertoire, and probably the earliest extant example of it. The fact that Mozart made the same interval mean something quite different at a later stage in *Don Giovanni* is neither here nor there, except as a further example of the composer's genius for making one musical phrase do the dramatic work of two.

The duet, which is notable for the imaginative use of the two flutes which give the score of *Don Giovanni* a peculiar warm colouring, is interrupted by a further short passage of recitative in which Don Ottavio solemnly swears by Donna Anna's eyes and their love for each other to avenge her father's death, and though the scene ends with a rather formal sequence of simple two-part writing for the voices the duet never quite loses the serious and purposeful D minor mood set by Donna Anna at the start.

Exeunt in the direction of the palace.

Scene 2: A street. Dawn.

Don Giovanni and Leporello appear, clearly in the middle of a conversation in which Leporello refuses to come to the point. Don Giovanni is getting impatient to know what is on his servant's mind. Yes, he promises not to be angry—provided it's not something about the Commendatore. After considerable prevarication Leporello tells his master point blank that he considers him to be leading a wastrel's life. Don Giovanni is about to box his servant's ears but on being reminded of his promise quickly changes the subject and asks Leporello to guess why they are where they are. Leporello doesn't know, but seeing that it is dawn supposes that his master is about to make a "new conquest" (an interesting sidelight on Don Giovanni's hours of business) and, if so, please could he know more so that the famous catalogue may be brought up to date.* Don Giovanni explains that he is in love with a beautiful young woman who, he is sure, loves him. Neither we nor Leporello learn any more about her, however, for Don Giovanni's attention is distracted by what he describes as "the smell of a woman—a beautiful one too!" ("What a nose! What an eye!" comments Leporello).

When the woman approaches Don Giovanni and Leporello hide in the doorway of a house and overhear her lamenting the treachery of a faithless lover. Perhaps "lamenting", which is sometimes used in connection with this aria, is not quite the right word. It is an angry as well as an humiliated woman whose singing is introduced by the determined orchestral phrase:

while she herself shows little trace of melancholy or grief in "Ah! chi mi dice mai quel barbaro dov'è?" ("Who will tell me where this monster is to be found?"):

Indeed, the more one considers the word "lamenting" the less appropriate it becomes. There is no feeling of despair discernible in a note of what the outraged woman sings; she becomes more and more the incarnation of the fury than which hell hath no greater as the aria progresses; when she finds him, she swears, and he does not come back to her, she

* The casual mention of the catalogue suggests that it was a familiar feature of the various Don Juan plays known to 18th-century audiences. To the member of a 20th-century audience, hearing Mozart's opera for the first time, the reference may pass unnoticed. Let it be said without spoiling anybody's pleasure, however, that it plays an entertaining part in the opera a few minutes after this first mention of it.

will inflict terrible torture on him ("orrendo scempio") and dig out his heart. And her threats are made to phrases like this:

When Don Giovanni has heard the motion before the house, as it were, he remarks to Leporello with a flippancy which is deliberately intended to reduce the whole affair to the level of farce: "Poor girl! Poor girl! We must console her!" To which Leporello in an aside adds the cynical observation that that's how eighteen hundred poor girls have been consoled already.

As the aria ends Don Giovanni comes out into the open and addresses the unknown woman. Before he can offer any form of consolation, however, he recognizes her as Donna Elvira, and she recognizes him with a command of epithet which leaves Leporello speechless with admiration. We are now right back in the *buffo* atmosphere again. Don Giovanni cannot get a word in edgeways; he tries to speak but Donna Elvira asks him what he can possibly have to say and proceeds to state her case at breakneck speed in a passage of recitative which takes her through the keys of G, C, E, A, D minor, C, B, E minor, D, G, E, A minor, D minor, and E before she pauses for breath and allows Leporello to remark that she talks like a printed book.

Don Giovanni takes advantage of the temporary lull in the conversation to say that he can explain everything; he had his reasons. He turns to Leporello for confirmation and his servant confirms, with considerable irony, that Don Giovanni most certainly had his reasons—strong reasons. Donna Elvira refuses to believe a word her betrayer says. Well, says Don Giovanni, at least she will believe *this* gentleman (indicating Leporello) who will speak the whole truth. Leporello looks a little sceptical at this, but Don Giovanni means what he says. Donna Elvira says very well; she will listen to Leporello but hurry up.

While Leporello is preparing to tell her everything Don Giovanni manages to escape unnoticed. When Donna Elvira eventually turns to find him gone, Leporello pleads with her to believe that he is really not worth bothering about; she is neither the first nor will she be the last.

"Look!" says Leporello, and he takes out a little book. This is the cue for the famous Catalogue Song—"Madamina! il catalogo è questo" ("Madame, this is the catalogue . . ."):

The little book which Leporello asks Donna Elvira to read with him is a catalogue of all the women Don Giovanni has ever seduced—six hundred and forty in Italy, two hundred and thirty-one in Germany, a hundred in France, ninety-one in Turkey. "But in Spain," says Leporello, "in Spain no fewer than a thousand and three"; and he announces it in a manner which can be interpreted as proud, or (which is how it has always struck me) as having just a hint of contempt in it for Donna Elvira that she should be one of the thousand and three.

Among this odd couple of thousand victims, Leporello explains, are peasants, serving maids and city girls, countesses, baronesses and princesses, women of every station, shape, size and age. Leporello runs through the list a second time and brings the first (Allegro) part of the aria to a close. The tempo changes to an Andante in 3/4 time in which Leporello elaborates on the characteristics of the various types of women and how Don Giovanni reacts to them—"Nella bionda egli ha l'usanza di lodar la gentilezza" ("With blondes he praises gentle manners . . ."):

In this section (notable particularly for the rich orchestral colouring of the accompaniment in which the violas are frequently divided into two parts) Leporello continues to describe his master's preferences, habits and idiosyncrasies. Among brunettes Don Giovanni finds an appealing constancy, among fair ones a sweetness of disposition.* Don Giovanni, Leporello goes on, likes plump ones in winter and slim ones in the summer, the tall ones must be stately and the small ones vivacious; he has included old ones for the sake of having them in the catalogue. But most of all Don Giovanni finds pleasure in the girl who is just beginning. Leporello's whole tone changes as he says this and his words are accompanied by a wonderfully effective four bars featuring the bassoon in yet another role created by Mozart's genius for instrumental casting—a role half sinister, half lascivious:

All in all, Leporello concludes in his summing up and with the bassoon

* Leporello makes a neat, almost tonsorial distinction between a blonde (*bionda*) and a fair one (*bianca*).

now in the major, Don Giovanni is content with anything in a skirt and, Leporello adds meaningfully to Donna Elvira, you know what happens then.

The aria ends with Leporello singing these words to an oddly seductive, lyrical little phrase which suggests that he has learnt a thing or two from his master in his time:

Scene 3 : The countryside around Don Giovanni's palace which can be seen in the background.

"Masetto, Zerlina; chorus of peasants who play instruments, dance and sing . . ." These are Da Ponte's original stage instructions which Mozart translates brilliantly into music with a most convincingly peasant-like opening chorus—a verse-and-refrain affair in which first Zerlina, then Masetto, then both together sing a series of nondescript praises of love, laughter and life in general:

Mozart's musical characterizations range in his operas from underdogs to demigods, but with none of them does he show a subtler, surer touch than with his peasants. Perhaps because there is nothing spectacular about the little choruses of peasants we encounter in *Figaro* and *Don Giovanni* we tend to take them for granted and regard them as no more than conventional opera choruses. One could make no greater mistake. Just as the drunken Antonio, in *Figaro*, is given full musical representation so equally are the other members of his class, even though their function in the action of the same opera is largely decorative.

Similarly in *Don Giovanni* the peasants can easily be overlooked, and while we are conscious later in this scene of Masetto's musical character, it is rarely noticed that this whole opening chorus (it is specifically labelled "Coro" even though the largest contribution is made by Zerlina and Masetto) is entirely in Masetto's own musical language, that—musically—he, Zerlina and their friends keep to their own class.

The peasant gathering is joined by Don Giovanni and Leporello. From Don Giovanni's opening remarks to his servant (they are clearly still in the midst of a conversation) it seems that "she", whoever she may be, has fortunately departed. We never learn "her" identity, however (Donna Elvira, perhaps?), because Don Giovanni abruptly changes the subject when he sees the crowd of pretty young peasant girls; he has no time for a bird in the bush if there are two almost in the hand. The sight

pleases his servant as well for Leporello is loudly hopeful that among so
many young women there might be something for him too.

Don Giovanni, full of gallantry, addressing Zerlina with the polite
"voi" but Masetto with the familiar "tu", asks what is going on and
learns that the approaching marriage of Zerlina and Masetto is being
celebrated. Generously—and gratuitously—Don Giovanni decides to
place the marriage under his "protection". He turns to give Leporello
instructions but finds him having fun with the girls.

"What are you doing?" demands Don Giovanni.

"Just bestowing a little protection, dear master," replies Leporello
blandly.

Don Giovanni, by now well accustomed to Leporello's fondness for
irony, ignores the gentle jibe and orders his servant to take everybody to
the palace, give them chocolate, coffee, wine, ham and show them the
gardens, the grounds, the rooms, the galleries and, in short, entertain
everybody—especially Masetto. Masetto says he will not go without
Zerlina. Leporello replies that Don Giovanni will take Masetto's place
and play his part perfectly. Don Giovanni personally adds that she will,
after all, be in the hands of a *cavaliere* and Zerlina echoes his words.

Masetto is about to continue his protests but is discouraged by Don
Giovanni's threatening gesture with his sword. The peasant decides that
perhaps discretion is the better part of valour and gives way in a surly
aria—"Ho capito, Signor, sì" ("I understand, my lord. . . .")—in which
Mozart makes a great deal of the orchestral figure:

20. Allegro di molto

It is a bitter, angular kind of song that Masetto sings, in which he
impatiently resists Leporello's efforts to drag him away while he abuses
Zerlina and sarcastically suggests that no doubt the *cavaliere* will make a
cavaliera of her. This passage has a peculiarly rough, rustic flavour to it—
a quality which is not softened in any way by the phrase occurring always
in unison:

21. Allegro di molto

Masetto and the other peasants depart with Leporello. The scene in
recitative which follows between Don Giovanni and the young lady whom
he now begins to address as "gentle Zerlinetta" (though still with the
formal "voi") is a masterly instance of insincerity and how to fall for it.
And fall for it Zerlina certainly does, for though she is clearly surprised
at Don Giovanni's suggestion that he should marry her (one suspects that
his "sposare" is a euphemism for something less permanent), she nevertheless believes all his highflown talk about the "nobility with honesty

painted in their eyes." To 18th-century audiences already very familiar
in theatre, fairground and puppet booth with the legend of Don Juan in
general and his personal character in particular, this scene must have been
hilariously *giocosa*, for it is a comic counterpart of the popular seduction
scene of Victorian melodrama. But whereas the Victorian audience
sympathized with the victim, the more cynical 18th-century audience
obviously tended to laugh at her innocence and gullibility, while reserving
the right, of course, to laugh at the villain's eventual discomfort as well.

Don Giovanni points to a little house on his estate, and telling Zerlina
that they will be alone and can "marry" there, begins the little duet
"Là ci darem la mano" ("There you will give me your hand and consent . . .") :

This is one of the most wonderfully sensuous scenes in all Mozart.
It is written in the "seduction" key of A major, like the duet between the
Count and Susanna in *Figaro*, but in such a way that this time both parties
are irresistible to each other. (I do not suggest for a moment, of course,
that there is any hint of a Great Love, merely that there is a strong mutual
physical attraction. Otherwise, why should Don Giovanni bother with
Zerlina or she with him?)

The subtleties of Mozart's characterization in this duet are to be
found—when they are analysable at all—in the little differences of
melody and phrasing that distinguish the vocal parts. The composer was
helped considerably in this by the librettist whose contribution should not
be underrated merely because we have come to regard the scene as being
principally a passage of exquisite music.

The "lyric" is noticeable for many subtle touches in its own right,
among them Don Giovanni's use for the first time of the familiar, intimate
"tu", and the fact that in the opening Andante section of the duet Zerlina
soliloquizes; she does not address a word to Don Giovanni, but reflects
on her own problems. She wants to, and yet she doesn't want to; she would
be happy, she says, but she might be making a fool of herself; she is sorry
for Masetto, but feels herself weakening. This indecision is superbly
expressed in the music by such phrases as:

It is only when Don Giovanni finally changes from the imperative
"Come!" to the exhortatory "Let's go" that Zerlina addresses him for the
first time. She echoes his "Andiam!" and as the time changes from 2/4 to

6/8 she sings the leading part in a thoroughly rustic expression of excitement and pleasure in what the lyric calls an "innocente amor":

This air of country-girl innocence is accentuated by the orchestra's introduction in this 6/8 coda of a bouncing dance rhythm which is ingeniously characteristic of Zerlina's mood:

Don Giovanni and Zerlina turn to go arm-in-arm towards the little house but unexpectedly find their way barred by the sudden appearance of Donna Elvira, who denounces Don Giovanni and congratulates herself on arriving in the nick of time to save an innocent girl, etc. Don Giovanni whispers to Donna Elvira: doesn't she see that he's only amusing himself?

"Amusing yourself is right!" she cries at the top of her voice. "And don't I know how you amuse yourself!"

Zerlina anxiously turns to Don Giovanni and asks him whether what Donna Elvira says is true. He replies, *sotto voce*, that Donna Elvira is a poor unfortunate woman who is in love with him and who has to be humoured by his pretending that he loves her.

"It is my misfortune to be a kind-hearted man," he sighs.

Donna Elvira now sails (there is no other word) into a short and indignant aria in which she warns Zerlina to come away from the man who would betray her with lying lips and worthless promises—"Ah, fuggi il traditor". The aria is based on a vigorous rhythm which pervades both the voice part and the string accompaniment of which this phrase is typical:

There has always been some doubt whether this aria is intended as imitation or parody of Handel's style, or whether in its deliberate use of what was already in Mozart's day an archaic idiom it can be regarded as a kind of musical sermon (Donna Elvira, after all, had been a nun in her time).

Whatever its original intention, however, it is by no means void of musical interest and its effect is dramatically revealing of yet another side of Elvira's intensely human, inconsistent, unpredictable and perplexed character.

Having said her angry say Donna Elvira sweeps out taking Zerlina away with her under her protection.

Don Giovanni is left alone on the stage, puzzling out why everything seems to be going wrong today, when he is joined by Donna Anna and Don Ottavio whose arrival he greets with a muttered aside that these two were the only two things hitherto missing from his day.

Donna Anna, who has not recognized her assailant of the night before, asks for Don Giovanni's friendship and help, a proposal which takes him a little unawares but from which he quickly recovers by declaring ("with much fire", says the libretto) that everything he has—his sword, his worldly goods, his very blood—is hers to command. Don Giovanni asks the reason for her request but before he hears the answer (which, one presumes, is that Donna Anna wants his help in finding her father's murderer) Donna Elvira makes a sudden reappearance with the dramatic cry: "So! I find you again, perfidious monster!"

I have always found this moment one of the most bewildering in the whole of *Don Giovanni*. On the one hand Donna Elvira's unexpected entrance creates a variant of the traditionally comic situation celebrated in *The Beggar's Opera* by the immortal "How happy could I be with either!"; on the other, Elvira herself is infinitely pathetic immediately afterwards when she starts the quartet by warning Donna Anna against the man "who has already betrayed me and now wants to betray you"—"Non ti fidar, o misera":

Donna Anna and Don Ottavio are moved by Donna Elvira's "noble mien and gentle majesty, her pallor and her tears." Don Giovanni tells them in an aside (which is nevertheless overheard by Elvira) that the poor woman is mad. Let them leave her to him, he says, and perhaps he can calm her. A great part is played in this quartet by a little cadence first sung by Elvira to the words "Te vuol tradir ancor" ("And he wants to betray you . . ."):

The phrase is subsequently used with great ingenuity of what one can only describe as "placing" in the course of the movement by violins, by a solo clarinet, a solo flute, or by flute and clarinet in octaves; and it is echoed, too, from time to time by the voices of one or other of the characters. It is a wonderfully characteristic example of Mozart's genius for economy of means.

Donna Elvira hotly denies Don Giovanni's accusation that she is mad and she does so in phrases which become increasingly florid and elaborate until Donna Anna and Don Ottavio admit they do not know whom to believe. One moment they are heard agreeing seriously with Don Giovanni's insincere assertion that his "soul is stirred with pity" by Elvira's misfortune—an assertion made reasonably convincing by Elvira's own extravagant protestations in phrases like this:

—while the next Don Ottavio announces in an aside his determination not to move until everything is clear, and Donna Anna, also in an aside, remarks that Elvira does not have the air of a lunatic either in her manner or her way of talking. Donna Anna and Don Ottavio eventually cross-examine the two parties.

"What about her?" asks Ottavio.

"Mad," replies Don Giovanni.

"What about him?" asks Anna.

"Traitor! Liar! Liar! Liar!" replies Elvira, which causes both Anna and Ottavio to begin to have doubts. Donna Elvira continues to rage at Don Giovanni who tries to pacify her, first by humouring her but eventually, as she refuses to quieten down, by appealing to her to behave in front of the others. It is the behaviour of Donna Elvira and Don Giovanni in this final sequence of the quartet which convinces both Anna and Ottavio that all Donna Elvira says about Don Giovanni is true.

This quartet which ends with Elvira storming off once more (though to a final *pianissimo* repetition, after seven consecutive playings, of the cadence quoted as Ex 28), is not only amusing, but unusually rich in Mozart's miraculous technical facility for characterization. Even Don Ottavio comes to life for an individual moment when he is not singing the same words in harmony with Donna Anna, while Donna Elvira and Don Giovanni are superbly preoccupied with their personal problems in a highly personal musical way. All in all, this movement is a gem of Mozart's unique understanding of the power that music has which drama has not: the power to present several points of view simultaneously.

At Donna Elvira's departure Don Giovanni quickly announces that he must follow the poor unfortunate woman, and assuring the "bellissima Donna Anna" of his service, help and attention at all times, he bids his friends adieu and leaves.

There now follows a moment of quite remarkable and dramatic discord in the orchestra's introduction to a recitative duologue between Donna Anna and Don Ottavio. For some reason the full harmonic impact of the

third bar is not indicated in any of the vocal scores of *Don Giovanni* I
have ever seen. In the orchestral score, however, Mozart wrote:

The effect of that clash in G and F sharp is so strong that, to me, it
stays in my ears in a curious way that colours the figure whenever it
occurs in the rest of the recitative, although the actual dissonance never
happens again. The forceful mood of this recitative is also enhanced by
the inclusion of trumpets who give a ferocious dramatic character to what
is in all conscience a dramatic enough episode: Donna Anna's recognition
of Don Giovanni as her father's murderer.

She also recognizes, of course, that it was Don Giovanni who had been
her assailant the night before, and Don Ottavio listens open-mouthed
to her narrative, adding suitably sympathetic remarks of indignation and
surprise as she tells the whole remarkable story—or nearly the whole of it.

Punctuated from time to time by variants of the figure in Ex 30
Donna Anna describes how a man (whom she has recognized by his voice
and manner to have been Don Giovanni) came into her bedroom at the
dead of night. He was wearing a cloak so that she could not see his face,
but she thought he was Don Ottavio. "But I learned later that I had
made a mistake" says Anna.

"Heavens!" says Don Ottavio. "Continue."

Donna Anna continues: "Silently he approached to embrace me.
The more I tried to free myself, the harder he held me. I cried out. No
one heard; with one hand he tried to prevent me calling out; with the
other he held me so that I thought I was lost."

"Scoundrel!" cries Don Ottavio. "And in the end?"

"In the end," says Donna Anna, "the grief, the horror of the infamous
attack gave me strength to struggle free."

"Oh dear," says Don Ottavio. "I breathe again."

"Then," Donna Anna goes on, "I shouted even louder, crying for help.
The culprit fled; I followed him out into the street, trying to stop him—"
and Anna concludes her narrative with a brief description of her father's
death.

Now, it is reported that 18th-century audiences found this a particularly
hilarious scene—especially Don Ottavio's line "Respiro!" ("I breathe
again"); it was obvious to everybody that Don Giovanni had, as they say,
taken his pleasure of Donna Anna for there are noticeable gaps and
discrepancies in a story which is far too much concerned with the attack
on Anna's honour and far too little with the killing of her father. Indeed,
it is almost as if Anna welcomed the purely incidental episode of her
father's death as an excuse to enable her to deal severely with her seducer
whose capital crime was otherwise scarcely worth noticing.

The most significant phrase in Donna Anna's story seems to me to be her statement that she learned "later" that she had made a mistake in thinking Don Giovanni was Don Ottavio. The word she uses for "later" in Da Ponte's book is "poi"—an ambiguous adverb in Italian which can mean "later", "then" or "afterwards". There is little doubt, I feel, that in this case it means "afterwards", for it was not until a struggle or two later that Donna Anna actually cried out for *help* and that Don Giovanni, with no further business to detain him, finally fled.

More important than any clues one may find in Donna Anna's account of the affair to Don Ottavio, however, is surely Don Giovanni's whole attitude towards her. If he had failed to seduce her he would still—since she was clearly a desirable woman—be pursuing her. But since he *has* seduced her he is completely indifferent to her—just as (and for the same reason) he is indifferent to Donna Elvira. He is interested only in Zerlina because, so far, she has eluded him. In short, Don Giovanni enjoys the chase and the kill but prefers not to be worried by what happens to the carcase.

By the end of this recitative, then, Donna Anna is understandably an angry, bitter and humiliated woman. Not only has her father been murdered but she has been seduced and then discarded by his murderer. (One suspects that as much as anything it was Don Giovanni's exaggerated politeness and his formally insincere your-devoted-servant attitude to the "bellissima Donna Anna" which finally convinced her that he was her betrayer. As an attractive woman she was naturally suspicious that a man of Don Giovanni's habits should not want anything of her; and as an intelligent woman she naturally reasoned—quite correctly—that if he wanted nothing of her it was because he had already had it.)

It is therefore a tragically bewildered Donna Anna who beseeches Don Ottavio to avenge her—"Or sai chi l'onore rapire a me volse" ("Now you know who laid hands on me and killed my father . . ."):

The determination of that opening runs through the whole aria and it is intensified a moment later when Donna Anna sings the word "vendetta" —saying to Don Ottavio that not only she but his own heart calls for revenge:

The astonishingly effective simplicity of that dramatic echo in the basses is typical of Mozart's masterly handling of the orchestra in this aria which is accompanied only by strings, horns, oboes and bassoons—and very rarely by all of them at the same time (to be exact, for fewer than fourteen bars altogether out of the total of 71 bars of intensely emotional music). It is a sobering thought to all with ambitions as orchestrators that Mozart can do with about 25 players what a so-called "master of the orchestra" cannot achieve with a hundred; for not all the bassethorns and heckelphones, E flat clarinets and contrabass tubas in the score of *Elektra* can ever enable Strauss' heroine to hold a candle to Donna Anna for sheer overpowering vindictiveness.

At the end of her aria Donna Anna stalks off leaving Don Ottavio to reflect in a scene which is constantly and almost universally condemned as an almost unforgivable anticlimax.

In a few bars of recitative Don Ottavio muses that he has never heard of a *cavaliere* capable of so black a crime and swears, by his duty as lover and friend, to vindicate Donna Anna's honour.

These admirable sentiments are followed by the aria "Dalla sua pace la mia dipende" ("On her peace of mind mine too depends; what pleases her gives joy to me . . .") :

There is no doubt, of course, that strictly speaking this aria *is* an anti-climax. But does it really matter? Personally, I do not think so, for it is such a beautiful aria in itself, with its wonderfully subdued opening accompanied by what one might call "motionless" strings, that—to me, at any rate—it comes as a great and welcome relief from the tension of what has gone before. Looking back over the immediate past of the score we have had Donna Anna's tremendous scene, the quartet before it, and Donna Elvira's vigorous aria before that. There has been no moment of relaxation for us since the seductive charm of "Là ci darem la mano", and although Mozart interpolated "Dalla sua pace" at this point in the opera because at the first Vienna performance the tenor found the later "Il mio tesoro" beyond his powers, I nevertheless do not regard it as an altogether unsatisfactory second thought.

I am probably alone in this for as a rule Mozart's second thoughts were not very happy, but if one can persuade oneself that with Donna Anna's aria a musical episode has come to an end and that a new one is beginning, rather than following on, with Don Ottavio's aria, then I think the feeling of anti-climax can be avoided and the aria enjoyed for what it is: an exquisite lyrical interlude.*

Even at risk of being accused of reading into the part of Don Ottavio something which neither composer nor librettist intended, is it so rare in real life to find a character as colourless and docile, worthy and well-meaning as Don Ottavio? Of course not. The world is full of voluptuous and desirable women who are accompanied by devoted dog-like followers to the exclusion of infuriated, because less successful, suitors. Such situations are not only common but are met with a shrug of the amazed shoulder and the comment so familiar as to be a cliché: "Well, I suppose he must have some hidden charms we know nothing about, because I can't see *what* she sees in him!"

Don Ottavio's unsuspected charm fortunately seems to be the highly commendable one to have in an opera—the ability to express his dog-like devotion in two quite beautiful arias. The only real mystery about Mozart's music for Don Ottavio is why, if an aria had to be substituted for "Il mio tesoro", it should have been interpolated in the first act (with first-act words to it, as it were) instead of being sung in the second act, which is where "Il mio tesoro" occurs. As it happens, by putting the substitute aria in the first act it has at least spared us all the difficult choice of having to decide which to omit. By having one in the first act and the other in the second, the tenor who can manage both (and what tenor will admit that he can't?) enables us to hear—rightly or wrongly—two lovely arias where the first Prague audience heard only one. (It occurs to me, of course, that the reason "Dalla sua pace" is where and what it is, is that Mozart himself had hopes that a tenor would arise capable of singing both arias.)

But all this, as I say, is very much a matter of personal opinion and preference, and so far as I am concerned I have never objected to the action being held up—or resumed—by the inclusion of something like "Dalla sua pace". How many operas, indeed, could do with being held up by anything half as interesting. However, perhaps I have a purely sensuous prejudice in favour of Don Ottavio's two arias: the first singer I ever heard in the role was Richard Tauber who demonstrated once and for all exactly how lovely these two arias can sound.

Anti-climax, colourless character or not, Don Ottavio sings his aria and departs, and Leporello returns to grumble to the audience telling us that whatever happens he is going to quit his master's employ: "And here he comes—look at him and his couldn't-care-less attitude!"

Don Giovanni enters in his usual hearty and irrepressible manner to be told by Leporello, that, so far from everything going well, everything is going badly. As instructed by "Don Giovannino mio" (he is fond of the

* It was only many years after I had first heard *Don Giovanni* that I encountered the theory that Mozart and Da Ponte had originally conceived Donna Anna's aria and exit as the end of the first of four acts. Thus my own instinctive inclination to regard "Dalla sua pace" as the beginning of a new chapter rather than as the continuation of an old one was not far out. If Mozart did not originally plan a tenor aria at this point but instead continued with the plot forthwith it does not alter what has always seemed unmistakable to me: that Donna Anna's aria, whatever follows it, marks the end of a dramatic and musical episode whether the curtain falls on it or not.

slightly sarcastic diminutive) Leporello took Masetto and the other peasants and entertained them, he explains to Don Giovanni, with the kind of "chatter and charming lies I have learned from you."

"Excellent!" says Don Giovanni.

"I said a thousand things to distract and pacify Masetto."

"Excellent!" exclaims Don Giovanni again.

"I made the men and the women drink and they're now all half drunk. Some of them started singing, others started joking, and the rest went on drinking. And then what do you think happened?"

"Zerlina."

"Excellent!" says Leporello. "And who was with her?"

"Donna Elvira."

"Excellent!" says Leporello. "And what did she say about you?"

"Everything bad she could think of," replies Don Giovanni.

"Excellent!"

"And what did *you* do?" asks Don Giovanni.

"Kept quiet."

"And she?"

"She began to rave and storm."

"And you?"

"Well," says Leporello, "when the storm seemed to have blown itself out I led her very gently through the door and locked her outside in the street."

"Bravo! Bravo!" cries Don Giovanni. "It couldn't be better! You have begun it for me, and I shall finish it off. We will invite all these worthy peasants to a party until night." (The action of *Don Giovanni* is designed to take place in the course of twenty-four hours; it is now late afternoon and Don Giovanni's invitation—which is for a party to take place at once—seems to be to some form of high tea.)

Don Giovanni now sings what is sometimes known as the "Champagne Aria". I imagine this derives from the quite hideous German translation that is still used in Central Europe—"Treibt der Champagner"—for there is certainly no specific mention of any particular wine in Da Ponte's original "Finch'han dal vino calda la testa" ("Prepare a feast to warm the head with wine . . ."):

34. Presto

No 12

The brilliance and exuberance of this vigorous, swaggering aria, which brings us back into the plot of the opera almost violently after the calm and contemplation of "Dalla sua pace", are matched by the brilliance and exuberance of the orchestration. Mozart uses strings, horns and all his wood-wind (i.e. flutes, oboes, clarinets and bassoons) for the first time since the overture and somehow manages to give the movement a glitter and sheen which one cannot anticipate by glancing at the full score. The very key of the aria, B flat, is not recognized as a "brilliant" tonality and one expects the orchestral texture to be comparatively heavy as a result of the violas being divided into two parts, the second violins, frequent use of double-stopping, thus contributing extra voices to a string section which is in consequence often divided into no fewer than seven different voices.

This sort of thing is one of the great and eternally mysterious aspects of Mozart's genius and I doubt if one teacher of orchestration in a thousand would do otherwise, if he encountered them in a student's exercise in a similar context, than strike out the divided violas and the full inner parts of the score on the ground that the result would inevitably be too "thick". But what in fact happens in the case of this aria of Don Giovanni's is that, by some inexplicable paradox, the orchestration of the whole movement is the most dazzling in the entire opera—a model of crystal clarity and elegant brilliance.

The dramatic purpose of "Finch'han dal vino" is to instruct Leporello to round up guests for Don Giovanni's party and to bring them to dance the minuet, the *follia*, the allemande, what they will. Don Giovanni is keeping open house and (he tells Leporello in audible confidence) he expects to increase the number of entries in the notorious *catalogo* by at least ten before morning—an estimate which gives an unexpectedly detailed though probably over-optimistic idea of Don Giovanni's conception of an evening's entertainment. At any rate, he mentions the target as a "decina", or half-score, no fewer than six times in the later part of the aria so it is obviously something he feels confident about. (The occurrence of the words "questa" and "quella" in the aria naturally strikes a chord in anticipation of the Duke in Verdi's *Rigoletto*. The difference between Don Giovanni and the Duke, however, is marked if very subtly so. The Duke sings of "Questa o quella"—this one *or* that—while Don Giovanni characteristically refers to "questa e quella"—this one *and* that. But then the Duke had no *catalogo* to fill.)

The score makes no provision for any change of scene to provide a setting for "Finch'han dal vino", though in practice sometimes a drop-curtain is used as a background for the scene between Don Giovanni and Leporello to enable the change to be made for the scene which follows.

*Scene 4: The garden of Don Giovanni's palace.**

In the midst of a crowd of peasants wandering about, chattering, or lying asleep on the ground, Zerlina and Masetto are heard in what is clearly the middle of an argument. Masetto is accusing Zerlina of being unfaithful to him and abandoning him on his betrothal day. If it weren't for the scandal it would cause, Masetto says he would—but Zerlina interrupts his threats and says that if he doesn't believe she is innocent then he may be as angry as he likes and punish her in any way he chooses; but

* The original Italian refers always to Don Giovanni's *palazzo*, the Germans call it a villa, while English synopses and programme notes describe it as a country house. It seems likely that Da Ponte visualized the kind of palatial country villa designed by Palladio which is found in Venetia; and since that sort of place—to me, at any rate—is a palace it is for that reason I have translated "palazzo" literally.

afterwards there must be peace and quiet—"Batti, batti, o bel Masetto" ("Beat me, beat me, dear Masetto"):*

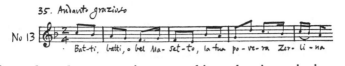

The orchestral accompaniment to this enchanting aria is another exquisite instance of Mozart's endless instrumental invention. An obbligato for solo violoncello runs through it from beginning to end, without a single bar's rest for the player: but even this unexpected garniture does not detract from the quite astonishing simplicity of the score and the economy of the part-writing. As with Susanna's "Deh vieni" in *Figaro* Mozart introduces a chamber-music quality into Zerlina's accompaniment, which consists of only one flute, one oboe and one bassoon in addition to the strings and two horns. For the most part the melody is supported in octaves either by 1st and 2nd violins, 1st violins and violas, or the three solo wind instruments.

In the first part of her aria Zerlina dares Masetto to beat her and gouge out her eyes as she stands before him like a lamb. But, she says, seeing him silent and ashamed, he hasn't the heart. The time changes from 2/4 to 6/8 and Zerlina, having won her point, cries "Peace" and promises that they shall spend their days and nights in happiness and contentment:

Masetto finds Zerlina's musical argument irresistible; she is a witch, he says, and he is weak in the head. All the good that her wheedling has done, however, is immediately dissipated by Zerlina's nervousness at hearing Don Giovanni's voice off-stage giving orders for the preparation of the feast. Masetto is suspicious at once when Zerlina looks for somewhere to hide, for he thinks she wants to avoid the embarrassment of meeting Don Giovanni in front of her lover, which would allow him to see her real relations with "monsù cavaliero".

The Finale to the first act now begins, which in its way is as full of movement and complications as the second act Finale of *Figaro*. Perhaps even more so, for the *Don Giovanni* finale suffers a physical change of scene in the middle apart from the purely musical changes of mood and varied characterization. To Mozart, however, the Finale was a musical whole,

---

* "Batti, batti" underwent one of the least appropriate musical translations in history when it was introduced into an English collection of "Sacred Melodies" compiled by William Gardiner in 1812, with the words "Gently Lord, O gently lead us through this lowly Vale of Tears" put to it.

beginning and ending in the key of C as the *Figaro* Finale begins and ends in E flat.

Masetto starts off the Finale by announcing that *he* is going to hide in order to see what goes on when Don Giovanni arrives on the scene. Masetto's music throughout the opera has a typical rugged, four-square quality and he points to the arbour where he is going to hide with an obstinate little phrase which recurs frequently in this first movement of the Finale:

Zerlina is appalled at the thought of Masetto hiding, not because she is afraid for herself, but for him. The poor thing ("poveretto") won't know what to do, she says, if he is discovered hiding Masetto retorts that all she need concern herself with is remaining where she is and talking to Don Giovanni in a clear, audible voice. (In this way, he says in an aside, he will know exactly how far the affair has gone—an aside which is matched by Zerlina's protest that her ungrateful and unkind lover seems determined to get into trouble today.)

Masetto hides himself in the arbour as a flourish of trumpets and drums added to the orchestra accompanies Don Giovanni's entrance. He is in an expansive and hospitable mood and arrives with four "nobly apparelled" servants to invite the peasants to his party—for it must not be forgotten that the peasants have been lying about on the grass ever since Masetto and Zerlina started quarrelling. Don Giovanni indeed has to greet them all with words "Wake up and let's laugh and enjoy ourselves!" He turns to his servants instructing them to take his guests indoors, and to the word-for-word echo of their master's invitation the servants lead the peasants into the house, their voices dying away in what must be one of the earliest operatic instances of the diminuendo of a receding chorus.*

When they have gone Zerlina, who has stayed behind, tries to hide from Don Giovanni among the trees, but it is obvious from the first note of the scene that she is not going to succeed. Mozart is not one to waste an opening phrase like this:

on a pointless situation. As Zerlina sings that she intends to hide, Don Giovanni sees her and catches her by the hand. She begs him to let her go,

* It is sometimes thought that this choral coda was entirely Mozart's idea, a spontaneous notion which occurred to him while he was composing, and that as he had no available words to set to music at that stage of composition he used Don Giovanni's opening invitation again, giving it by mistake to the four servants to repeat in full instead of to the chorus of peasants to whom the sentiments would have come more naturally—that part of the invitation, at least, which follows the imperative "Wake up!"

but with seductive and unequivocal words he tells her that he is "all love" and wants to "make her happy" in the arbour. Zerlina, as we know, is less anxious about her own fate than about what will happen if Masetto is discovered. Don Giovanni leads Zerlina into the arbour and is surprised and disconcerted to discover Masetto there. The situation is a little reminiscent of the great *Figaro* finale, but instead of being confronted by the wide-eyed innocence of a Countess's maid or the humiliating revelation of an eavesdropping page, Don Giovanni is faced with a very surly and implacable peasant indeed. Don Giovanni plays for time, and recovering himself blandly implies that he had been looking everywhere for Masetto because Zerlina was feeling lonely and "cannot exist without you"—a glib remark,

which Masetto throws back, note-for-note, with the ironic assurance ("un poco ironico") that he understands perfectly:

At this moment the sound of music is heard coming through the windows of Don Giovanni's palace, a welcome diversion which enables Don Giovanni to change the subject and suggest that he, Masetto and Zerlina should all go indoors and join the party, a suggestion accepted with quite remarkable eagerness and alacrity by the two peasants.

This little scene ends in an F major which the composer immediately transforms into the ominous relative D minor, to bring in Don Ottavio, Donna Anna and Donna Elvira "in maschera"—that is, in those all-enveloping cloaks and masks familiar from the Venetian carnival scenes of Guardi and Longhi.

The conspiracy of the three masks to expose all Don Giovanni's wicked deeds is rather surprisingly led by Donna Elvira in a vigorous and determined tune echoed by Don Ottavio and accompanied by a busy string figure:

The appearance of Donna Elvira as ringleader is a little unexpected, one feels, because it was only such a short while before that we were listening to one of the greatest of all vendetta arias from Donna Anna.

Now it comes to it, however, it is Donna Anna whose courage needs
screwing to the sticking-place and it is Don Ottavio who has to help her
to it, by pointing out that their friend Donna Elvira is right and that
sorrow and fear must be forgotten.

Donna Anna is not at all convinced. She foresees danger and complications, and she fears not only for Don Ottavio but for all of them. Before
the enthusiasm of the unpredictable Donna Elvira can have any effect on
Donna Anna, however, the window of the palace is opened from inside
by Leporello and the sounds of a minuet are heard coming from Don
Giovanni's party—the Celebrated Minuet, played by strings, oboes and
horns back stage:

Leporello looks through the window and seeing the masked trio draws
Don Giovanni's attention to them; their presence is clearly as unexpected
as it is impressive. Don Giovanni looks through the window and immediately tells Leporello to invite them in. He retires to leave his servant to
attract their attention a little unceremoniously with "psst! psst!"

The three masks, who have recognized Don Giovanni by his face and
his voice as The Betrayer, look up at Leporello's greeting, and the two
women delegate Don Ottavio to answer. Leporello repeats his "psst!
psst!" and adds his master's invitation, which Don Ottavio accepts on
behalf of himself and his companions. Leporello acknowledges the acceptance and disappears, closing the window behind him and so shutting in
the sound of the minuet.

The musical action now returns to the orchestra in the pit with one of
those remarkable, ominous modulations which Mozart uses from time
to time. Like the modulation in the finale of *Figaro* to which I referred and
which it closely resembles (see *Figaro*, Ex 58, p. 77), it is a phrase which
means little on paper and even less out of its context. But for all its apparent
simplicity there is never any question *in the theatre* of the effect of:

This modulation now leads to one of the most overwhelmingly effective
moments in all opera: a short passage of some twenty bars in which the
three masks, accompanied only by the wind instruments of the orchestra
(flutes, oboes, clarinets, bassoons and horns), stand and reflect in their
individual ways before entering Don Giovanni's palace. Donna Anna has
recovered some of her courage and with Don Ottavio supporting her
implores heaven to protect her "zealous heart"; while Donna Elvira
prays that heaven will avenge the betrayal of her love. The couple of lines
in which these two prayers are expressed provide the sole text of this trio.

Don Ottavio sometimes sings in sixths with Donna Anna, but for the most part he provides the bass to the women's voices which weave in and out in a superbly decorated arabesque of which every note is completely personal and peculiar to the character which sings it. The trio begins:

For the student of orchestration the accompaniment is of particular interest; it is limited to wind instruments throughout, as I have mentioned, and makes particularly effective use of arpeggios in the low register of the clarinet to give an unusual depth of instrumental colour which persists, without benefit of strings, until the end of the scene.

Scene 5: A brightly lit room prepared for a lavish ball.

The scene opens with Don Giovanni and Leporello showing their guests to their seats at the end of a dance; Don Giovanni is attending to the girls and his servant to the men. Stage "business" and conversation, which includes offers of coffee, chocolate, ices and sweets (the host obviously considered his guests had had more than enough strong liquor in the scene before), are carried on to the activity and brilliance of:

Masetto begs Zerlina to be careful, an admonition which Zerlina ignores but she joins her lover in an aside observation that the scene has begun so sweetly that it may well end in bitterness. Don Giovanni, unaware of Zerlina's apprehension, flirts openly with her while Leporello imitates his master's habits and mannerisms with two other peasant girls. Masetto's reaction to all this is, to say the least, unfavourable and his "ugly look" is noted and commented upon by Zerlina as well as by Don Giovanni and Leporello.

The atmosphere is immediately changed, however, by the arrival in a stately tempo with trumpets and drums of the three masks. They are welcomed with ceremony first by Leporello and then by Don Giovanni; they reply in formal terms that they are grateful for so many signs of generous hospitality and together with their host and his servant join in echoing Don Giovanni's cry of "Viva la libertà!"—an admirable sentiment but rather puzzlingly irrelevant just at that moment.

Don Giovanni, having persuaded his guests to join him in his praise of liberty, gives orders for the musicians to strike up and there follows a scene of immense technical ingenuity.

It begins with the Celebrated Minuet, played by an orchestra of oboes, horns and strings on the stage, this time in G major instead of the F in which it was played before. Don Ottavio and Donna Anna take the floor; Anna is in a highly nervous state but her companions encourage her, though Donna Elvira does not exactly cheer her up by pointing out Zerlina with the ominous words: "That is the peasant girl!" Anna's reaction to this is to cry out in despair "I shall die!"

Don Giovanni occupies himself with the seduction of Zerlina, and the general situation, according to both him and Leporello, is deemed to be going well. Masetto overhears this remark and with heavy irony echoes a growling "Indeed, everything is going fine!" Don Giovanni instructs Leporello to entertain Masetto and a second orchestra of violins and basses is heard tuning up over the music of the first.* While Leporello is busy with Masetto, Don Giovanni is luring Zerlina to the dance,—not to the minuet, which Don Ottavio and Donna Anna continue to dance, but to a country dance now struck up by orchestra No 2.

Leporello's efforts to persuade Masetto to dance with him are finally rewarded and a third orchestra tunes up before launching into a waltz. "Waltz" is a rather loose term to describe the dance in 3/8 time played by the stage band in this scene. In the score Da Ponte's stage directions state that Leporello forces Masetto to dance "la Teitsch" with him. "La Teitsch" was a phrase that puzzled me for a long while until it occurred to me that it was Da Ponte's phonetic transcription of the way Mozart pronounced "deutsch." Mozart frequently wrote "deutsch" as "teutsch"; his famous German Dances were referred to by their composer as "Teutsche Tänze", and as an Austrian he naturally changed the *eu* diphthong to *ei*—making the word sound like "tÿtch" instead of "toytch". The reason for the feminine article in "la Teitsch", of course, is that in the Italian *danza* is implied which is a feminine noun.

With Leporello and Masetto joining Donna Anna and Don Ottavio, Don Giovanni and Zerlina on the various dance floors (Donna Elvira is left to play the part of wallflower) we have three different dance rhythms going on at once, and at the start of the Teitsch they occur in this fashion:

*The effect is carefully written in the score but in all honesty it must be admitted that it is very rarely audible in practice—mainly, I think, because the strings on the stage are usually too few to make any impression against the minuet orchestra and the singers.

With the introduction of the waltz to the ensemble Mozart begins to reinforce his two strings-only orchestras from time to time by the oboes and horns of the original minuet-band. The oboes support occasional melodic phrases of the *contradanza* (the Italian corruption of the English "country dance"), the horns play a series of triplet figures to underline the rhythm of the waltz. While the tune of the minuet has become familiar enough to the audience by repetition for it no longer to need instrumental reinforcement from the oboes, the tune of the waltz has to make itself heard without any outside assistance at all.

Perhaps ideally this three-dances scene would be played in three different rooms with the action in each visible through wide doors to those dancing in the other two. Something of the kind seems to have been in the mind of both composer and librettist, for the dances are carefully divided into "classes"—the minuet for the aristocracy, the waltz for the lower classes with the country dance, less stately than the minuet but more dignified than the Teitsch, performed as a compromise by an aristocrat dancing below his station with a peasant girl who is dancing above hers.

Exactly how this scene should be staged is fortunately the director's worry and need not concern us. Somehow or other, however, Don Giovanni must be able in the course of dancing with her to abduct Zerlina from the ballroom without being noticed by anybody but Leporello. As Don Giovanni and Zerlina disappear through one of the doors of the ballroom, Leporello stops dancing with Masetto and hurries after them. Donna Anna, Donna Elvira and Don Ottavio, who have witnessed none of this, remark that the culprit is running into his own trap—an assertion which looks like being proved right almost immediately, for the dance music is interrupted by cries for help coming from Zerlina off-stage. The dance orchestra musicians (and the "crowd" players whom Da Ponte includes among "the others") hurriedly leave the scene, and the orchestra in the pit takes over once more with agitatedly dramatic music as the three masks excitedly try to break down the door to a phrase which occurs in both major and minor in the course of the next minute or so:

That short phrase is virtually the last easily-remembered tune in the Finale, for while a great deal goes on in the drama the music which goes with it is singularly uninteresting and not at all what we would expect from the composer of a movement like the second act Finale of *Figaro*. It is conventionally "brilliant", conventionally noisy, and—for Mozart—most unconventionally devoid of any character-drawing or subtle dramatic comment.

The first sensation in the action is the return to safety of Zerlina, followed by Don Giovanni, who grabs Leporello with him and (according to Da Ponte's stage direction) "making as though to stab him, but the sword does not leave its scabbard." Don Giovanni's pretence does not deceive the three masks, however; Don Ottavio pulls out a pistol and covers Don Giovanni with it, at the same time taking off his mask. The two women also unmask and as Don Giovanni recognizes them, Donna Anna, Donna Elvira and Don Ottavio are joined by Zerlina and Masetto in denouncing him as a deceiver and telling him that since they now know everything his number is up.

"Tremble!" they cry. "Soon the whole world will know of your black and terrible deed and of your inhuman cruelty. Hark to the thunder of vengeance! Its lightning will strike you down ere long!" Because of the general din of this finale there have sometimes been producers who have engaged a thunderstorm to accompany these words, but the thunder and lightning are, of course, purely figurative although it must be admitted that the nature of most of the music is stormy enough as it sweeps faster and faster to the fall of the curtain.

Exactly what is supposed to happen in the final stages of this closing scene neither Da Ponte nor Mozart gives any clear indication. Don Giovanni declares, in answer to the company's threats and invocations, that he fears nothing and nobody. One thing is certain: as the curtain falls not a hair of Don Giovanni's head has been touched, though for details of how he escapes from the menace of Don Ottavio's pistol one may consult any one of the variety of published opinions ranging from acting editions of the vocal score to the stories of the opera printed in opera house programmes. A Gallup Poll would reveal that the majority view (although there is quite a high percentage in the Poll who answer "Don't know") is that Don Giovanni draws his sword and thrusts Leporello into the threatening crowd, making his escape in the subsequent confusion. This seems a suitable solution on the whole (even though "the crowd" had been sent off by Da Ponte with the dance band musicians), but whether this is what happened in the original production of *Don Giovanni* or not is another matter. One is a little sceptical of these helpful suggestions on reflecting that almost without exception these same sources ignore Da Ponte's specific instructions that when Don Giovanni emerges after Zerlina's escape he threatens Leporello with an *undrawn* sword and treat us to a complicated and detailed description of how he should have a drawn sword in his hand.

A drawn sword might possibly have added colour to Don Giovanni's story: an undrawn sword obviously gave him away at once. Da Ponte does not write many stage directions in his libretto; it is remarkable, when he does, how little notice anybody seems to take of them.

ACT II

Scene 1 : A street; on one side of it Donna Elvira's house with a balcony.

No curtain in all opera rises in such a nonchalantly businesslike manner as this one on the second act of *Don Giovanni.* In a single introductory phrase Mozart takes his audience unmistakably back into the world of *opera buffa:*

The bouncing impertinence of that introduction has always reassured me that there is nothing to worry about where the inconsistencies of Don Giovanni's escape from the dilemma of the previous scene are concerned. Like the hero of the serial story written by the office boy, Don Giovanni was left in a hopeless mess at the end of one instalment to be disembarrassed in the next by the simple device of starting the sequel with the words: "With one bound our hero leapt to freedom."

So it is that Don Giovanni is as free as the air at the beginning of this scene in Act II, his only care in the world the obviously familiar and monotonously recurrent situation of Leporello's threat to leave his service. The matter is discussed with remarkably few words (though with a frequent repetition of them) in this opening duet. Don Giovanni says Leporello is mad; Leporello says he is not. Don Giovanni asks what he has done that his servant should want to leave him; Leporello answers "Nothing". He is just fed up. And there, it seems, the matter is likely to rest as the duet ends and Leporello moves off.

Don Giovanni calls him back, suggesting they should make it up and be friends. Leporello, with feigned reluctance, accepts Don Giovanni's offer of money (about £4) with all the practised assurance of one who has gone through what he calls the "ceremony" many times before. "But you can't seduce me like you can seduce your women," he adds.

"Think no more of it," says Don Giovanni. "Will you do as I tell you?"

"Yes," replies Leporello, "—provided we leave women alone."

"Are you mad?" exclaims Don Giovanni. "Don't you know that they are more necessary to me than the bread I eat, the very air I breathe?"

This resounding expression of his philosophy in a thrown-away line of recitative has in its time been regarded with quite overwhelming awe by eminent students of this eternally perplexing opera of Mozart's. They see in it the answer to the whole enigma of Don Giovanni's character, the reason for Don Giovanni's "tragedy"—the tragedy of sexual obsession, etc. Unfortunately what is overlooked is Leporello's immediate comment on a blatantly insincere, unserious and characteristically flippant remark: "And you still have the heart to deceive them?" and Don Giovanni's unconvincing and thoroughly unprofound reply to show that no man can fool his valet: "If you're faithful to one, you deceive the others. I, who am generous by nature, wish to be fair to all. But there are women who do not appreciate this and think me deceitful." In this context, it will be seen, all the profound psychological revelation promised by that one line about women being more necessary to Don Giovanni than the air he breathes is deflated at once, and is about as worthy of serious study as almost exactly the same remarks made by Macheath in *The Beggar's Opera*. Unhappily, it is often difficult to convince some people that because something is said in a Mozart opera it is not necessarily of greater philosophical and social significance than the same thing said in a ballad opera by John Gay nearly sixty years earlier.

Leporello loyally replies that he has never encountered a character more generous or kind than Don Giovanni. These *complimenti* at an end, servant and master get down to business, with Leporello abruptly asking what he can do for his employer and Don Giovanni answering: "Listen! Have you seen Donna Elvira's maid? No? Well, you've never seen anything more lovely!"

With relations between master and servant clearly on a normal footing once more Don Giovanni starts to plan a seduction with Leporello's help. It is dusk and convinced that the girl's appetite would be more easily whetted if she thought Leporello was courting her, Don Giovanni arranges to change clothes with his servant—"a gentleman's clothes don't have a very good name with girls of her class," he explains. Leporello objects, but Don Giovanni overrides him angrily and hats and cloaks are exchanged. His plans are delayed for a moment, however, by the appearance at her window of Donna Elvira. She reflects on her bewildered feelings bidding her heart be silent and not yearn for the man she knows is a liar and a deceiver, but whom she still loves and cannot give up.

Donna Elvira's words are sung to what may be called the "first subject" of a movement which expands into a trio and into what is perhaps the most beautiful musical scene in the opera. The scene opens like this:

The instrumentation of this trio is for flutes, clarinets, bassoons and horns in addition to strings, and the omission of the oboes avoids any element of harshness in a wonderful orchestral colouring. Leporello and his master first make their musical presence felt sharing a little phrase which is bandied about between bassoons, violas and basses, clarinets and flutes:

This is used with such remarkable ingenuity by Mozart that it is played eight times running on one occasion and nine times on another without for a moment becoming monotonous or—more important—ever losing its point. It is not played for a moment too long or too little.

When Leporello reports that he can hear Donna Elvira's voice Don Giovanni tells him to stay where he is and taking up a position behind his servant (who is dressed in his master's cloak and hat) answers Donna Elvira in the same musical terms as she has been using.

Donna Elvira is at her most vulnerable and Don Giovanni knows it; he echoes her tune as seductively as he knows how, flattering her with endearments, prayers for forgiveness and promises of true love. She, poor woman, imagines that the voice she hears belongs to the figure she mistakes for Don Giovanni and her resistance inevitably breaks down in the end. An unexpected and surprising modulation

leads to Don Giovanni anticipating in a curious way, if in a different key, the kind of tune he sings in the scene immediately following this, when— once again—he is thoroughly occupied with the mechanics of seduction. The blood relationship between "Deh, vieni alla finestra" and Don Giovanni's C major lure in the trio is not easy to mistake:

There is no need to attach any deep importance to this coincidence, although it would no doubt be easy to prove by some teutonic ingenuity that Don Giovanni is obsessed in his mind, not with the Elvira he is seducing with Leporello playing the visual part of Don Giovanni, but with the maid he will shortly be seducing while visually playing the part of Leporello. Whatever the significance of the similarity, in this present context it has the effect of breaking down Donna Elvira's defences, and though she protests that she doesn't believe Don Giovanni's threats to commit suicide her protestations grow feebler until, at the end of the trio (during a great deal of which Leporello is helpless with *buffo* laughter), Elvira leaves her balcony to come down and join the man she thinks is her lover.

The purely sensuous beauty of this trio can have a most unbalancing effect. The dramatic situation itself does not deserve music of such an absorbing and overwhelming character, for the dramatic situation, after all, is flippant, comic and not to be taken seriously unless we wish to charge both Da Ponte and Mozart with an almost unforgivable lapse of taste.

And yet how is one to regard this trio? Elvira's longing to resume her love-affair with Don Giovanni is as clearly apparent as any emotion in the whole opera. Don Giovanni's sincere insincerity is equally obvious. If he sings the same sort of tune as Donna Elvira he does so because he wants her to believe that he feels the same way about things as she does.

I would like to state here that I do not subscribe to the common English view of "sincerity" as a virtue in itself. Don Giovanni to me is just as sincere in everything he does (which may be evil) as Don Ottavio is in everything that he does (which may be good). The English interpretation of "sincerity"—particularly when applied to the arts—is limited and implies only good. Don Giovanni I believe is sincere in his exploitation of insincerity because he is sincere in his *aims*, which can be gained only by insincere methods. Don Giovanni is the archetype of Shakespeare's men who were deceivers ever; he cannot resist indulgence in deception for the sheer joy of deception for its own sake. Though we know that his first object is to get Donna Elvira out of the way in order to seduce her maid undisturbed, there is little doubt that Don Giovanni enjoys the process of removing Elvira. It is the thrill of the chase again, and he enters into the spirit of it as instinctively as a kitten will play with a ball of wool even though, in this case, the whole process is merely an expedient and he does not propose to enjoy the usual excitement of the actual kill.

In the second half of the trio, indeed, once he sees that Elvira has fallen into his trap, Don Giovanni gives up his wooing tactics and reflects to himself what a fine coup this is going to be and what a fine fellow he is— "nobody has a more fertile talent than mine. . . ."

When Donna Elvira has disappeared from view at the end of the trio, Don Giovanni turns to Leporello to ask what he thinks.

"I think you must have a soul of bronze," replies Leporello.

Don Giovanni calls his servant a ninny and gives him his instructions. When Elvira arrives Leporello must run towards her and embrace her, kissing her four times, and, imitating Don Giovanni's voice, must somehow contrive to take her away to leave the coast clear for his master.

"And if she recognizes me?" asks Leporello.

"She won't—unless you want her to," replies Don Giovanni.

Don Giovanni moves into the shadow to watch Leporello make love to the hapless Donna Elvira, who now arrives excitedly on the scene. There should be no possible fear in the recitative which follows of taking the dramatic situation seriously, even if one is a little bewildered by the contradictions provided in the trio by the supreme quality of the music and the deliberate low-comedy of the action.

The scene between Leporello and Donna Elvira is short, and can be extremely low and extremely comic. All Elvira's seriousness is offset by Leporello's obvious enjoyment of the whole charade and his amusing impersonation (or what he considers to be an impersonation) of his master's mannerisms and language: Elvira is addressed as "my life", "pretty face" and "my Venus". Don Giovanni, at the side of the stage, creates a disturbance by having an imaginary sword fight with an imaginary adversary whom he kills. This provides Leporello with his cue to take the frightened Elvira to safety, and Don Giovanni is left alone on the stage to serenade Elvira's maid in peace.

Don Giovanni now sings the Canzonetta, "Deh, vieni alla finestra" ("Come to the window") which, we have heard, was oddly anticipated in the trio (Ex 52):

The pizzicato accompaniment to the serenade is decorated by a mandoline obbligato which, according to the experiences of some of my English and American colleagues, seems to be more usually performed by pizzicato violins in the orchestra. If this be true then I must count myself luckier than they in the performances I have heard of *Don Giovanni*, for I have always heard it played on the mandoline—a practice which I am glad to note is followed in recordings of the opera.

The German translation of *Don Giovanni*, however, confuses the whole issue altogether, for whether the obbligato is played on a mandoline, pizzicato on a violin, or on a harp with its strings damped with tissue paper, the German words tell us to "Hark to the sound of the zither!" Could anything be more typically unimaginative than giving a Spanish aristocrat a zither to play on—the national peasant instrument of Bavaria and the Austrian Tyrol?

Whatever the instrument supplying the obbligato, however, we never know what effect the serenade has on Donna Elvira's maid, for when he has finished singing Don Giovanni is interrupted by the arrival of Masetto ("with arquebus and pistol") leading a band of armed peasants on the prowl in search of Don Giovanni, whom they propose to kill.

In the dusk and wearing Leporello's hat and cloak Don Giovanni is mistaken for his servant, and in this guise offers to help Masetto in his search.

"One half of you go that way," says Don Giovanni, pointing in one direction, "and the rest of you go the other."

Don Giovanni gives these directions in his servant's voice. Mozart sets them to Leporello's music, for in the aria which begins "Metà di voi quà vadano" ("Half of you go in that direction . . .") he makes a point of stressing Leporello's familiar patter-mannerisms and characteristically angular musical accent. So long as Don Giovanni remembers he is supposed to be Leporello the accompaniment features a sly little figure which is first heard at the beginning of the aria:

For a few bars, however, Don Giovanni reverts to his own elegant type. Having dispersed the other peasants he is left alone with Masetto and in a wheedling phrase takes him by the arm and assures him that they will see the matter through at their leisure.

The first Leporellian figure (Ex 54) returns at the end of the aria and Don Giovanni leads Masetto away. They return a moment later, however, and Don Giovanni proceeds to cross-examine Masetto on his intentions—which are that, armed with a musket and pistol, he proposes to leave Don Giovanni in little pieces. The peasant hands Don Giovanni his arms to look at; yes, they are all he has. Once he is assured of this Don Giovanni sets about Masetto, beats him with the flat of his sword and departs, leaving a badly battered peasant moaning painfully on the ground.

Zerlina, carrying a lantern, appears on the scene to discover her unhappy lover groaning with pain. A gently comic little scene ensues in which Masetto exaggerates his injuries and Zerlina consoles him. She will take him home and care for him, she says, if he promises to be less jealous in future; and she tells him of the cure she knows which will restore him to health—"Vedrai, carino, se sei buonino" ("You will see, beloved, if you are good, what a fine remedy I have . . ."):

Zerlina's "cure", of course, is her love for Masetto and she describes it in an aria of surprising depth and tenderness, a depth which is accentuated by the richness of the scoring (clarinets taking the place of oboes in the wood-wind) and a warm tenderness which suggests that Zerlina and the Susanna of "Deh vieni" in the last act of *Figaro* are very much sisters under the skin. The second part of the aria introduces an ingenious "heart-beat" effect which Zerlina exploits with irresistible charm. The scene ends with Masetto being helped off by Zerlina—a piece of stage "business" which is accompanied by an unusually long coda consisting of a *forte* reprise of the opening phrase of the aria and ending with the "heart-beats" dying away to a final *pianissimo*.

Scene 2: A dark courtyard with three doorways in Donna Anna's palace.

Leporello leads Donna Elvira hurriedly into the courtyard to avoid a company of people carrying lanterns and torches in the street outside.

Donna Elvira is a little puzzled by Leporello's behaviour (she still imagines he is Don Giovanni, of course, which is precisely why he is so anxious not to be discovered) and asks anxiously what he is afraid of. Nothing, nothing, he replies; if she will only stay there he will go and see if the coast is clear ("How on earth can I get away from her?" he asks in a ferocious aside), and making use of the general darkness of the surroundings he succeeds in escaping—though not, as we shall see, either very successfully or very far.

Donna Elvira cries despairingly and vainly after him not to leave her, and it is her apprehensive reflection which begins the famous sextet which now follows—"Sola, sola, in buio loco" ("Alone in this darkness I feel my heart beating . . ."):

This sextet is another of those great musical sequences found in Mozart's operas in which one is provided with a kind of panorama of action, emotion and character without interruption of the continuity or over-all conception of the musical thought, although there may be changes of key, time and tempo.

Donna Elvira's long opening phrase—her only contribution to the sextet for some time—is followed by a harassed passage from Leporello whose inability to find his way out of the dark courtyard (he keeps coming across the wrong door) is expressed in his familiar frustrated comic-patter way. Leporello's desperate repetition of his conviction that it is time to escape leads to a modulation which while perhaps not the most unusual sound in opera is surely the most surprising and unexpected. So surprising and unexpected, so quickly come and gone, indeed, that I cannot resist quoting the six bars in question in full, in the hope that by my doing so the listener who is not prepared for them will not let them slip by unnoticed:

The real unexpectedness of this passage is in the astonishing orchestra-tion of the last three bars: the sudden introduction of a drum roll and the scoring of a lyrical *melody* on the open notes of the first trumpet—an instrument which Mozart otherwise almost invariably uses for fanfares or dramatic emphasis with sustained notes (as in the overture to *Don Giovanni*).

The trumpets, which take the place of the horns throughout the D major section which now follows until the original E flat returns, herald the arrival of Donna Anna and Don Ottavio accompanied by servants carrying torches and lanterns. It was obviously these lights that had caused Donna Elvira and Leporello to seek refuge in the dark palace courtyard which, as Da Ponte would have known from his native country* is often used as a public thoroughfare, and two of the three doors mentioned in the stage directions of this scene would probably lead to the private apartments of the palace, while the third would lead out into the street.

Donna Anna and Don Ottavio are dressed in mourning, for we must not forget that it is the death of her father which is the starting point of the whole action of the opera. Don Ottavio, whose function becomes increasingly that of consoler-general and less of possible husband-to-be, sings first begging Donna Anna to wipe the tears from her eyes—"Tergi il ciglio, o vita mia":

Donna Anna begs him to allow her at least the relief which tears can bring to her sorrow, and with a long and dignified phrase she brings the music into C minor and to a miraculously effective figure in the violins which plays an important and moving part in the sextet until the final Molto Allegro:

We now hear coming from the darkness the voices of Donna Elvira, wondering where her "lover" can be, and Leporello, still vainly trying to find a way out. Donna Elvira and Leporello both see a doorway at the same moment and make towards it. When they reach it, however, the door is opened by Zerlina and Masetto who prevent Leporello leaving and cry "Stop villain! Where are you going?"

In unison (which is unusual, for Don Ottavio usually follows Donna Anna's voice around at the safe and faithful distance of a sixth or tenth below) Donna Anna and Don Ottavio point to the supposed Don Giovanni with "There is the blackguard! How did he get here?", and join Zerlina and Masetto in a common demand for "death to the perfidious one who betrayed me"—curious words for Don Ottavio and Masetto to sing in all conscience.

This unanimous if somewhat prejudiced view of Don Giovanni's shortcomings brings Donna Elvira out into the open. To the accompaniment of the pathetic figure quoted in Ex 60 she pleads for mercy for the man whom she now describes in so many words as her husband—"mio marito"—in

* It is no use pretending that *Don Giovanni* is really set in Spain; if it were we should not be hearing a mandoline, for a start.

the hope, one can only suppose, that by doing so she may soften the hearts of those who are set on punishing the man who has made an honest woman of her. Donna Elvira's appearance amazes everybody, but their amazement does not run to regarding the idea of a married Don Giovanni as funny, nor to preventing a united and forcefully expressed refusal to show any clemency. All Elvira's entreaties are rejected with the firm decision that her "husband" must die.

Don Ottavio draws his sword and is about to kill Leporello when the unfortunate servant falls to his knees and tearfully begs for mercy. Leporello's pleas and protestations are serio-comic in effect, for while Mozart adds a tearful little chromatic phrase which gives the scene a comic grotesqueness, there is a genuine pathos in the characteristically mournful G minor of the passage with its divided violas and generally dramatic orchestral colouring:

Ironically there is a quaint nobility about these phrases of Leporello's which makes him sound more aristocratic, more genuinely like Don Giovanni than at any other time during the whole masquerade. His pleas, however, leave no doubt of either his innocence or his identity in his accusers' minds and they are left, if not speechless, at least pretty perplexed by the unsatisfactory turn things have taken and there is a return to the figure in Ex 60 which dies away on an unmistakable question mark.

The question is not answered so much as shelved as the mood reverts to the opening E flat and the vigour of a Molto Allegro. The assembled company reflects on the extraordinary day it has been and on the unforeseen novelty of the situation ("che impensata novità"). It is a typical and brilliant movement building up to a sparkling and exciting finish and in which only Leporello, with his reiterated passages of anxious patter expressing the opinion that it will be a miracle if he can get himself out of *this* mess, receives any individual attention as a musical character and he holds on grimly to his own words, singing them against the other five singers who combine to sing about something quite different. At the end of the number Donna Anna leaves, taking her servants and—one presumes—all the available light with her.

If ever there was an ensemble intended and conceived and only logical as the finale of an act it is this sextet in *Don Giovanni*. Just as there is every musical argument in favour of Donna Anna's "Or sai chi l'onore" (No 10) as the finale of a first act, so it is obvious that the sextet should bring down the curtain on a third act. One of the principal points to support this is the purely physical one of the presence on the stage of six characters who would not, in the ordinary operatic way, be gathered together for any other purpose but that of providing a finale.

Exactly what happened and when it happened in the course of the creation of *Don Giovanni* that Mozart and Da Ponte had to compress an opera conceived in four acts into one with two long ones is unfortunately not known. It is only by the "feel" of the music that we are entitled to consider the idea at all, for it is otherwise the merest conjecture. Something, nevertheless, must have occurred to have made librettist and composer change their plans, for neither Da Ponte nor Mozart was one to countenance willingly, let alone deliberately, the kind of dramatic and musical anti-climax which inevitably results from the way the opera has come down to us.

As in the case of the scene which followed Donna Anna's fierce dramatic exit in Act I the best thing for the listener to do is to take a deep breath and imagine that a new stage in the story begins with the conclusion of the sextet and avoid the feeling of anti-climax by treating what follows as a kind of interlude, if not as a new and madly exciting development of the plot. For what now occurs is all fairly irrelevant, though much of it is entertaining.

When Donna Anna has left, Donna Elvira, Don Ottavio, Zerlina and Masetto turn on the wretched Leporello. First Zerlina attacks him for beating up Masetto (as she thinks); Donna Elvira is angry because she fell into the trap; Don Ottavio is convinced, as a matter of unswerving principle, that Leporello is up to no good (Ottavio is clearly opposed to the whole conception of Habeas Corpus). Only Masetto has no viewpoint to put forward but suggests that they should all punish the unfortunate fellow nevertheless, and there follows a characteristically *buffo* number for Leporello in which he begs his tormentors to have pity on him—"Ah pietà, Signori miei!"

Where earlier in the opera Mozart made lyrical use of the drop of the seventh (see Ex 10) he uses the same device in this aria of Leporello's to give a grotesque and comic quality to the vocal line, and we have sequences like

and

Evidently Mozart associated the idea very closely with Leporello's character, especially when the servant was frightened or in an awkward situation, for it occurs yet again later on in the opera.

In the course of his aria Leporello addresses a number of plausible arguments to Zerlina, Donna Elvira and Don Ottavio (in that order—he ignores Masetto altogether) and as the music dies away he manages to escape, muttering the phrases

which have already been heard from time to time and now supply the material on which the music fades. Only Donna Elvira considers it worthwhile to shout "Stop!" after him; it is evidently an automatic and habitual reflex action on her part, for she doesn't press the point.

Don Ottavio now addresses the assembled company with one of the most remarkable passages of logic and reason even the operatic stage has produced in its time.

"My friends!" he declares. "After the enormous excesses that have been committed we can no longer doubt that it was Don Giovanni who killed Donna Anna's father. Wait here in this house. I shall communicate with the proper authorities and in a few moments I promise you shall be avenged. Duty, pity and affection demand that this be done."

Don Ottavio, who cannot be considered very bright at any time, has taken an unusually long time to reach a conclusion which Donna Anna reached by first hand experience in Act I, and now that he has reached it he has scarcely made much of a case for the prosecution. Evidence based on the unsuccessful seduction of Zerlina, the beating of Masetto and the practical joke played (with Leporello's initially enthusiastic co-operation) on the unhappy Donna Elvira, would scarcely cause a police court magistrate to commit Don Giovanni for trial on a charge of murder. Ottavio's behaviour, indeed, is pretty odd altogether, for he now sings an aria in which he begs his listeners—Donna Elvira, Zerlina and Masetto—to go and console Donna Anna, dry her tears and tell her that he is going to avenge all the wrongs that have been committed.

All in all, it is a pretty comical situation, but we can forgive it all since, now left alone and prior to proceeding to see the police (we cannot conceive him simply "going"), Don Ottavio delivers himself of the exquisitely lovely aria—"Il mio tesoro" ("Meanwhile, go and console my dear one . . ."):

The action and continuity of the drama has now got into such a muddle that there is nothing for it but to sit back and enjoy Mozart for the sheer sake of the music he makes and consider ourselves lucky that we are not the Viennese audience of 1788 when the aria had to be cut because the tenor was incapable of singing it.

At that performance the general air of interpolating a diverting interlude after the sextet was maintained by the introduction in the place of Don Ottavio's aria of a comedy scene for Zerlina and Leporello. Zerlina has somehow managed where the others have failed to catch Leporello single-handed and waving a knife in her hand she drags him on to the stage by his hair. She threatens him in a pseudo-recitative in which she echoes ironically the final phrases of Leporello's aria (Ex 65) in the same key. The passage is marked *a tempo*, so it was obviously intended to follow immediately on Leporello's escape. This means that Donna Elvira's cries of "Stop!" and Don Ottavio's great bit of detective work are cut (which suggests that Ottavio's reasoning was not considered convincing enough without his aria to take our minds off it), and by some extraordinary means Zerlina is able unaided to capture the fugitive and bring him back on to the empty stage, the others somehow having wandered off in unspecified directions meantime.

The "business" of the scene is performed in normal recitative once Zerlina has got Leporello where she wants him, and she proceeds with the help of a peasant, who happens to be passing, to tie him to a chair, which in turn is fastened by a rope to one of the windows of the palace.

The duet which follows, like the rest of this whole substitute scene between Zerlina and Leporello is, of course, omitted from normal performances—though not from all recordings of the work.* Most vocal scores of *Don Giovanni* include it, however, as No 22b and it is worth more than a moment's passing study; it is a charming little duet and except that the whole action of the opera would become hopelessly entangled if it were included as well as Don Ottavio's aria there have been times in all our lives when we could have done without "Il mio tesoro" sung indifferently and would willingly have exchanged it for an acceptable alternative like this duet.

At the end of the number Zerlina abandons a thoroughly well-trussed-up Leporello and gaily leaves the scene. With no help at all from another passing peasant Leporello manages to escape—dragging with him both the chair and the palace window which is torn out of its frame.

Zerlina returns with Donna Elvira to show the noble lady how the rascally Leporello has been punished. Finding that her prisoner has escaped Zerlina is understandably indignant. Donna Elvira remarks that no doubt Don Giovanni is at the bottom of all this. Zerlina agrees and goes off in high dudgeon proclaiming that Don Ottavio shall hear of this— for Don Ottavio, Zerlina leads us to believe, will fix everything and avenge all who need avenging.

Though Zerlina's exit brings to an end what might be considered the interlude within the interlude of this part of the opera, we are still not yet back where the Prague audience was at the first performance of the opera: for Donna Elvira's presence alone on the stage at this point is due

* It is included in the RCA–Victor set conducted by Erich Leinsdorf (1960).

entirely to the insistence of Mlle Cavalieri during the Vienna production (she was the original Constanze—see p. 31) on being given a *scena* worthy of her talents and artistic importance. Mozart gave her one—a long and fascinating, if dramatically entirely irrelevant scene beginning with a particularly moving recitative accompanied by strings and including such poignant un-18th-century passages as:

Donna Elvira's mood is, once again, one of self-pity and it seems that, in the phrase of an old Scots nurse I knew of, she's "aye complainin'." But having resigned ourselves to the acceptance of so much of what goes on in this act as being directly unconcerned with either the plot or with the development of character we are able to continue our relaxed attitude towards the whole "joyous drama" and enjoy Donna Elvira's aria— "Mi tradì quell'alma ingrata" ("I was betrayed by that ungrateful soul"):

A peculiar and enthralling feature of this aria is that the 8/8 rhythm of the first full bar of the tune persists unceasingly for all but two of the 129 bars of the aria (excluding the two signing-off bars of the short coda). It is an *ostinato* which is quite fascinatingly distributed between the voice and the individual orchestral parts and accentuated by a busy and important part for the violoncellos who are rarely honoured in Mozart's scores by permission to occupy a separate stave in the score. We had the solo violoncello obbligato to "Batti, batti"; in "Mi tradì" the whole section is allowed to shine in a manner which did not occur with any regularity in the orchestra until Beethoven got to work to divide the classical bass part into its two independent components—violoncello and double bass.

With the end of what is in all conscience a magnificent and beautiful aria which it does nobody any harm to hear in an opera house, the interlude invented to pass the time between what surely should have been the end of Act III and the beginning of Act IV comes to an end. The curtain falls and the scene changes.

Scene 3: A cemetery with equestrian statues, among them the marble statue of the Commendatore.

The action of the opera starts up again at once in recitative as the curtain rises on this scene. Don Giovanni still disguised as Leporello, leaps breezily over the wall into the cemetery remarking that the moonlight is as clear as day and altogether it is a night made for the pursuit of love. It is still early it appears from Don Giovanni's announcement that it is "only two o'clock at night". This does not mean 2 a.m. although we know that Don Giovanni tends to feel at his best as a lover at dawn. Italian standard time is not recognized very strictly on the operatic stage, and "two o'clock of the night" can mean either 8 p.m. or two hours after dark —which might be 10 or 11 at latest. There are still clocks in Italy which never strike more than six strokes, a habit which those who know Verdi's *Ballo in maschera* will remember from the second act of that opera when midnight is indicated by a clock striking six.

I mention this question of the time of night because the whole of the action of *Don Giovanni* is supposed to take place in the course of 24 hours. We can ignore the raising of a statue to the Commendatore as being of any consequence because either it is a piece of permissible poetic licence, or— more likely—the statue was put up before the Commendatore's death. Da Ponte's exact description of what we commonly call the Cemetery Scene is "An enclosed space in the form of a 'sepolcrato' "—which can mean a vault or a tomb on the grandiose and elaborate scale found in Italy where vast stone canopies supported by pillars are a common sight. It was common practice until even later than the 18th century for family burial sites to be decorated with effigies of one kind or another not just in commemoration but also in anticipation of the death of those concerned.

In the case of Donna Anna's father it would not have been at all unusual for his statue to have been raised in what was obviously a *private* family mausoleum—one has only to consider the original commission by Pope Julius II of Michelangelo to erect a Sepulchral Monument during the Pontiff's lifetime. The presence of a carved inscription on the statue which is noted in the action of the scene is also easily explained if we go back to the libretto by Bertati on which Da Ponte based so much of his *Don Giovanni*. In Bertati's original the scene begins with Don Ottavio arriving with a stone-mason and instructing him to carve an inscription on the base of the monument. Da Ponte omits this incident altogether, but the fact of its omission does not mean that the inscription could not have been added in the time, although if Don Ottavio had to live according to both Da Ponte and Bertati's requirements he would have had a very busy day indeed. Bertati's preoccupation with the inscription, however, does suggest more than ever that the statue had long been erected and that the inscription was a topical addition occasioned by recent unhappy events.

Meanwhile, one of the reasons Don Giovanni is pleased that it is still early in the evening is that he is anxious to hear all about his servant and Donna Elvira. It is not long before Leporello turns up; he is on the run (having—if that scene was played—rid himself of the chair and window frame he was tied to by Zerlina) and takes refuge in the graveyard. He is in a grumbling mood, and his surprise at coming across Don Giovanni in such unfamiliar surroundings is far from pleasant.

Indeed, he becomes less and less pleased as time goes on. He changes clothes with his master and asks him what he has been doing since he last saw him. Don Giovanni replies that most of it will keep, but he must tell him the best one of all—namely, that he has only just come from meeting a pretty young girl in the street whose hand he had taken and who had tried to run away from him until she had suddenly thought that he was—guess who? Leporello! This little anecdote doesn't please Leporello at all, particularly as it looks as if there is worse to come. But it seems that the girl had somehow recognized Don Giovanni, and screamed and the would-be seducer had had to run for it, and that is why he was where he was.

Leporello is far from amused. "Supposing it had been my wife?" he asks his master, sullenly. Don Giovanni roars with laughter: "Better and better!"

Don Giovanni's laughter is cut short by the sinister voice of the Commendatore's statue proclaiming: "You will not laugh after dawn!" The effect of this sudden interruption of the gay dialogue recitative by a formal, declamatory vocal passage is immensely dramatic, particularly because Mozart introduces a sound completely new to the opera with which to accompany it—the solemn tones of three trombones.

The sound of trombones, associated in the mind of the 18th century audience with the supernatural and the solemnly religious, is introduced into *Don Giovanni* only so long as the Statue is in action. While it is said that Mozart had trouble with the trombone players at rehearsal and added wood-wind parts to the two pronouncements made by the Statue in this scene in case the trombones went wrong, I think it is only fair to point out that equally if the oboes and clarinets went wrong there would be no "top" to the tune or instrumental support for the Statue's vocal line. Basses and bassoons double the three trombone parts in case of accidents, but the oboes and clarinets have an important and independent part of their own to play.

It is fairly obvious, I think, that these instruments accompanying the Statue's warning phrases are meant to be played either off or under the stage, and I deduce this not from precedents to be found in Purcell's music to Shadwell's Don Juan play, *The Libertine*, but from observing in the score of *Don Giovanni* that when Mozart has instruments playing on the stage they are written into the score *without any suggestion of dynamics or expression marks of any kind*. This may be seen in the music for the three dance orchestras in Act I and in the accompaniment to the Statue in this present scene. Immediately the main orchestra takes over again we encounter expression marks once more.

I do not know the reason for this absence of dynamics unless it was that Mozart considered that to have it otherwise was entirely superfluous: music on the stage or behind the scenes was beyond the control of the conductor and had to be played as loudly as possible to be heard at all; there was certainly no time to indulge in the luxury of fancy nuances. Whatever the reason, however, this will be found to be a peculiar fact which cannot be entirely accidental.

Hearing the Statue's voice Don Giovanni asks quickly who is speaking.

"Oh," says Leporello, casually, "somebody from the other world who knows you well."

"Be quiet, you fool!" snaps Don Giovanni and drawing his sword he prods about among the headstones and statues. Once more the Statue speaks, warning Don Giovanni to let the dead rest peacefully.

This time Don Giovanni shrugs his shoulders; it is obviously somebody outside the cemetery playing the fool. Then he notices the Commendatore's statue for the first time. "See what the inscription says," he tells his servant. Leporello begs to be excused; he has never learnt to read by moonlight. Don Giovanni repeats his command.

Leporello reads: "Vengeance here awaits the villain who took my life." Leporello is terrified.

"The old fool!" laughs Don Giovanni ("o vecchio buffonissimo!"). "Invite him to supper this evening." (This phrase in itself surely sets the time of the scene as the early evening.)

The unfortunate Leporello is forced to relay his master's invitation, which he does unwillingly, with exaggerated politeness and with frequent grotesque protestations of helplessness and terror—his terror being expressed repeatedly by the characteristic Leporellian drop of a seventh at such words as "Padron, mi trema il core", an interval which is stressed by the unison legato orchestral accompaniment to the phrase:

Every time he hesitates Leporello is prodded with his master's sword to pull himself together. The Statue is eventually seen to nod his head in acceptance of the invitation. This action impresses Don Giovanni, and in a sudden change of key from E major to C major he extends the invitation personally for the first time:

The Statue accepts with a solemn "yes". There are no trombones to accompany him this time as presumably the players are on their way down from the stage to take their places in the pit for a later scene in which their presence is required in the orchestra; but it is a supernatural-sounding affirmative nonetheless and leads to a quite remarkable passage of six bars or so in which Mozart anticipates a whole century of sinisterly dramatic music as Don Giovanni reflects on how bizarre the whole scene is ("bizarra è inver la scena") to an orchestral accompaniment which, it has been said, seems to have strayed into the wrong century:

The music quickly returns to the grotesque and frightened chattering of Leporello's sevenths, however, and master and servant jump over the wall and are gone to a final fading couple of bars in which divided violas suddenly play an unexpected and important part.

Scene 4: A gloomy room.

"Camera tetra" is the sum total of Da Ponte's stage direction for this scene and since the rise of the curtain reveals Donna Anna and Don Ottavio in—we presume—Donna Anna's palace, it is easy to understand why. Donna Anna, in mourning, gets more and more gloomy as the opera proceeds—but only to look at. Her music, curiously enough, gets increasingly cheerful. At the beginning of this scene Don Ottavio is doing his best to console her, offering (in recitative) his love, his life—but Anna rebukes him. How can he say such things at such an unhappy time? This is almost too much for the patient Don Ottavio and he accuses her of being cruel.

This causes Donna Anna to reflect seriously in an orchestrally accompanied recitative which quotes a couple of times the first theme of the aria which follows. We need not take what Donna Anna tells us in this introduction too seriously, however, for it is none of it anything more than an imposing-sounding excuse to lead into a lovely, irrelevant and quite indispensable aria, entirely different from anything we have heard from

Donna Anna before—"Non mi dir" ("Do not tell me, beloved, that I am cruel to you . . ."):

Superficially this aria, described as a Rondo in the score, is strangely unemotional for the Donna Anna we have come to know for her outbursts earlier in the opera, and yet it has an elegance and assurance that suggest something of the character of Donna Anna as it is in normal circumstances and not as we know it under the abnormal, exaggerated and excited conditions created by the drama and hurly-burly of the story so far.

A faster section follows the leisurely opening of the Rondo and with restrained and unexpected, but thoroughly effective, coloratura decoration Donna Anna suggests to Don Ottavio that perhaps heaven will one day feel pity for her:

And having delivered herself of a beautiful and remarkably self-centred aria (she virtually thinks of herself and only herself throughout it) Donna Anna leaves the room for an unspecified destination. The unfortunate Don Ottavio, if he follows the score too closely, is left with a couple of lines of recitative in which he announces that he must follow Donna Anna to share her suffering ("with me her sighs will not be so deep"), and he too leaves the room. Merciful producers, however, usually cut these remarkably superfluous bars so that Donna Anna can bring the curtain down to such applause as she may have earned and the opera can proceed with its Finale with the change of scene.

Scene 5: A brightly lit room in Don Giovanni's palace; a meal is laid out on the table.

A characteristic flourish of trumpets and drums added to the orchestra prepare us to discover Don Giovanni in the expansive and hospitable mood with which this particular instrumental colouring is so often associated in Mozart. Hospitable he may be, but Don Giovanni is nevertheless oddly impatient, for having invited the Statue to supper he makes very little effort to wait for his guest's arrival. Perhaps he is convinced that the whole business is improbable, and since he has worked up an appetite for his supper one way and another during the past 24 hours he casts all ceremony aside and rubbing his hands he notes with relish that his meal is ready, bids the musicians of his private band strike up, adding rather bluntly that he expects to be well entertained for his money. Don Giovanni's first words are "Già la mensa è preparata" ("The meal is ready") and they are set to a swaggering phrase full of healthy anticipation:

The comedy scene which follows seems to have been a traditional feature of most Don Juan plays long before Bertati's and Da Ponte's time; as in *Don Giovanni* a great deal of fun is had, for instance, in Molière's *Don Juan* (1665) with the comic servant's attempts to filch tit-bits from his master's dishes. But where Molière's Sganarelle is finally and generously invited by his master to sit at table with him (although his plates are always being taken away from him by footmen before he can eat), Leporello is not so favoured and is consequently always being caught with his mouth full at the wrong moment.

This simple comedy is performed principally to the accompaniment of music from Don Giovanni's private band, who entertain him with "selections" from operas. It is obvious from the context that these musicians should be playing on the stage (Don Giovanni would hardly come so far out of character as to lean over to the pit and tell the musicians to earn the money he is paying them), but the score gives no indication that this is what is intended. Indeed, there is what I consider a strong contraindication inasmuch as the parts for 2 oboes, 2 clarinets, 2 bassoons, 2 horns and a violoncello to help the bass part along are all carefully written with expression marks which, as we have seen, are absent from passages intended for extra-orchestral performance in this opera.

The most common explanation put forward for the absence of Don Giovanni's private band from the stage is that the stage in the original Prague production was too small. Without knowing exactly what the scene looked like, nor how cluttered up the stage became with Don Giovanni's supper table, side tables and other properties this might well be the answer, were it not that three orchestras totalling at least 13 players (if only one player is required for each string part) were able to find room to play on the stage in the ballroom scene at the end of the first act, whereas there is apparently no way of accommodating a modest ensemble of eight wind-players and a violoncellist in the finale of the second.

My view is that the whole thing was dictated by the simple mechanics and economics of the opera house: there were no clarinets available for the stage band. That there were extra oboes and horns at the theatre's disposal I deduce from the use of these instruments on the stage in the ballroom scene—a scene which is both preceded and immediately succeeded by the pit orchestra using a full complement of oboes and horns so that there is no question of the players having time to dash backwards and forwards between pit and stage.

In the graveyard the extra oboes were again available and presumably also an extra pair of bassoons to support the shaky trombones if necessary; but the inclusion of clarinets in this scene is made possible only by the time provided for them to get up on the stage by the change of scene to the cemetery and by their omission from the duet (No 24) which follows. Before the clarinets are wanted again in Donna Anna's Rondo (No 25) there is another change of scene which gives the players ample time to return to their seats in the orchestra. When we come to the beginning of the Finale (No 26) Mozart uses his full orchestra—i.e. double wood-wind, horns, trumpets, drums and strings—and though he may have extra oboes, horns and even bassoons to spare for stage use, he still cannot lay hands on a pair of clarinets to include in a separate band on the stage; so the "stage" band is incorporated in the orchestra pit where, coming under the control of the conductor, they are given dynamic markings to observe.

It is plain from the libretto, however, that a band is meant to be on the stage and obviously Mozart hoped that in later productions it would be practicable; otherwise, I feel, he would have written the supper music for the combination at hand—namely, that which played for the earlier ballroom scene. It is obvious, in short, that Prague presented practical difficulties which, while they may present problems to Mozart scholars, are only too familiar to all of us who have ever had first-hand experience of the theatre in the provinces.

Don Giovanni's private band plays items from three operas, and as they occur so Leporello—at least, according to most full scores, though not apparently to all copies of the libretto—makes indirect reference to the tune we are listening to. The first tune is from the finale of Act I of Martín y Soler's opera *Una cosa rara*:

If there was any particular significance in the inclusion of this tune in the scene it does not seem to be known; for us at this stage in history however, there is a certain irony in it inasmuch as it was *Una cosa rara* (libretto by Da Ponte) which made such a success in the autumn of 1786 with its first performance in Vienna that it virtually displaced *Figaro* from the repertoire. As it was it was only the success of *Don Giovanni* when it arrived in Vienna which restored its composer to favour sufficiently to revive interest in *Figaro*.

The next supper tune comes from Sarti's opera *I due litiganti*—the so-called "Scoffing Song" which had first been heard in Prague in 1783, "Come un agnello":

The third interpolated item is one which almost certainly brought the house down as its first bars were recognized by the Prague audience. Whether Mozart included it as a gesture of gratitude and a compliment, or as what might today be known by that repellent word, a "gimmick", there is no doubt that the unexpected introduction of the tune of "Non più andrai" in a quaintly busy instrumental arrangement must have had a delighting effect on the public which had so firmly taken the music of *Figaro* to its heart:

The tune is played through twice to accompany the stage business demanded by Don Giovanni's supper and Leporello's endeavours to get his share of it, when the action of the drama begins again in a drastic fashion with the entrance of Donna Elvira.

The poor lady enters in a state which Da Ponte describes as "disperata" and in a determined phrase she announces that she has come to give one further proof of her love for Don Giovanni by forgiving him and begging him to change his way of life:

Don Giovanni, rising from the table and dismissing the musicians with a sign (a last and indisputable indication of where the wind band is meant to be) shows considerable surprise, which is shared by Leporello, and they both ask what is the matter.

To Don Giovanni's even greater surprise Donna Elvira falls on her knees to continue her entreaties. Don Giovanni remarks that if she will not rise then he had better go down on his knees too; and does so. Donna Elvira, whose sense of humour is not at its strongest just at this moment, accuses Don Giovanni of making fun of her.

"I? Make fun of you?" protests Don Giovanni as he lifts her to her feet. "Whatever for?" He continues to treat her with exaggerated courtesy, but as she persists in mixing abuse with her pleading he loses patience and begs to be excused while he returns to his supper. Would she care to join him? But he gets no kind of coherent reply and while Elvira repeatedly calls him a "horrible example of iniquity" Don Giovanni sings irrelevantly the praises of women and wine as the foundation and glory of humanity. The recurrent phrase which accompanies these noble sentiments has always struck me as one of the queerest in all music. It is a passage written in two simple parts which bristle with the most unexpected, barely concealed consecutive open fifths:

The starkness of the implied consecutive fifths which I have indicated above is something which never fails to send a shiver down my spine. There are many academically more correct alternatives to that bass part, but none of them so effective as Mozart's astonishing unorthodoxy.

With a final repetition of her line about Don Giovanni being a "horrible example of iniquity" Donna Elvira goes to the door to leave. She lets out a piercing scream and staggers back into the room to make her escape by another door. Don Giovanni, who is puzzled by this further interruption of his meal, sends Leporello to the door to see what it is all about. Leporello too lets out a yell and staggers back speechless into the room, locking the door behind him. The tempo changes from the versatile 3/4 in which so much has been happening and a breathless Leporello relates what he has seen in an agitated passage which begins:

He tells Don Giovanni of the "stone man", the "white man" he has seen outside and begs his master not to go out of the room; and he gives a grotesquely graphic description of the approaching Apparition's relentless and terror-striking steps. Don Giovanni doesn't understand a word his servant is saying and considers him quite mad. A knocking is heard at the door. Don Giovanni orders Leporello to open it; the knocking becomes more insistent as Leporello grows more terrified and firmly fixed to the spot. Don Giovanni goes towards the door himself, while Leporello hides under the table saying that he does not want to look at his "amico" any more—an unexpected and rather touching insight into a generally perplexing master-and-servant relationship. Don Giovanni opens the door and returns followed by the Statue of the Commendatore whose entry is accompanied by this slight harmonic alteration of the first bars of the Overture:

That opening chord of the diminished seventh still succeeds in providing a remarkable element of surprise which could never be achieved by a literal return to the first bar of the Overture (Ex 1), even though the "tune"—i.e. the 1st violin part—is the same in each case. (In practice, of course, it is not until one hears the third and fourth bars of Ex 82 that association with the overture is complete in one's mind, anyway.) In addition to the harmonic variation there is the instrumental one of the inclusion of what we may now regard as the Statue's bodyguard of trombones in the orchestra.

I do not think we need worry for a moment, as some scholars do, whether in this Finale these three instruments should be played on the stage (as they were in the Cemetery scene) or not, for the simple technical reason that if they were played back-stage, off-stage or below-stage they would be quite inaudible and therefore useless for all practical purposes. The trombones are meant to be part of the pit orchestra; they are carefully decorated in the score with dynamic markings, which means that they are the immediate concern of the conductor and, as such, intended to fit in with the other instruments of the orchestra. The Statue is now mobile; he is no longer making sinister announcements in the middle of a *buffo* recitative. He has entered the general action with (literally) a vengeance and though he may bring his peculiar and personal instrumental colouring with him he is now sharing the musical plot and dialogue with others; he is no longer a remote marble figure perched on a marble horse, for he has left his horse behind him. Presuming that Mozart intended to have trombones at all in this scene (former doubts about that now seem to have been mercifully cleared up), it seems incredible that anybody should ever have credited him with so little professional nous as to imagine that he would have them in some remote, invisible and certainly inaudible position to take part in an orchestral ensemble of considerable complexity and difficulty.

From the initial hearing of the opening chords which attend the Statue's appearance it must not be thought that we are in for a note-for-note reprise of the overture. We get far more than that, for Mozart develops his stern Andante-in-D-minor mood far beyond anything we hear in the overture. He makes use of the same figures, phrases and dramatic ideas but builds them up relentlessly and without the relaxation of tension provided in the overture by the introduction of the principal D major section (Ex 2).

The two main figures featured in this scene are:

and the *crescendo-piano* runs in violins and flutes:

The variety of dynamics throughout this scene is astonishingly effective, particularly in the use of sudden alternations of *forte* and *piano*, which Edward J. Dent has so graphically said "disconcert the nerves like the pitching of a ship in a storm."

Against this remarkable and superbly dramatic musical background the action of the opera continues a little leisurely, perhaps, but in an undeniably impressive manner.

"You invited me to supper," says the Statue. "Here I am."

"Well, I must confess I didn't believe you would come," replies Don Giovanni, "but I will see what can be done. Leporello! See that another supper is brought at once!"

A terrified and trembling Leporello emerges from under the table and muttering "Oh master! Master! We are all dead!" is about to make a dash for it when he is deterred by the Statue proclaiming: "Wait a minute!" and indicating in a stately and ponderous manner that as one accustomed to celestial fare, mortal food no longer agrees with him, and anyway it is another, more serious matter which has brought him to Don Giovanni's palace.

"Well, come on!" says Don Giovanni, with ill-concealed impatience, "What do you want?"—a question which Don Giovanni asks in the course of a remarkable chord sequence characteristic of the numberless details of a scene which still retains its power to surprise and astonish the listener:

The orchestration of this whole scene is unfortunately a subject too big and too fascinating to discuss in as much detail as it deserves, for in addition to the trombones there are endless subtleties such as the writing for the two bassoons (particularly in the harmonic sequence I have indicated above in Ex 85), and the sinister *pp* notes for trumpets and drums.

Don Giovanni's impatience with his guest is understandable and it obviously begins to try his courteous nature when the Statue keeps repeating himself by singing, like an after-dinner speaker who is not going to keep us long, "I speak. Listen: I have no more time."

"Speak! Speak!" urges Don Giovanni, "I am listening!"

The Statue takes his time, having—as we feared—more of it than we were led to hope. "You invited me to supper. You know your duty. Answer me, answer me: will you come and dine with me?"

The first person to react to this unexpected turn of events is Leporello, who quickly speaks on behalf of his master who—excuse, please—is very busy.

Don Giovanni ignores his servant's protests, however, and replies that nobody shall accuse him of discourtesy.

"Decide!" proclaims the Statue.

"I have decided," answers Don Giovanni.

"Then you will come?"

"Say no, say no!" pleads Leporello, but in a final defiantly heroic phrase unlike anything we have heard from him before, Don Giovanni declares that his heart is steadfast and he fears nothing. He will go with the Statue.

The Statue takes Don Giovanni's hand and as the unfortunate mortal cries out in its icy grasp, the Statue a little cynically asks what's the matter.

"Repent and mend your ways!" thunders the Statue. "It is the last moment!"

The tempo has now become faster as Don Giovanni struggles vainly to free himself.

"Repent!" commands the Statue.

"No!" cries Don Giovanni.

Six times the Statue's command is met with the same answer as the basses in the orchestra introduce a series of fierce stormy phrases which give added emphasis to the *f-p* of Professor Dent's pitching ship.

It is interesting to note how until this point in the scene the trombones have been virtually silent whenever Don Giovanni has sung; in fact, up to the moment when the Statue grasps his hand there is only one bar in which the trombones play while Don Giovanni is singing, and that is to provide a crescendo leading to the Statue's refusal of his offer of supper. Now, however, as Don Giovanni becomes more and more in the Statue's power the trombones tend increasingly to add their solemn and sinister tones to the orchestral accompaniment until their contribution is incessant.

At Don Giovanni's final "No!" (which is the eighth in all) the Statue accompanied by a remarkable *pianissimo* unison passage for strings, oboes, bassoons, trombones and eventually flutes, disappears. Da Ponte's laconic stage direction reads: "Disappears. Fire from different directions; earthquake."

This concisely described scene quickens the tempo once more to Allegro, and as the flames begin to engulf Don Giovanni we are reminded of the inexorable fate which overtakes the dissolute by the repeated unison hammering of the orchestra already anticipated in the Statue's approach at the start of the scene:

From under the earth opened up by the earthquake a chorus of demons is heard—unison male voices denouncing and calling Don Giovanni in a sinister near-monotone. (For the sake of poetic justice surely the tormenting demons should have been female, not male?) Leporello supplies a counterpoint of quite unusually vernacular commentary as he watches his master's torment and refers, in the Italian equivalent, to Don Giovanni's "desperate 'phiz' "—hardly a respectful way of describing the face of a generous if rapidly disintegrating employer. But Leporello is no longer in the state of abject terror he was before; the Statue has gone and he is strangely composed when confronted by the spectacle of Don Giovanni's end. There are no chattering grotesque expressions of fear in his music; instead he provides an almost solemn underlining of the orchestral bass parts, and although he assures us in the words he sings that the gestures, cries and lamentations of the *dannato* Don Giovanni strike him with terror he is most uncharacteristically calm and collected and in no way suggests that the final destruction of his dissolute *padrone* is at all far enough out of the ordinary to comment on.

Don Giovanni goes to hell with a final despairing "Ah!" and the orchestra resolves into a more placid D major for a final eight bars to bring the personal history of Don Giovanni to an end.

With scarcely a moment's pause, however, a brisk Allegro brings in Donna Anna (who doesn't sing with the rest to begin with), Donna Elvira, Zerlina, Masetto and Don Ottavio (accompanied by officers of the law) excitedly looking for Don Giovanni:

While her companions are unanimous in their lustful eagerness to show their contempt and hatred for the perfidious and shameful one, Donna Anna maintains her typically individual and remotely detached, upper-class attitude towards the situation and tells us in a solo phrase that she will be happy only when Don Giovanni is in chains. Leporello spoils these bloodthirsty dreams of revenge, however, by emerging from under the table and announcing a little grimly that the gentleman they are looking for has gone away—a long way away. The angry party turns on Leporello and demands to know what he means. He starts to tell them, but they don't listen because they are so busy shouting at him to hurry up with the story. At last Leporello gets a word in edgeways and gives a recognizable if understandably not very coherent account of what has happened.

Donna Elvira recognizes from Leporello's description that she has already met the Statue earlier, when he was coming to supper. She has no sooner got out the first three words of the phrase "Ah, it was the ghost that met him", when first Donna Anna, then Zerlina and Don Ottavio together, and finally the slower-witted Masetto are all saying the same thing in the same words as Donna Elvira—a remarkable instance of either telepathic anticipation or parrot-like echo, for by the time she is first interrupted Donna Elvira hasn't been able to say more than "Ah, it was . . ."

As for where or whether anybody but Elvira and Leporello ever saw the Statue I do not think we need worry too much or regard their words as anything more than an expedient to provide Mozart with a musical transition to the passage which follows. This begins as a duet between Donna Anna and Don Ottavio which is started off by Ottavio suggesting that now all their troubles have been solved by divine intervention Donna Anna should no longer keep him in suspense and languishment—"Or che tutti, o mio tesoro":

89. Larghetto

Or che tut-ti o mio te- so - o, ven-di-ca-ti siam dal cie-lo

Donna Anna replies in even more florid terms that she will remain in mourning for a year, then perhaps the matter of marrying Don Ottavio can be considered again. Thus, in a somewhat leisurely fashion, a decision is reached to postpone the final decision affecting the lives of two of the characters—with Donna Anna showing strong signs of that approaching return to normality already hinted at in "Non mi dir" (No 25).

Donna Elvira, in one single melancholy sentence, announces that she will retire to a convent for the rest of her life, and we hear the last of this perplexing, moving and intensely human character as an individual in the phrase:

90 Larghetto

Io men va-do in un ri- ti-ro a fi-nir la vi-ta mi-a

Zerlina and Masetto switch the tune of Donna Elvira's renunciation into D major and echo it as they decide to return home and "dine in company" (so much has happened in the 24 hours in which the story of *Don Giovanni* is meant to take place that we tend to forget that the unfortunate peasants began the day celebrating their forthcoming marriage).

Leporello declares philosophically that, for his part, he will go to the tavern to find himself a better master, and joins his two fellow-proletarians in a unison proclamation that as far as Don Giovanni is concerned "Let the rogue rest with Proserpine and Pluto."*

That admirable sentiment expressed in what may be regarded as operatically sacred and profane—or legendary and realistic—language, Zerlina, Masetto and Leporello invite us all to join them in repeating joyfully the "oldest song"—"Repetiam allegramente l'antichissima canzon" —words which end with a colon and lead us back to the D major of the overture and the final musical sequence of the opera.

The first to give us the words and music of the "oldest song" are Donna Anna and Donna Elvira. Stating the theme of what promises to be a stupendously constructed fugue they tell us: "This is the end of the wrongdoer." It is 32 bars before we hear the next lines of the lyric, but then that is always likely to happen when fugues are set to words. In due course, however, we are given the final instalment of the *antichissima canzon* and learn in poetic language what amounts—freely translated—to a reflection that the mortal punishment of the wicked fits their crime.

Purely as an essay in counterpoint which seduces the listener into believing it is far more profound than it really is (the quickness of Mozart's hand deceives the ear), this stimulating, trumpet-and-drums epilogue (the trombones went underground with Don Giovanni) is an unanswerable assertion that the opera is a *dramma giocoso* for there is surely little in music more aggressively unsolemn and optimistic than the opening subject:

The contrapuntal dexterity with which this tune is treated is fascinating, entertaining and exhilarating, and the curtain falls after a quite unexpectedly quiet passage for first and second violins only has led to a characteristically definite and final Mozartian signing-off. Five bars of rapid and loud *tutti*—and what is there left to say anyway? Only in the scores of Mozart himself is there anything to be found to approach the masterly apt, unanswerable coda of *Don Giovanni*.

A tragedy? A comedy? If so, whose tragedy? *Don Giovanni*, once scholars and theoreticians get at it, can be made to mean anything,

---

* Molière's *Don Juan* ends with Sganarelle bewailing the non-payment of his wages. It is a very French play.

everything or nothing. Let us look for a moment at the case put by those who ask us to regard it as a tragedy.

The argument they use most strongly to support their case is the omission at the first Vienna performance of the final sextet. It was omitted for the best, most practical and most common of all theatrical reasons: there was no time for it. Mozart had had to write another aria for the tenor ("Dalla sua pace"—No 11) and in place of the aria which it replaced ("Il mio tesoro"—No 22) had added a comic duet for Zerlina and Leporello introduced, as I think I suggested, in circumstances of charming but quite ridiculous improbability. It is perhaps too easy to suggest to the Don-Giovanni-for-tragedy party that it is a little inconsistent if Mozart, having carefully deleted the gay, untragic final sextet so that the opera might finish on a sombre note with the destruction of Don Giovanni, should then proceed to fill the vacant time with a *comic* scene and thus give the "tragic" Vienna production additional opportunity for laughter denied to the public of Prague who were offered the work as a *dramma giocoso*.

A century of German romanticism inevitably resulted in an insistent form of propaganda which even today, in our more Mozart-enlightened days, has a deceptively plausible sound to it. Leaving aside the purely practical-professional reason for its omission—the time factor—Mozart, we are told, cut the final sextet in Vienna because he wanted his opera to be regarded as a tragedy. Well, supposing he did cut the sextet for that reason: the omission of an expression of a reasonably happy ending for six characters still does not make a tragedy for the seventh.

The truth is that, sextet or no sextet, nothing on earth can ever make an opera described by its composer and librettist not only as a *dramma giocoso* as well as independently by its composer as an *opera buffa*, but given as its first title something which might have as its English equivalent "The Libertine Chastised" ("Don Giovanni" was only an alternative) into a tragedy or anything like it. An opera called *Il dissoluto punito* might, at best, be regarded as a morality (which the Don Juan story was originally), but that surely must be the limit of its Significance. With characteristic woolly-headedness it is the Germans who have failed to perceive that while what is tragic is often dramatic, what is dramatic is not necessarily always tragic. A Mozart opera with a violent death in the first scene and spectacular mortal retribution in the last is perhaps unusual; but it doesn't automatically make it a tragic opera.

The answer to the whole question, surely, is in the original description of the opera: it is a *dramma*, and it is *giocoso*. There are dramatic moments of sadness, squalor and violence, and there are moments of charm, comedy and gaiety. If there is any possible tragic aspect of the story it is the purely cynical one of Don Giovanni's recurrent failure to seduce anybody at all (that is, if we accept—as I personally do not—that he failed to seduce Donna Anna). Regarded in that light, perhaps it is a tragedy that the last hours of that Don Giovanni we have heard so much about, and from whom we expected so much, should show the Great Seducer, the owner of the famous *catalogo*, going to eternal damnation with devils, flames and hidden choirs for no more vicious or inexcusable a crime than the killing in a duel of an old man whom he tried his hardest to dissuade from fighting at all and, in fact, killed in self-defence. The *dissoluto* is *punito* for crimes and vices the audience is expected to know by heart, but none of which occurs in the course of the action of *Don Giovanni* (even the seduction of Donna Anna must, for decency's and probability's sake, be considered to have taken place during the overture).

None of this, however, is particularly tragic; it has something of the frustration of poetic injustice, maybe, but little more, for the possibilities of the genuinely tragic elements of the story—the characters of Donna Elvira and Donna Anna and what happens to them after Don Giovanni's death—have no further place in this particular drama.

More convincing to me than any reflection on the fate of the individual characters, on the other hand, is the purely musical evidence of Mozart's score. As a boy in Vienna I continually heard *Don Giovanni* in its truncated form (from which the Zerlina-Leporello duet had also been cut, of course), for the 1788 Vienna version without the final sextet (but with "Il mio tesoro") still prevailed as the official form of the opera in the early 1920's. The sextet in spite of its bright and so obviously right and satisfying D major finish was to me no more than an appendix at the end of the score, something which, without bothering to question its necessity or authenticity, I had somehow been led to dismiss as an unimportant, and indeed probably spurious, interpolation. As a result of this I never ceased to find the Vienna ending unsatisfying and illogical. A mere eight bars of D major after Don Giovanni's final destruction did not convince me that enough had been said. It was one of the least conclusive passages in all music, and if I tolerated it then it was because I was young and accepted the Vienna Opera's way of doing things.

There was never any question that Mozart felt something was needed after the disappearance of Don Giovanni, for although he cut the sextet in Vienna he still brought his six surviving characters on to the stage to let out piercing, bloodcurdling yells when they saw the dissolute one punished by hell-fire and devils in the final eight bars following his last despairing cry. The exigencies of the production may have temporarily affected Mozart's method; they did not alter his intentions.

Finally, there are inevitably those who, having failed to persuade us that *Don Giovanni* is a tragedy, will insist that the inclusion of the sextet is an anti-climax anyway. Again I do not think this feeling is inevitable if one regards the whole episode as an epilogue, as a little scene in its own right which ties up not only the dramatic loose ends of the action but with its sustained movement in D major gives a final flourish to Mozart's musical handwriting as he writes "The End".

In the past quarter of a century those who provide opera for us have undergone a considerable change of heart, and it is now the rule rather than the exception for *Don Giovanni* to be played with the final sextet intact. In this way one of the most remarkable of all Mozart's operas ends with a convincing and full-blooded Presto instead of with a half-hearted and rather dragged-in D major afterthought to a scene which had been predominantly in D minor from the moment the Statue entered. If I have seemed to be anxiously preoccupied with the rights and wrongs of this Finale it is because it has taken so long to re-establish Mozart's original ending. As I have pointed out, the Vienna ending was still current in my own boyhood and, while I think we may count on at least a few generations without interference with Mozart's first thoughts, there is always a danger that somebody may decide that *Don Giovanni* is a tragedy again and omit the final pages which confirm so conclusively the type of opera this is meant to be. The description of a work as a *dramma giocoso* was not a term invented by Mozart or Da Ponte. What they invented was the unique variety of mood and scene, tears and laughter, wit, drama and excitement that could be included in the simple and all-embracing framework of a *dramma giocoso* called *Il dissoluto punito, ossia Il Don Giovanni.*

COSÌ FAN TUTTE

Or *La scuola degli amanti.* "Dramma giocoso" in two acts by Lorenzo da Ponte. First performed at the Burgtheater, Vienna, on 26th January, 1790, conducted by the composer. First performance in England: 9th May, 1811, Haymarket Theatre, London. First performance in the United States: 24th March, 1922, Metropolitan Opera House, New York.

LET it be said at the outset that *Così fan tutte* is a supremely lovely, funny and enchanting comic opera. That, at least, is the conclusion we have reached in the 20th century. Indeed, so certain are we today of the quality and greatness of the opera that some have come to adopt a frighteningly familiar attitude to the work and refer to it even in print by the single adverb "Così". This example of the typically English love of nicknames and abbreviations is pronounced, of course, to rhyme with "posy", and nothing can persuade them that it is a laughable habit comparable to speaking of Shakespeare's three famous plays as "All's", "As" and "Much".

However, this idiosyncrasy is in itself a reassuring sign; for it means that Mozart's opera is deemed to be instantly identifiable by its original (or in this case, part of its original) Italian title and that all attempts to anglicize any more of it than its pronunciation have at last been abandoned. The phrase "Così fan tutte" is not untranslatable, of course, for it means literally "Thus do all [women behave]", but nobody has so far succeeded in finding anything but a clumsy English, French or German equivalent for a title which is characteristically neat, to the point and essentially Italian. The suggestion that Da Ponte's subtitle, "The School for Lovers", should be used for English versions of the opera makes at least for tidiness and is a phrase that falls easily on the ear of those familiar with the language of Sheridan, but its greatest disadvantage seems to me to be that even the most knowledgeable opera-goer may have to scratch his head for a moment before it dawns on him that he is being offered not an unfamiliar Mozart work, but a famous and highly entertaining and satisfying comic opera called *Così fan tutte*.

The libretto to *Così fan tutte* was the last and perhaps most nearly perfect of the three librettos Da Ponte wrote for Mozart. Paradoxically, the subject was the choice of neither poet nor composer, but of the Emperor Joseph II who, as a result of the renewed interest in *Figaro* which had been stimulated by the performances in Vienna of *Don Giovanni* in 1788, decided to commission Mozart to compose another comedy for the Court Opera.

Where *Figaro* and *Don Giovanni* had been adaptations of already existent stage works—Beaumarchais' play in one case and Bertati's opera in the other—*Così fan tutte* was what would nowadays be called an "original".

The tradition is that the Emperor commanded Da Ponte to collaborate with Mozart using as the theme of their comic opera the true story of a series of scandalous events which had amused and startled Viennese society not long before. That is the traditional tale. My own belief, recalling that the same theme, with barely enough variation to satisfy a Hollywood story conference, was used in Molnar's comedy, *The Guardsman*, is that the plot of *Così fan tutte* was a product of the highly productive Budapest dramaturgic industry which has flourished for centuries and shows every sign of continuing to do so for many more. If the events of *Così fan tutte* did, in fact, occur in Vienna then, at best, I feel it was only another instance of nature imitating art.

The essence of good comedy, however, is surely not that it *has* happened necessarily, but that it *could* happen. Unless there is that link with reality comedy degenerates into farce, though even farce, heaven knows, sometimes cannot compete with the things that happen in real life. The situation of *Così fan tutte*, in which two young women, A and B, are respectively engaged to lovers C and D who pretend to leave for the wars but instead return, disguised, and prove their mistresses' infidelity by each seducing the other's fiancée, is a situation which if it did not in fact happen in real life is certainly good enough to have done so.

The *dramma giocoso* which Da Ponte and Mozart made out of this real or imagined incident was at all events such a convincing affair and so horrified the Germans by the immorality of the situation and its treatment, by the disrespect shown for the sacred and noble figure of Woman, that they spent the best part of the 19th century "improving" the libretto and making it suitable for family audiences.

The opera must indeed have seemed to them sadly untypical of the Divine Mozart, who not only seemed to enjoy the trivialities, not to say indecencies, of an exquisitely constructed libretto, but even went so far as to squander an unending stream of lovely music on worthless characters and contemptible situations. It is this second aspect of Mozart's opera, indeed, which may well have been the greatest shock of all to the solemn German mind, for Mozart convinces us that, although we are concerned with an artificial comedy, *if* human beings ever found themselves having to express the emotions they feel in *Così fan tutte* then they would do so to the highly expressive and often moving music found in this score.

It is perhaps for this reason personally I have always found *Così fan tutte* a perplexing work—amusing, entertaining, witty and certainly gay, but because of the contextually unexpected beauty and depth of so much of the music inclined to prove an experience of such artistic richness and perfection that the effect can be almost oppressive and exhausting. It seems to me, in other words, that *Così fan tutte* suffers from an *embarras de richesse* without parallel among Mozart's operas. The invention and urgency of its music is almost superhuman in its unrelenting intensity and consistency, and in consequence there are times when as ordinary human beings ourselves we could wish for a few human failings from the composer.

Così fan tutte has been described as a perfect work of art, and that, in the end, is perhaps all that is the matter with it. It is a readily forgivable fault, after all.

There is perhaps one particular aspect of *Così fan tutte* for which the newcomer should be prepared: Mozart's habit of switching without warning from parody of the grand tragic manner of *opera seria* to moments of music as movingly and intentionally *seria* as almost anything he ever wrote. The dividing line between parody and sincerity is so narrow, so difficult to distinguish sometimes, that one hesitates to draw attention to it lest the listener spend his time waiting for subtle twists and musical quips in passages where they do not occur and so miss them altogether when they do.

Because the whole pattern and construction and final effect of *Così fan tutte* is a magnificent monument to the invention and ingenuity of the greatest musico-dramatic partnership in the history of opera, there has been an increasing tendency in recent times to attribute far more to both music and libretto than I believe either composer or poet intended. The modern attitude to the opera, in other words, has in it more than a hint of intellectual snobbery. It is a perfect comic opera; because it is perfect it must be full of subtleties which are above the heads of the common people. It needs musical education and scholarship to appreciate such subtleties. Q.E.D.

Twelfth Night is Shakespeare's perfect comedy, but one does not need to have taken a "first" in the English Tripos to recognize that, or enjoy it.

And so it is with Mozart and *Così fan tutte*. The comedy of his last great comic opera is comic *in itself*; the fact that we may never have heard a single note of an 18th-century *opera seria* is not going to lessen our enjoyment of the evening's entertainment for a moment. The immediately comic things will always strike us as their composer intended. We are wasting our time, and Mozart's, I think, if we worry about the things that don't make us laugh, for it is highly probable that the composer meant us to take them seriously. As we know from *Don Giovanni*, Mozart was a bewilderingly unpredictable and nonconformist composer. He is still the same composer in *Così fan tutte*.

CHARACTERS IN ORDER OF APPEARANCE:

FERRANDO, *an officer in love with Dorabella* . *Tenor*
GUGLIELMO, *an officer in love with Fiordiligi* . *Baritone*
DON ALFONSO, *an elderly philosopher* . . *Bass*
FIORDILIGI ⎱ *sisters from Ferrara, living in* . *Soprano*
DORABELLA ⎰ *Naples* . . . . *Soprano*
DESPINA, *servant to the sisters* . . . *Soprano*
Soldiers, servants, sailors, guests, townspeople.

Scene: Naples. Time: The 18th century.
The action takes place between early morning and midnight.

ACT I

The overture, in C major, begins with a short Andante in which the oboe, associated frequently in the opera with the cynical chuckling of Don Alfonso, plays a couple of phrases which have little dramatic or musical interest but lead to a passage which has both. This is the presentation of a theme which is sung later in the action to the words which give the opera its title:

The Andante now changes to Presto and the business of the overture proper gets under way in a manner which can be described only by the over-worked term "bubbling". Mozart makes use of three themes, twisting them characteristically to give an impression of symphonic development but in fact doing nothing more than creating an atmosphere of general good humour and exuberance to put us in a receptive mood for the story which follows.

Whether one agrees or not with the suggestion sometimes made that this Overture is commonplace—and deliberately so—is a question of personal taste in such matters. I should have thought that far too much ingenious construction went into this piece ever to justify the accusation of commonplaceness, and in any case I fail to see what dramatic purpose Mozart had in mind that he should necessarily want to write a commonplace introduction to a sophisticated comedy.

However, of the three themes in question, the first sets the tempo of the Presto and is less a theme in effect than a figure which Mozart uses subtly as a means of varying key and mood:

The second tune is perhaps the greatest delight of the whole Overture, for it forms the subject of a many-sided and chattering conversation in the wood-wind, a joke whispered, chuckled over and passed on by oboe to flute, from flute to bassoon, from clarinet and bassoon in octaves, oboe and bassoon in octaves, to flute and clarinet in octaves. It is a phrase of virtually one bar which thrives on repetition and modulation:

From time to time the easy progress of the Overture is disturbed by some fierce and loud *tutti* chords, and the rather unexpectedly sinister intrusion of this sequence in various minor-key forms:

Towards the end of the Overture there is an unheralded repetition of the "Così fan tutte" theme (Ex 1), the *piano* section divided from the *forte* section by a long pause bar but otherwise played without any alteration of the basic tempo, thus showing once again* that the fast movement of the 18th-century overture is intended to be played at twice the speed of its slow introduction. There is a short coda based on the figure in Ex 2 and the Overture to *Così fan tutte* comes to a formal and final close like that to *Figaro* and so spares everybody the trouble of having to fix a "concert" ending as they had to with *Die Entführung* and *Don Giovanni*.

Scene 1: A café.

The curtain rises during the introductory bars of a brisk and business-like Allegro to show Ferrando and Guglielmo seated at breakfast with Don Alfonso:

Ferrando sings first, continuing a conversation which seems to have been going on for some time and in its most recent stages has obviously led to Don Alfonso saying something derogatory about the young ladies to whom the two officers are engaged.

"My Dorabella," protests Ferrando indignantly, "is quite incapable of such a thing. She is as faithful as she is beautiful."

"And my Fiordiligi," insists Guglielmo, "would not know how to deceive me."

Don Alfonso replies with what must be a repetition of his original unpopular assertion: that he knows from experience of the world what he is talking about, and he is not going to argue any more. But the two young men refuse to let the matter rest there. Either Don Alfonso must prove his

* See p. 32.

charge or pay for his calumnious gossiping with the sword. The trio
rattles fiercely to a menacing end and the argument and threats are continued in recitative in which, at one point, Ferrando and Guglielmo show
a united front by expressing themselves in harmony.

A second trio starts up with Don Alfonso quoting an old proverb to his
obstinately unconvinced young friends:

"The faithfulness of woman," he says, "is like the phoenix: everybody
has heard about it, but nobody has ever actually seen it." Don Alfonso's
mocking little jingle is supported by some spirited comment in the same
vein from a single flute and bassoon.

Ferrando and Guglielmo maintain their indignant refusal to believe
anything that Don Alfonso can say, varying their intransigence with
reflective sighing of their mistresses' names.

Once more the conversation is continued in recitative, but this time
Don Alfonso is able to restore a little order and reasonableness into the
proceedings. He is willing to stake a hundred guineas on his certainty that
Fiordiligi and Dorabella, where fidelity is concerned, are no different
from other women. The two soldiers accept the wager eagerly and with
brash self-confidence, and promise to accept the two conditions attached
to it: not to tell what Don Alfonso calls their two "Penelopes" of the
wager, and to do everything that Don Alfonso tells them to do during the
next twenty-four hours.

The third trio of the scene begins with Ferrando deciding how he will
spend the money he is going to win. He will arrange a serenade for his
"Goddess", he says, and tells us about it in a fine broad and romantic
phrase:

Guglielmo, being a baritone, is a little more realistic and decides in a
matter-of-fact, no-nonsense-in-the-Army manner that he will give a
dinner party "in honour of Cytherea". (Both these young officers have
had a classical education and are rarely at a loss for the apt quotation or
allusion in any situation.) Don Alfonso pricks up his ears at Guglielmo's
mention of a dinner party. Whereas, in the unlikely event of his losing his
bet, there would clearly be nothing for him to enjoy in Ferrando's
serenade, a dinner party could be a different matter altogether.

"Shall I be one of the guests?" asks Don Alfonso.

The two officers promise he will be invited (since he will obviously
have to pay for it) and the scene ends with the three men anticipating the

toasts they will drink to the God of Love to a tune which assumes a slightly martial air as trumpets and drums are added to it:

This theme is extended into an elated coda which allows for such stage business as accompanies the general exit—Ferrando and Guglielmo above themselves with cocky self-assurance, Don Alfonso laughing to himself—and the curtain falls.

Scene 2: A garden by the sea shore

Sitting in their garden, each gazing at a portrait of her lover which hangs on a chain at her side, are Fiordiligi and Dorabella, the "two sisters from Ferrara, living in Naples."

The point of the sisters being *dame ferraresi* had a particular significance at the first performance of *Così fan tutte* in Vienna, for one of the parts was sung by a singer who did, in fact, come from Ferrara. This was not a matter of type-casting such as we might expect of managements anxious for a publicity angle in our own day, but of Da Ponte having what might be considered private fun in public. The part of Fiordiligi was taken by Adriana Ferraresi del Bene, *née*—at Ferrara—Francesca Gabrielli. (Though one more usually encounters the name as "Ferrarese del Bene", I have adopted "Ferraresi" because that is the form used by Mozart in his letters. I like to err in good company if I am wrong.) Adriana Ferraresi del Bene was Da Ponte's mistress and had been for a couple of years or more. She also (which was Mozart's immediate concern) had a most unusual type of voice, as we shall discover when we come to study some of the music which occurs later in *Così fan tutte*.*

Scarcely half a minute of this scene in the young ladies' garden elapses before we have our first perplexing example of Mozart's habitual juxta-position in this opera of the serious and the comic. The orchestral intro-duction is a neat little instrumental landscape full of southern warmth and colour, largely obtained by the use of the clarinets and bassoons:

These introductory bars may be said to provide us with our first experience of the second and preponderantly characteristic mood of *Così fan tutte*. The first scene opened very much in keeping with the *buffo* atmosphere created by the Overture—a bright key and a tempo full of sparkle, vitality, and fun, a mood sustained by the other trio movements which followed and presented the buoyant, masculine aspect of the opera.

The soft A major which introduces the second scene reveals the lyrical, feminine side of the work, and it is this side which in the end seems to prevail more strongly. This may be only a personal reaction, but it is the graciousness and elegance of *Così fan tutte*, demonstrated so typically in this opening to Scene 2, which I remember long after the more obvious bustle and *buffo* incidents are forgotten. (If this means that ultimately it is the feminine element in the music which triumphs, then there is nothing wrong about that. The whole opera, from title page to final curtain, is about women, after all.)

A powerful factor in the creation of this feminine atmosphere is what may be called the prevailing wood wind of the opera's whole climate. Mozart uses the clarinets in *Così fan tutte* in a way which gives the opera a distinctive and peculiar instrumental character, and in this introduction to Scene 2 we have an effective instance of the *dolce* nature of the instrument exploited by the composer to such a degree that it seems to colour the whole work.

The serene, charming atmosphere of the instrumental introduction is a deliberately deceptive device, however. Its serenity and charm serve largely to prepare the comedy and anti-climax of the duet started by the voices of Fiordiligi and Dorabella. Against the background of a delightful and varied orchestral accompaniment the two sisters sigh their hearts out over the charms of their lovers, gazing rapturously at their portraits as they sing of the beauty of Guglielmo's mouth and the flames that burn in Ferrando's eyes.

Here, by gentle mockery, composer and librettist have created the pair of love-sick maidens to end all love-sick maidens. The young ladies, with an occasional, discreetly florid run to show they are of gentle birth (only the gentry and *poules de luxe* ever indulge in coloratura in opera), first state their cases separately and then, as the tempo changes to Allegro, in thirds and sixths to indicate that they are in harmonious agreement on the subject.

The new tempo is interrupted a couple of times for the sisters to sing a short and suitably ecstatic cadenza together on the word "amore"—a pause for reflection on which the bassoon, very much the comedian again in this opera, makes audible and delighted comment.*

No sooner have Fiordiligi and Dorabella come to an end of their protestations than they both declare—a little surprisingly—that they are in the mood for some excitement. Fiordiligi tells her sister's fortune and sees an unmistakable M and a P in her hand, which can only stand for

* The orchestral accompaniment to this whole duet is unusually effective; in addition to the soft colouring of the clarinets and the rather ribald contributions of the bassoon, we encounter once more Mozart's ingenious and characteristic use of divided violas.

"matrimonio presto". The mere mention of the word matrimony sets the sisters impatiently wondering why their lovers are so late: "it is six already."*

There is movement off stage, but it is not their lovers who arrive. It is Don Alfonso, alone, agitated and apparently in tears. He makes an attempt in 38 bars of what is rather grandly described in the score as an Aria (the nearest he gets to one in the whole opera), to tell them what has happened, but he hasn't the heart, he says; the words stick in his throat— what a disaster!—nothing worse could have happened!

Don Alfonso stammers his way through a series of broken phrases in a poignant minor key—the same F minor which was so incongruously used for Barbarina's lament, and as in the little scene in *Figaro*, there is just that touch of caricature which is doubly effective for being so restrained. Don Alfonso sings his unhappy and tearful "aria" to an agitated accompaniment of strings only in which divided violas wail sadly and the violins sob:

Don Alfonso's deliciously comic simulation of grief and anxiety, which is one of the few solo moments of music enjoyed by the plausible old cynic whose personality so unmistakably dominates the action if not the music of *Così fan tutte*, has the desired effect on the love-lorn young ladies at once and he takes his time deliberately in telling them the worst.

Ferrando and Guglielmo, he explains, have been posted on active service with their regiment—an item of news which comes as such a shock to Fiordiligi and Dorabella that, although the scene is played in recitative, they react simultaneously and in harmony.

Don Alfonso announces enigmatically that the two officers haven't the courage to come and see their mistresses, "but if you badly want to see them, they are here"—and the officers enter immediately on Don Alfonso's invitation.

With five people now on the stage Mozart deals with the whole situation in a quintet, one of those wonderfully conceived ensembles which are almost impossible to quote from, for the mere words and notes of them give no idea of the practical effect of what Mozart has written. This is particularly the case in this quintet where it can be said there are three points of view shared and put forward simultaneously by five people; but whereas the sentiments of two of the characters are genuine and sincere, those of the others are entirely feigned and hypocritical. How this is achieved in music is one of the secrets of Mozart's genius as a composer for the theatre.

After an almost bare beginning in which Ferrando and Guglielmo sing nothing more startling than a phrase each based on the notes of the chord

* That is, noon. See p. 124.

of E flat the ensemble opens slowly like a luxuriant flower. The hypocrisy of the two officers with their assumed sadness and Don Alfonso's praise for their heroic bearing in such sad circumstances gives place to the sisters, whose (apparently genuine) grief is expressed in tearful broken phrases urging (in thirds) their lovers to draw their swords and plunge them into their hearts.

This show of heartbroken emotion delights the two young men, who nudge Don Alfonso and tell him they told him so. The wily old philosopher smiles and tells them to wait and see; there is plenty of time yet.

The five characters, having said their say on the situation in general (unless the repeat is cut in performance they say it all again later to fulfill the conditions of sonata form), now settle down to reflect on the harshness of destiny which so ruthlessly destroys all mortal hopes.

This development of the quintet, which is marked to be sung *sotto voce*, is begun to a burbling accompaniment by Fiordiligi and Dorabella:

Ferrando, who intends to spend his winnings on a serenade, naturally plays a lyrical role in the ensemble; he echoes the young ladies' sentimental tune with such apparent conviction, indeed, that one suspects he almost believes it himself.

Guglielmo, in accordance with his temperament, mutters away with Don Alfonso and so helps us to remember what the sheer sensuous beauty of the music might lead us to forget: that there are two distinct sides to this present question.

The ensemble is succeeded by a recitative of tears, tender embraces and consolations and a passage in two parts in which the soldiers express well-drilled sentiments with ludicrously comic effect.

The discipline of the two officers is shown in a delightful *duettino* which occurs at this point but which, for some unexplained reason, is nearly always cut in performance.

Apart from its purely musical charm and gaiety and the rigidly formal two-part singing throughout (neither singer ventures a note unless the other is there to support him), the duet throws a reassuring light on the character of Ferrando who is too often dismissed as a sloppy effeminate figure and on no stronger evidence as a rule than the lyrical part he plays in the quintet we have just heard. Not only does Ferrando have a heartily virile part to sing in this duet, but his one decorative run is repeated note for note by Guglielmo, which surely suggests that it is healthy and soldierly to add a little colour to a melodic line occasionally.

The delicately scored accompaniment, which has been such a feature of *Così fan tutte* so far, makes typical use of divided violas again and gives a pleasant warmth to contrast with the stiff-upper-lip attitude of the two officers whose hopes of a safe return are expressed in the sturdy tones of:

What Ferrando describes as the "fatal drum" ("tamburo funesto") is now heard in the distance and an equally fatal boat approaches the shore to take the officers away to the wars. The regiment approaches to the strains of a good trumpets-and-drums march to which a chorus of towns-people sings the praises of a soldier's life:

It says a great deal for the almost unquestioning acceptance of Da Ponte's conventions in Così fan tutte that few people ever seriously raise the matter of the mechanics of Don Alfonso's plot at this point of the opera, for one is surely entitled to be intrigued by the quite outrageously con-venient turn events take to suit the philosopher's scheme.

Either the long arm of coincidence has become telescopic almost to infinity, or Ferrando and Guglielmo are higher-ranking officers than we have been led to believe their age and charm entitles them to be, but to oblige Don Alfonso it seems that a war—or at least a military operation—has suddenly been arranged so that Ferrando and Guglielmo are enabled to take heart-breaking leave of their young ladies with full military hon-ours, merely to win a wager.

If it is not coincidence, or the personal authority of Ferrando and Guglielmo which brings about this fortunate movement of troops, then Don Alfonso's stage management must be regarded as so brilliant that the two officers must have been out of their minds ever to enter into any form of wager with him at all.

A puzzling situation is confused slightly further by both officers missing the boat, which sails away with the regiment leaving them behind to follow, Don Alfonso suggests, in a smaller vessel "with a few friends". Neither pair of lovers takes much notice of any of this, however, and after a couple of phrases of duet-recitative they join forces in an ensemble which Don Alfonso's barely controllable laughter turns into a quintet.

This, for all its caricature and comedy, is an enchanting little movement started by Fiordiligi and Dorabella, tearfully making their lovers promise to write to them every day, and developing into a strangely moving and beautiful sequence which seems to have strayed from the more serious pages of *Figaro* and *Don Giovanni*. A gently throbbing string accompaniment is sustained throughout, but we tend to forget its original comic purpose as it is overshadowed by long, romantic phrases like Fiordiligi's

The emotional mood is disturbed once more by the military chorus. Ferrando and Guglielmo board the little boat and sail off into the distance, leaving behind them an apparently stunned Dorabella, for when she comes round she has to ask where the men have gone; Don Alfonso tells her. Fiordiligi, on the other hand, needs no prompting; she just waves sadly as the boat disappears far too quickly.

The *terzettino* which comes now, as the two ladies and Don Alfonso wave their final farewell to "lovers and friends", is one of the most remarkable pieces of music in all Mozart's operas. I do not believe that we are not intended to take at least two-thirds of this little trio seriously—the two-thirds supplied by the voices of Fiordiligi and Dorabella; and if we are also inclined to take even Don Alfonso seriously for a moment then that is not surprising either, for although he is a cynical and, at times, start-lingly fierce misogynist, Mozart convinces us by purely musical means that Alfonso is a sentimentalist at heart and sincerely moved, not by the departure of Ferrando and Guglielmo, which he knows to be "fixed", of course, but by the sight of the genuine sorrow felt by Fiordiligi and Dorabella. And there is no doubt at all, from what the composer tells us, that they are extremely sad at this parting from their lovers.

Mozart's treatment of this sentimental moment in *Così fan tutte* has no parallel so far as I know anywhere else in his music. As the three characters wave sadly to the boat sailing away, praying for a calm sea and a safe return, he creates a quite remarkable "forward-looking" atmosphere which has been the unmistakable prototype of all the undulating water music, forest murmurs and sundrenched seascapes of music ever since.

As one would expect, the effect is created by miraculously simple means—muted first and second violins with a gentle rippling figure which is maintained off and on throughout the trio:

So far as the words and sentiments are concerned this trio is unusually unanimous, in that nobody goes off at a tangent. The two sisters cling together in thirds and sixths, and Don Alfonso supports them with a gentle and intensely singable bass line to the tune which starts "Soave sia

il vento, tranquilla sia l'onda" ("Let the wind blow gently and the sea
be calm . . ."):

The phrase immediately following this may strike the ear of the English
listener as familiar and perhaps raise his eyebrow:

It is unlikely, I fear, that Mozart had any intention of quoting (even in
such a cynical context) that part of the English folk song, "Early one
morning", which has the words

Oh, don't deceive me; Oh, never leave me!

In addition to the murmuring violin figure the orchestration of this
terzettino (was there ever a more wonderfully thrown-away description for
a movement of such prodigious originality?) is characterized by five bars
in which the three voices are accompanied only by clarinets and bassoons.
It is the restraint of these five bars (the accompaniment does no more than
double the voices, note for note) which makes quite startlingly effective
the new and unexpected orchestral sound which is heard at the fourth
bar of the following phrase:

This, seemingly like every other bar in this *terzettino*, is quite remarkably
"forward-looking", for at this point, and again three bars later when the
word "desir" recurs, the wood-wind chords give us a first glimpse of the
fairy-tale world of Mendelssohn's *Midsummer Night's Dream* music and
the last scene of Verdi's *Falstaff*. Once again the means are quite
ridiculously simple: for the first time since the Overture and the general
fife-and-drum noisiness of the military chorus (No 8) Mozart uses the
flutes of his orchestra and the effect is magical.

The *terzettino* dies away and the young ladies leave Don Alfonso alone
on the stage. The philosopher's mood changes completely in a recitative
which begins with self-congratulation on his gifts as a comedian and ends
with an outburst accompanied by strings of quite surprising vehemence
as he spits out his contempt for women in general and the idea that
anybody should risk losing a hundred guineas in their cause.

Don Alfonso, so recently the gentle cornerstone of the *terzettino*, storms
off and the scene changes.

Scene 3: An elegant room in the sisters' house, furnished with various chairs and a small table; there are three doors, two at the side, one in the centre.

Despina is discovered preparing chocolate for her employers and in the true tradition of the servant of *opera buffa* she is inevitably complaining about her lot. Like all the more important servants of Italian comedy too, she is eternally hungry and only just escapes being found tasting the chocolate when Fiordiligi and Dorabella arrive. The "business" of surreptitiously sneaking delicacies from the tables of the rich is a convention to inform the audience at once that we are in the presence of a quick-witted servant and not of the other familiar figure of 18th-century Neapolitan comedy, the "servo sciocco", or stupid servant, who is too slow and unintelligent to realize that there are such things as "perks" at all.

Fiordiligi and Dorabella enter, but refuse Despina's offer of chocolate with such dramatic expressions of horror and revulsion that even their servant, for all that she is accustomed to tantrums and displays of temperament, is a little surprised.

"Bring me poison! Bring me a dagger!" wails Fiordiligi.

"Close the windows!" cries Dorabella. "I hate the light!" she continues, in an accompanied recitative of quite remarkably ridiculous tragic proportions. "I hate the air I breathe! I hate myself! Go away and leave me alone!" And the dark sombre recitative, which would have fitted Donna Anna like a glove, leads into an aria of an appropriately dark, sombre and *agitato* order—"Smanie implacabile" ("Relentless madness"):

In this aria of Dorabella's we have a first-rate instance of the purely musical comedy of *Così fan tutte*, of the effectiveness of the ludicrous juxtaposition of what might pass for genuinely tragic music and a completely incongruous situation. Da Ponte's words add a touch of literary burlesque, for they are just that tiny bit too poetic in their expression of Dorabella's threat to show the Eumenides themselves the meaning of tragic love—if she survives the horrible sounds of her own sighs. These sighs Mozart interprets in the conventional manner:

The aria remains, indeed, a hilarious example of operatic parody, differing from all other parodies in that its perpetrator was himself the greatest composer of opera who ever lived.

The grand tragic scene ends and Despina asks what is the matter. On learning that the young ladies' lovers have left Naples she laughs: "Is *that* all?" They'll come back, she assures her despairing mistresses; if their lovers survive the war they will return covered in glory; if not—well, there are plenty of other young men.

Fiordiligi and Dorabella are shocked almost speechless by this attitude. "Why don't you go out and amuse yourselves?" asks Despina.

"Amuse ourselves?" cries Fiordiligi indignantly.

"Of course," replies Despina, "like your dear lovers are doing at this moment."

"Don't you dare insult those noble models of fidelity and undying love!" storms Dorabella.

"Oh, come, come!" retorts Despina. "That's nursery stuff." Despina breaks into a cynical little aria in which she asks her two listeners whether they really believe that of men—and soldiers at that? A half-skittish, half-mocking introductory passage in 2/4—"In uomini, in soldati sperare fedeltà?"—leads to the aria proper which is in that simple, bouncing 6/8 so characteristic of the peasants in Mozart's operas. Though she is a knowledgeable young woman, with her sophisticated views and obvious experience of men, Despina is still a peasant in domestic service, and it is in the accent of her class that she sings that all men are made of the same stuff—"Di pasta simile son tutti quanti":

21. Allegretto

No 12

Di pa-sta si-mi-le son tut-ti quan-ti

For the first time in the opera since the Overture and the military march the acid tone of the oboe is heard. Despina has little in her nature that is suggested by the sentimental gentleness of the clarinet, and as on a couple of occasions before in "Deh vieni" in *Figaro* and "Batti, batti" in *Don Giovanni*—the peasant-servant girl's music is given a characteristic instrumental colouring by featuring *one* flute, *one* oboe and *one* bassoon, the three instruments often playing together in octaves.

At the end of Despina's aria Fiordiligi and Dorabella sweep out of the room indignantly as their servant runs off giggling.

Don Alfonso arrives, on a visit of condolence, to find the scene deserted. "What silence!" he reflects. "What an air of sadness in these rooms!" He calls for Despina and holds up a gold coin as an inducement to collaborate with him in his plan and keep a dead secret just that much of it as he intends to tell her: that he proposes to bring two foreign gentlemen to divert her unhappy employers.

Despina, having been reassured that the unknown foreign gentlemen are young, rich and handsome, agrees to play her part. The orchestra takes over from the recitative and the foreign gentlemen enter—Ferrando (fair) and Guglielmo (dark), heavily disguised in grotesquely exotic costume and affecting long moustaches. Don Alfonso introduces them to Despina, saying that they may depend on her to be of service to them. The two foreign gentlemen kiss Despina's hand gallantly and plead with her, by the hand they kiss and the kind looks she gives them, to contrive that the ladies to whom they have come to pay court shall turn their lovely eyes in their direction.

It is not until we get to the phrase in which Ferrando and Guglielmo give voice to these sentiments that we encounter anything much in the way of a memorable tune in the voice parts. The movement is started off by some prosaic, matter-of-fact declamation by Don Alfonso and for some time thereafter the conversation piece is framed by a series of figures and phrases in the orchestra. Ferrando and Guglielmo come in at the cadence of one of them when we hear the gentlemen—in admirably courteous and gallant harmony—singing the florid passage:

Despina laughs happily to herself—"What clothes! What faces! What moustaches! Are they Poles or Turks or what?" It is a typical peasant reaction to the foreign and unfamiliar. The most important thing, however, is that Despina doesn't recognize Ferrando and Guglielmo through their disguises; this comes as a considerable relief both to them and Don Alfonso.

Despina's chattering disturbs her mistresses and they call for her from their room. Despina takes no notice; Don Alfonso hides away behind a door where he is audible and visible only to those (which includes the audience) whom he intends shall hear and see him, and the two sisters enter as the tempo changes to a characteristically "angry" 3/4 like Osmin's famous outburst in *Die Entführung*.

Significantly, since they are in no sentimental mood as a result of having their siesta disturbed, the sisters' music for the first time is coloured by the piercing and petulant sounds of oboes. The clarinets return only when Despina, Ferrando and Guglielmo fall on their knees and beg the sisters' forgiveness in a passage for clarinets, bassoons and violoncellos which introduces another deliciously incongruous serious note in a burlesque situation ending with the melancholy cadence:

Another outbreak of oboes in place of clarinets accompanies the renewed fury of Fiordiligi and Dorabella at this indignity, an outburst which is answered on each occasion by plaintive phrases in the same vein as that quoted in Ex 23.

Suddenly there is another change of tempo to a hectic Allegro Molto. Trumpets and drums add their arresting tones and prepare us for the news that the patience of Fiordiligi and Dorabella is obviously exhausted —a state of mind which they lose no time in announcing in the most rapid and determined manner—"Ah, che più no ho ritegno' ("I can contain myself no longer . . ."):

The reaction of the onlookers to this display is immediate and intriguing. Ferrando and Guglielmo, sticking *sotto voce* to their two-part way of musical life, are extremely satisfied and reassured by the "rage and fury" of their young ladies. Despina and Don Alfonso, equally unanimous in their view, express the opinion that the same rage and fury are highly suspicious, but being cynics of different sexes and generations they react to the situation independently and not at the same moment, until the sextet gets going as a furious ensemble and we begin to hear everybody's point of view at once at dynamic levels ranging from the original *sotto voce* to a general *forte*.

At the end of the sextet Don Alfonso, who has contributed some audible and apposite words and music from his hiding place, appears with all the air of having just arrived on the scene and asks what all the fearful din is about. Dorabella points angrily: "Look! Men in our house!"

"What's wrong with that?" asks Don Alfonso mildly.

"Wrong? On a day like today?" snorts Dorabella.

Don Alfonso turns round. "Heavens!" he exclaims. "Am I dreaming? These are my very best friends! How on earth did you two get here (back me up, come on!)—why?—where?——"

Ferrando and Guglielmo play their parts well and after being formally introduced to the young ladies pay compliments of such extravagance that the orchestra has to support a recitative which grows more elaborate and dramatic with each ardently expressed sentiment. Ferrando and Guglielmo make a duet of their recitative, Fiordiligi the beginnings of a *scena* in which she rebukes her vacillating sister with such violence that Despina leaves the scene in terror.

Fiordiligi warms to her subject and develops her thesis with such determination that her increasingly dramatic declamation leads us to expect exactly what we get—an aria on a very grand scale indeed.

The original singer of the part of Fiordiligi at the first Vienna performance was, as we know, Mme Ferraresi del Bene whose remarkable voice
was capable of all, if not more, than is asked of the average soprano and
contralto combined. Her range—or at least such of it as she was asked to
use in *Così fan tutte*—was

and it was a phenomenon that obviously tickled Mozart's sense of humour
considerably. Fiordiligi's "Come scoglio" ("Firm as a rock") is not only a
parody of a particular form of florid and pompous operatic aria but
provided an opportunity for the composer to have fun at the expense of
a singer he did not greatly care for. Mozart's fun did not consist of
demanding long runs or flourishes from top to bottom register of Ferraresi
del Bene's voice and back again, but of writing single notes separated by
such wide intervals that the singer was constantly having to alternate
between the soprano and the alto colouring of her voice with hilarious
results. It is the comic effect of this which makes me doubt a recent
theory that in performance Mme Ferraresi filled in the gaps with roulades
and arpeggios; it would have spoilt the whole idea.

In practice Mozart is very sparing of this particular joke; he gets his
laughs by tactical surprise in the Maestoso introduction and by an
unexpected repetition in one passage of the Allegro that follows; but that
is all. Mozart was far too fine and experienced a musical comedian to
overdo a gag, and in fact in the course of the entire long aria there are
exactly—and only—seven instances of the exaggerated jump of anything
more than an octave. I mention this because it is one of the illusions of
our time that "Come scoglio" consists of nothing but caricature and
coloratura; there is certainly something of both, but not nearly so much of
either as some would have us believe.

The vocal part of the opening Andante is certainly spectacular:

But in the end it is not its more obvious eccentricity and absurdity which
makes this aria a gem of musical comedy so much as the pompous
banality of its sentiments and the solemn coloratura in which they are
expressed. It is an aria of intriguing paradox, because for the very reason
that it *is* largely parody and caricature, like all good examples of that
form of humour it demands first-rate performance; the clown whose act

depends on burlesquing an acrobat, or failing to juggle, is always a first-class acrobat and juggler himself. This aria of Fiordiligi's needs a first-class vocal acrobat and juggler. But it is Mozart who is the real comedian in this aria; not the singer. The singer has to sing as well as she ever knew how to, with a dead straight face, and if she acquits herself well she will satisfy the composer, herself and us in the audience who are thereby enabled to appreciate the intentions of both of them.

After her first angry protestations of immovable fidelity Fiordiligi settles down to a no less menacing Allegro, in the course of which, in addition to a number of other admirable assertions, she repeats her initial sentiments. The new theme is

which, after suitable decoration and recapitulation, leads to an even faster movement in which the vocal line grows increasingly florid and difficult to sing, beginning with the opening

and landing the singer in concerto-like passages such as

The instrumentation of the accompaniment to "Come scoglio" is worth noting. Trumpets are included to add their occasionally ominous note and lend authority to Fiordiligi's important pronouncement. But though the deceptively soft tones of clarinets accompany her "Così ognor quest'alma è forte nella fede", it is the peevish sound of the oboes which indicates clearly what frame of mind she is in. There is no other opera of Mozart's in which the peculiar use of wood-wind instruments is such a clear barometer of emotion or guide to character as *Così fan tutte*.

At the end of her exhausting and impressive aria Fiordiligi not unnaturally turns to go, accompanied by her sister. But the young men and Don Alfonso beg them to stay, Don Alfonso asking them to be a little more charming towards such well-mannered, well-intentioned suitors, and Guglielmo adding his pleas on behalf of himself and his friend. Guglielmo develops his theme in a charming and carefree aria of quite captivating directness and simplicity. This is the confident extrovert speaking who, even when he is play-acting as a lover, is not out of character. He composes no fine poetic phrases but concentrates on the purely physical attraction of his friend and himself—their shapely legs, their fine eyes and triumphantly manly moustaches—"Non siate ritrosi, occhietti vezzosi" ("Do not spurn us, O charming eyes . . ."):

The instrumentation, indeed, underlines Guglielmo's clear-eyed honesty and lack of cunning admirably, for the accompaniment is for strings, solo flute and solo bassoon; the cynical character of the oboe and the sentimental warmth of the clarinet are carefully omitted.

Originally at this point in Mozart's first conception of the opera there was another aria altogether—a long, ambitious and magnificently effective *buffo* number for Benucci, who had created the part of Figaro and who was cast as the first Guglielmo. Mozart's decision to leave out this aria on second thoughts (it is included as No 15a in some scores and listed as K.584 in Mozart's complete works) was obviously the right one. Not only would Benucci's show-piece have held up the action at a moment when one most wanted to know what was going to happen next, but it would have been entirely out of character. Guglielmo, for all his gaiety and apparent experience, is a simple soul at heart and the Benucci aria would have involved him in moments of wit, bravura and general sophistication foreign to his nature, inclination and whole personality.

The two arias have one thing in common, however: before Guglielmo can finish either of them Fiordiligi and Dorabella walk out on the scene. The only difference is that whereas in the first "Benucci aria" they leave 67 bars before the end (and miss a long and brilliant coda by doing so), in the second they miss no more than eight bars—three of which they have heard before, while the remaining five are not meant for their ears anyway as they are filled with Guglielmo's delighted laughter at the way things are turning out. He laughs partly at the indignant departure of Fiordiligi and Dorabella and partly with satisfaction at the way he is convinced things are progressing to Don Alfonso's disadvantage.

Guglielmo's aria leads directly into a trio in which he is joined by Ferrando in hearty laughter so loud that Don Alfonso has to warn them not to be so noisy or they'll give the game away. Don Alfonso also has his laugh, but it is the quiet laugh born of wisdom and experience and the certainty that the last laugh is always the longest. On paper this trio is remarkably unremarkable; in practice it is extremely funny. Consequently there is virtually nothing that is really worth quoting from it except perhaps the revolutionary use Mozart makes of a syncopated figure to suggest the two lovers' scarcely controllable laughter—a figure which set a pattern of syncopation for such later masterpieces of their kind as the last movement of Schumann's Piano Concerto and Arditi's immortal song, "Il bacio":

Ferrando and Guglielmo are by now convinced that so far as Don Alfonso's wager is concerned it is almost a shame to take the money. They make a magnanimous offer to accept twenty-four of the originally staked 100 guineas and call the whole thing off. Don Alfonso reminds them of the conditions of the wager: that they shall do what he tells them for 24 hours and there is still plenty of time to go.

Don Alfonso tells the two officers to wait for him in the garden, where he will send his orders. Guglielmo turns ruefully to his friend and asks: Don't we eat today then? Ferrando replies that when the battle is over the victory dinner will taste better than ever. Guglielmo, who keeps a stiff upper lip in all circumstances, makes no further comment, but stands rigid and silent while Ferrando sings an entirely superfluous but indispensably lovely aria reflecting poetically that a breath of tenderness from the loved one is all the food the heart desires—"Un'aura amorosa":

Ferrando sings, and departs with Guglielmo.

Don Alfonso is left alone on the stage to have another long talk with Despina, who seems to be hatching some sort of plot which she shares neither with us nor with Don Alfonso. Her only public concern is that the two young foreign gentlemen are rich. Don Alfonso once more reassures her on this point and she makes a promise that before morning her ability to deal with a mere couple of women will have brought victory to the picturesque suitors.*

Scene 4: A small garden, with grassy banks at the side.

Fiordiligi and Dorabella are discovered, as Despina warned us in her recent conversation with Don Alfonso, "telling their troubles to the breeze and the midges." It is in this mood that the finale to Act I begins—to ravishingly idyllic music in which the two sisters (closely bound in their

---

* In their disguises Ferrando and Guglielmo are usually described as being "Albanians". There is no direct mention of this either in the libretto or in the stage directions when they first appear in costume. We are no wiser even after Despina's puzzling over whether they are "Poles or Turks". Specific mention of their being "Albanians" is not made until very near the end of the whole opera. On the face of things it seems Da Ponte took a Shakespearean view of producers and designers by hiding his clues in the text and giving no direct help. On the face of things. The other side of the question will be raised later in this chapter.

troubles by thirds and sixths) lament with singularly little grief in their voices that things have changed so suddenly, and that before their true loves went away the stars were kind—"Ah! che tutto in un momento":

33. Andante

No 18

Ah,   che   tut-ta in un mo-   men-to   si cau-gio la for-te   mi-a,

Mozart imbues his summer-afternoon scene with a gentle shimmering heat-haze suggestion of Despina's breezes and hints that the midges were really benevolent enough to have been butterflies, for there is nothing malicious or—in the literal sense—piquant about the evocative little figure shared by flutes and bassoons in the course of this exquisite duet:

34. Andante

No 18

Ft.

p

Bassoons

The serenity of the scene is rudely interrupted, however, by an outbreak of considerable musical violence and the agitated cries off stage of Ferrando and Guglielmo, whose threats to kill themselves are answered by Don Alfonso's appeals to reason and moderation. The two sisters' alarm is increased as Ferrando and Guglielmo enter, each carrying a phial of poison and followed by an apparently panic-stricken Don Alfonso.

The music to which this scene is played is quite remarkably dramatic and convincing in its seriousness. The general mood of high tragedy is further sustained by Mozart's use of his most *serioso* key—G minor—and the sincere concern of the two sisters at the unexpectedly disconcerting turn of events. For the two sisters, of course, it is indeed a serious situation and the comedy of the action lies in everybody else on the stage, as well as in the audience, knowing that the whole thing is a put-up job. Does Mozart parody himself at this point? It is hard to say. The sisters, as we know, are sincerely affected; equally, the two practical jokers must sound no less sincere, otherwise their play-acting will not be convincing. In short, the comedy is mostly in the ear and eye of the beholder who is best placed to sit back and enjoy the incongruity of words, situation and music.

From the moment it gets really under way with the entrance of Ferrando and Guglielmo we are inextricably involved in a tremendous Mozart finale, the sort of finale which defies detailed quotation on paper because its greatness lies not in its themes but in their development, and their ability to sweep us along by the sheer force of an unending flow of rich musical invention almost without parallel even in Mozart's own operas.

Ideas—comic, serious, irrelevant and surprising—tumble over each other with immense and fantastic spontaneity and profusion, so that at one moment we might be listening to the development section of a great symphony, at another dragged without warning from broad Neapolitan daylight to the blackness of a tragic Seville night when we hear the assembled quintet express communal horror at the situation with

This phrase is surely a thoroughbred full-brother to Donna Anna's outburst in *Don Giovanni* quoted in Ex 8 on p. 86. While the contexts may differ, the similarities between the two phrases at least indicate the class of music into which *Così fan tutte* falls happily and naturally.

Now while all this is leading to wonderful music, as Don Alfonso points out in a matter-of-fact change to E flat, it is not doing the dying young men much good if Fiordiligi and Dorabella stand there and do nothing. The two sisters immediately panic and cry out, with magnificent ineffectualness: "People! People! Come here!"; and as nobody answers in the space of a couple of bars they call instead for Despina.

Despina enters and seeing Ferrando and Guglielmo lying in mortal agony on the ground quickly deduces that they are in need of medical attention, and taking Don Alfonso with her departs to fetch a doctor and an antidote in a deliciously mischievous phrase:

The two pairs of lovers are now left alone, Fiordiligi and Dorabella to reflect despairingly and helplessly on the implications of Despina's shattering diagnosis, Ferrando and Guglielmo to enjoy the sisters' discomfort as they writhe and groan at their feet. The earlier business-like E flat gives way to a more dramatic and earnest C minor in which Mozart gives symphonic status and treatment to the figure

The development of this provides a background for the sisters' anxiety and helplessness. When in a moment of characteristic weakening Dorabella remarks that she thinks the young men are rather handsome, the

rock-like Fiordiligi firmly suggests that they should do something definite; so they feel the suffering Albanians' pulses, their cold foreheads and observe what are clearly unmistakable if slightly premature signs of the setting in of *rigor mortis*. The seriousness of the mood is sustained by Ferrando and Guglielmo, who note *sotto voce* and with considerable satisfaction that the young ladies are growing tamer and more tractable (the original Italian has the delightful phrase, "più domestiche e trattabili"):

The prevailing air of pathos is exaggerated by a typically Mozartian use of chromatics as this second sustained section comes to an end with Fioridiligi and Dorabella admitting that they are moved to tears. In the course of the long cadence to this quartet, Ferrando and Guglielmo are heard to wonder whether the young ladies' new sympathy may not ripen into love. Why they should wonder this, if they do not also hope it, is an intriguing subject for cynical discussion, but not relevant to this study; though perhaps we may be permitted to wonder why the lovers suddenly seem so pleased at the prospect of losing their bet.

Key, tempo and time change suddenly as Don Alfonso enters accompanied by the Doctor whom he presents with

The Doctor is immediately recognized by Ferrando and Guglielmo in an aside to be Despina "in maschera", who greets the assembled company with "Salvete amabiles bones puelles", a form of easily understood near-Esperanto not far removed from the present-day dialect of Udine and (for some reason) of Sardinia, but which is double-Dutch to the two sisters. The Doctor, an obliging little figure, offers to speak in any language they may choose to name—Greek, Arabic, Turkish, Vandal, Swabian or Tartar. Don Alfonso interrupts the recital to point out that it is of more immediate importance to know what can be done for the patients who have taken poison. "What can be done?" echo the two sisters.

"First," replies the Doctor, "we must know what manner of poison this was and why it was taken. Was it hot or cold? Was it a little or a lot? Did they take it in one or more doses?" Fiordiligi, Dorabella and Don Alfonso reply with admirable promptness that it was arsenic, the motive was love and the poison was swallowed in one gulp.

The Doctor, satisfied by the answer given, produces the cure in the form of a "mesmeric stone which originated in Germany and later became famous in France":

The "stone" is nothing more or less than a magnet, its mesmericness a little joke at the expense of Dr Mesmer, an old friend of the Mozart family who, among other things, was the original investigator into the subject of animal magnetism and in whose garden in Vienna the twelve-year-old Mozart's opera, *Bastien und Bastienne*, had first been performed.

The Doctor runs the magnet up and down the prostrate bodies of the two poisoned lovers, who twitch convulsively as the mysterious "stone" revives them—an action which is underlined with enchantingly comic effect in the trilling of flutes, oboes and bassoons in the orchestra who echo Despina's phrase in Ex 40.

The twitching becomes so violent, however, that the sisters are ordered by the Doctor to hold the patient's heads to prevent them breaking their skulls on the floor in their convulsions. Miraculously the poisoned lovers are restored to life and they stare around them, as if in a dream, to a gentle figure for strings:

In hesitant, bewildered phrases Ferrando and Guglielmo ask where they are. Are they in Heaven? Is that Pallas and Cytherea they see before them? No, the ladies are their own beloved goddesses, and there is romance in the air once more as the clarinets return to the orchestra to support the lovers in their declaration:

The ladies are not a little appalled by the fervour with which their hands are held, but Despina explains that it is only the after-effect of the poison; there is nothing to be afraid of. Fiordiligi and Dorabella observe that that's all very well, but it isn't exactly proper behaviour.

An ensemble quietly develops with the ladies protesting in their usual harmonious way, Despina and Don Alfonso repeating the tale of the after-effects of the poison, and the two men alternating their ardent pleas with asides telling us they are bursting with laughter.

Fiordiligi and Dorabella find their resistance weakening and it affords them little comfort to be told by Despina that the effects of the animal magnetism will restore the young men to normal health in an hour or two. Towards the end of this little movement, however, it is clear that Fiordiligi is feeling herself again, for she opens her lungs in a highly characteristic outburst in the cadence to the tune of:

There is a sudden change of key and tempo to a vigorous Allegro and in surprisingly commanding tones Ferrando and Guglielmo demand a kiss or they will die. There is nothing gently pleading about their threatening cries of

The ladies are horror-struck and the music stops dead in its tracks, resuming only as Despina and Don Alfonso urge the two sisters to grant the young men's request as a gesture of kindness. The indignation which greets this "excessive demand of a faithful heart" is stupendous and threatens to dissolve the four onlookers in uncontrollable laughter, though Ferrando and Guglielmo are not certain whether the fury is genuine or put on.

The sisters' threats grow more violent as Mozart lets us hear their anger growing in a rising chromatic sequence with stormy pitching-and-tossing dynamics. Fiordiligi's personal indignation naturally takes the form of some hair-raising *fioriture* which she stops only when, on the request for a kiss being repeated, she is once more left open-mouthed at the impertinence of it all. But she soon gets up steam again and as the finale builds up to a brilliant climax she sits on a fierce top A while Ferrando indulges in a little mimicry and has some spectacular moments of *fioriture* of his own.

The curtain falls on a fine noise coming from all concerned, though whether the kisses are given or not we do not learn.

ACT II

Scene 1: A room in the sisters' house.

Così fan tutte being an *opera buffa* it is in order that a new act may start
with a scene in recitative. In this case we discover Fiordiligi and Dorabella
being lectured by Despina (now no longer the Doctor) who tells her mistresses to behave like grown-up women and not to sit around moping; and
she reiterates her philosophy that they should behave as their soldier-
lovers (and indeed *all* soldier-lovers) behave when they are out of sight.
"Are you flesh and blood, or what?" asks Despina, breaking into a frank
exposition of the correct behaviour expected of correct young ladies
in their position—"Una donna a quindici anni" ("At fifteen a girl should
know. . . .") :

The first impression we have of Despina during the opening couple of
phrases of this aria is that she is more sophisticated than we might expect;
but after an intriguing instance or two of unexpected harmonic colouring
the number settles down as one of characteristic grace and charm in the
Susanna-Zerlina tradition. And in accordance with that tradition we
encounter yet another case of Mozart's peculiar use of a single flute and
a single bassoon to play an important part in the orchestral accompaniment. The tempo of Despina's aria quickens from Andante to an Allegretto which might have come note-for-note from a Donizetti or Rossini
comic opera:

Mozart not only anticipated Donizetti and Rossini in the tune, the
harmony and the rhythmical "chuck-chuck" of the accompaniment of
this section of Despina's aria, but in the orchestration as well; by no means
the least considerable and original contribution to an enchanting and
sparkling item is made by the wonderfully effective—and almost incessant
use of the flute and bassoon playing the tune two octaves apart. Here we
have the orchestral blue-print of some of the wittiest and gayest moments
in *Don Pasquale* and *L'Elisir d'amore*, in *La Cenerentola* and *The Barber of*

Seville. It is what one might consider this "modern" quality that makes so much of the music of *Così fan tutte* unique among Mozart's operas.

Despina, after singing her own praises with "Viva Despina! who knows how to make herself useful!", leaves on as applause-provoking a musical exit line as an artist could wish for. She also leaves behind her two young ladies who are pleasantly puzzled to wonder whether, after all, there isn't something in what Despina says. It couldn't do much harm to flirt a little—provided, of course, one is discreet and careful about it—and it is not long before they are deciding in a duet how they will pair off. Dorabella will take the dark one and Fiordiligi is happy to laugh and play with the fair one. In the duet which follows it is characteristically Dorabella, the more adventurous of the two sisters, who opens the proceedings —"Prenderò quel brunettino" ("I will take the dark one. . . ."):

There is little in this whole exquisite score to match the purely sensuous beauty of this scene for the two sisters as they settle down to pleasant anticipation of the joys ahead. Mozart still has a little fun at the expense of Fiordiligi's vocal range, but for the most part it is a straightforward exercise in ingenious writing for two voices in canon, in imitation, in duologue, in thirds and sixths, in excited breathless phrases and the long lines of graceful runs and communal cadenzas.

The curtain usually falls as this lovely movement comes to an end, but should by rights remain raised for a few moments to allow Don Alfonso to appear and invite the two sisters to come into the garden and hear some music.

Scene 2: Garden by the sea shore with grassy seats and two stone tables. At the landing stage is moored a flower-decked barge, on board which are Ferrando, Guglielmo, singers and a band of musicians.

The curtain rises on a serenade (the day is wearing on by now) played by the small band of wind instruments on the barge—flutes, clarinets, bassoons and horns. At least, we are meant to believe the music is actually coming from the barge; in fact there is no indication in the score that any instruments other than one solitary military drum is to be heard on the stage during *Così fan tutte.* Wherever the music comes from, however, it is a sound of quite remarkable beauty and serenity, having something of the air of calm and peaceful eternity evoked by Gluck in his music for the Elysian Fields in *Orpheus.*

Twenty-four introductory bars in this vein are played by clarinets, bassoons and horns (the flutes do not come in until the chorus sings later on) to accompany the arrival of Fiordiligi and Dorabella as they are led in by Don Alfonso. When the audience is in a receptive mood (Despina is also present, of course) the serenade proper begins with Ferrando and Guglielmo, still disguised as Albanians, beseeching—to the same thoroughly un-Balkan tune—the zephyrs to bear their sighs to their souls' beloveds. For all its unseriousness it is an exquisite little serenade; it ends with a short reprise of the first theme by the chorus as the lovers, wearing chains of flowers, step ashore.

At this point of the story what is perhaps one of the least expected situations arises: *both* pairs of lovers are tongue-tied and bashful. One might have expected the sisters to be shy and awkward but not, surely, the young men who have so far entered into the spirit of the masquerade with such verve and enthusiasm. The awkward silence, however, enables Don Alfonso and Despina to take over the stage management of events and in what is virtually a duet, though the half dozen bars contributed by Ferrando and Guglielmo make it technically a quartet, they edge the two pairs of lovers if not quite into each other's arms, at least somewhere in that direction. The music which accompanies this conspiracy is of remarkable gaiety. To mention that it is marked "Allegretto grazioso" is not the half of it, for its effervescence and general sense of elation and mischief are heightened by Mozart's surprisingly unconventional instrumentation—two flutes, two bassoons and two trumpets added to strings to give a quite astonishing lightness to the orchestral texture of a movement which is naturally *leggerissimo* from the start:

The theme is transformed in a brilliant Presto to give Don Alfonso and Despina a few moments of patter-comedy before they leave the stage to a couple of pairs of embarrassed young people.

If ever there was a moment in comic opera when recitative was the only possible means of expression it is now; for how else could a composer do justice to the monumental anti-climax of the first four lines of dialogue spoken by the four lovers?—

Fiordiligi: What a lovely day!
Ferrando: A little warm, I think.
Dorabella: What sweet little trees!
Guglielmo: Yes, yes, indeed. Very pretty. With more leaves than fruit.

The first positive gesture comes rather unexpectedly from Fiordiligi who takes Ferrando off for a walk in the grounds. Guglielmo makes the most of his opportunity and within a comparatively few bars of recitative has Dorabella accepting a tiny golden heart from him, which he hangs round her neck, at the same time taking her portrait of Ferrando in exchange.

Dorabella, as we have come to expect by now, does no more than go through the most empty motions of resistance to all this, and she is by no means unresponsive by the time Guglielmo begins his duet with her—"Il core vi dono" ("I give you this heart . . .") :

For the opening couplets of the lyric Guglielmo and Dorabella use the formal "voi" in addressing each other, but thereafter they lapse into the familiar "tu"—a significant detail which explains (or perhaps excuses) the development of the duet along the line of the age-old routine of feeling and listening to the loved one's heart beating loudly and passionately in his/her breast. Guglielmo is the first to introduce this tactic and within less than a bar of his mentioning it Dorabella echoes it, and two bars later both of them are being as coy and graphic about heart-beats as Zerlina in "Vedrai carino".* This simple singing game provides no more than an interlude in the duet, however, and the scene ends with the music suggesting that there is likely to be just as much between Dorabella and Guglielmo as meets the ear.

The relatively placid air of Mutual Regard Ripening into Love which Dorabella and Guglielmo leave behind them is rudely shattered by the agitated entrance of Fiordiligi, followed by Ferrando. It is a highly dramatic entrance worthy of the forceful orchestral support and comment also given to the recitative that explains it. Ferrando, in an unusually spirited frame of mind, is full of ardent speeches and passionate declarations (he uses the familiar "tu", and Fiordiligi rather surprisingly does too) and in an aria which is rarely performed or even recorded these days he notes happily that he succeeds in drawing sighs and longing glances from her. The aria, which is No 24, is to be found in most vocal scores of *Così fan tutte* and is a cheerful episode, as the first bars may suggest:

51 . Allegretto

No 24

Ah! io　veggio quell'a- ni- ma　bel-la　al mio pian-to re-si-ster non sà,

The aria ends with an Allegro section based on a speeded-up version of the opening tune and Ferrando leaves the stage to a bewildered Fiordiligi.

As we learn now from another dramatic recitative Fiordiligi's bewilderment is one of conflict between her desires and her conscience. She is in love with the Albanian stranger, but she is betrothed to a soldier away at the wars. She makes peace with her conscience by singing an elaborate

* See p. 116.

rondo of immense difficulty and unusual brilliance and beauty—"Per pietà, ben mio" ("Pity me, my dear one, and forgive the error of a loving heart . . ."):

In this scene for Fiordiligi Mozart is in a more staid frame of mind. He is still writing for the remarkable voice of the original singer of the part, but this time—perhaps a little grudgingly—he is admiring Mme Ferraresi's range rather than mocking it. At all events, while occasionally in this long and lovely Adagio introduction to the rondo he exploits the wide leaps and bounds of which the singer was capable, it is not with the suggestion of malicious intent which got the laughs in "Come scoglio". Whether Mozart's decoration of the orchestral accompaniment with complicated solo passages for horns is to be enjoyed for its own musical sake, or whether we are to take it as comedy, regarding the spotlighting of these instruments as the audible symbols of cuckoldry they were in Figaro's "Aprite un po' quegli occhi" (Ex 50, p. 74), it is difficult to decide. Personally I believe that in this instance we are confronted with a composer completely absorbed in the joys of occasional virtuosity made possible not only by the presence of a remarkable prima donna, but also of an unusually fine horn player at the first performance of the opera.

The general *concertante* spirit of the Adagio is continued in the rondo which follows:

Fiordiligi's words are of little importance, for they are merely a poetic paraphrase of her sentiments in the Adagio; but the music she has to sing to them is stirring and brilliant. With all its flourishes, trills and vigorous decoration, by the time flutes, clarinets and horns have performed their final runs and Fiordiligi the last of her determined shakes, one feels that one has listened to the finale of an impressive concerto. With this and, one trusts, our applause ringing in her ears, Fiordiligi leaves the stage.

The two young men now enter and in an amusing recitative sequence compare notes on their activities. Ferrando is extremely pleased with the state of affairs so far; the money is as good as in their pockets, for Fiordiligi has proved herself a model of impregnable fidelity—an item of news, which, Ferrando is sure, will give considerable satisfaction to his friend. It does indeed give satisfaction to Guglielmo, but the mood of general complacency is rather disrupted by Guglielmo having to break the embarrassing news of Dorabella's inconstancy by showing Ferrando the locket she has given him.

This is more than Ferrando can bear. The satisfied smile leaves his face and in a moment he is in the midst of an angry accompanied recitative. The more Guglielmo reasons with him not to waste his time on a worthless woman, the more desperate Ferrando becomes. He bears no ill-will towards Guglielmo. It is Dorabella's behaviour which shatters him. How can all those vows and sighs be forgotten in so short a time—in one day!—in a few hours!

Guglielmo, whose advice to his friend has become increasingly unhelpful during Ferrando's outburst, signs off with a little masterpiece of fatuous verbosity as he remarks that "this is certainly a case to cause astonishment".

Guglielmo, one begins to suspect, is not altogether displeased at the way things are turning out. He did not appear tremendously enthusiastic, or indeed even relieved, by Ferrando's report that Fiordiligi was still faithful. He took it all very much for granted; and there is the first hint of a note of Don Alfonso's cynicism to be detected in his voice which suggests that he is quite happy to have his cake and eat it. At any rate, Guglielmo is content to be cheerful about it all and breaks into an aria in which he addresses the women of the audience—"Donne mie". The gist of this bustling song is that since women are so fickle one can hardly blame lovers for complaining. It is a burden which Guglielmo sings with *buffo* good humour and with no trace of either sorrow or anger, although in the course of a superbly light fingered accompaniment in which the strings play passages of almost unceasing semi-quavers, there are moments in the minor and the addition of trumpets and drums to give an air of dramatic determination. The predominance of the acid tone of oboes, too, suggests that Guglielmo has been partially converted to the philosophy of Don Alfonso, whose rather angular type of tune is more than just echoed in the theme of the aria:

A distraught Ferrando is left alone on the stage to reflect his unhappy lot in an agitated orchestrally-accompanied recitative. In spite of the way Dorabella has treated him he is still sincerely in love with her, and his cavatina which follows is a serious soliloquy on what Ferrando feels is his betrayal and deception by a faithless heart which—in spite of everything— he still adores: "Tradito, schernito, dal perfido cor"

After this rather melancholy opening protest in C minor the main tune

of the cavatina is introduced in E flat by clarinets and bassoons, which
Ferrando takes up after them:

When a little later this tune occurs in C major the same four bar
introduction is played by oboes and Ferrando continues uninterruptedly
on his way to end a charming scene which is far too often and quite
unreasonably omitted from performances of the opera.

During the final stages of the cavatina Don Alfonso and Guglielmo
have appeared in the background. When Ferrando has finished Don
Alfonso comes forward to congratulate him. "That," he says, "is real
constancy!" Ferrando is not at all pleased to see him ("cause of my
misery") but Don Alfonso reassures him that there is nothing very
unusual about it; circumstances often alter cases: Fiordiligi is faithful to
Guglielmo, whereas Dorabella is not faithful to Ferrando. Guglielmo chips
in with the superbly conceited assurance that of course things couldn't
really happen otherwise. What woman, asks Guglielmo, would ever dream
of being unfaithful to *him?* He's not blowing his own trumpet, but—
strictly between friends—one has certain advantages, you know.

Guglielmo turns to Don Alfonso to claim his half-share of the wager,
but the philosopher reminds him that time isn't up yet and they mustn't
count their chickens before they're hatched—a little maxim which Don
Alfonso utters unexpectedly in six bars of a 6/8 tune to end the recitative.

Scene 3: A room in the sisters' house with several doors, a mirror and a small table.

Despina is discovered busily congratulating Dorabella on being a
sensible woman at last. Dorabella replies that she tried hard to resist the
handsome stranger but his cunning, eloquence and charm would melt a
heart of stone. Fiordiligi enters in great distress, blaming—a little illogic-
ally—both Despina and Dorabella for the state she finds herself in. She is
in love, and her love is not just for Guglielmo, she adds. This information
delights Dorabella as well as Despina. Fiordiligi is shocked by the way her
sister receives the news. "What about our lovers who left for the front
this morning?" she asks.

"Listen," says Dorabella. "How do we know they won't be killed at the
war? A bird in the hand's worth two in the bush."

"But supposing they come back?" cries Fiordiligi.

"We shall be wives by then—and a thousand miles away," replies
Dorabella casually. Fiordiligi is appalled. "But I don't understand how
one can change one's affection in a single day."

"What a ridiculous remark!" exclaims Dorabella. "We're women, and
after all, what have you done?"

"I know how to control myself."

"You don't know anything"—a comment which comes a little unexpectedly from Despina.

"You'll see!" counters Fiordiligi, haughtily.

Dorabella asks her sister to believe her that it's much better if she does give in, and sings an enchantingly gay, rather Despina-like aria to illustrate her point—"È amor un ladroncello" ("Love is a thief and a serpent . . ."):

57. Allegretto vivace

Nᵒ 28

È a-mo-re un la-dron-cel-lo, un ser-pen-tel-lo è a-mor.—

As this is a new and different Dorabella, so her music takes on a new and different instrumental colour, and whenever she sings her opening phrase it is to the accompaniment of wind instruments only, which in this number consist of a single flute, two oboes, two clarinets and two horns used in various combinations and permutations. The wind section, indeed, dominates the whole aria in an intriguing way, leaving the strings with a completely subordinate part to play. Apart from its refreshing and purely musical attraction this number is important as a stage in the development of Dorabella's character; there is therefore less excuse than ever for omitting it, as too often happens, from performances and recordings of the opera.

Dorabella and Despina leave the room and Fiordiligi is alone with her thoughts once more, but as she speaks them out loud in recitative she is naturally overheard by Ferrando, Guglielmo and Don Alfonso who stand out of her sight in a doorway and see everything that goes on. Fiordiligi is resolute once more and announces that she will not see her strange lover again ("Bravissima!" comments Guglielmo. "Do you hear that? My chaste Artemisia!"). She calls for Despina and sends her to fetch a couple of "the many uniforms", two swords and two helmets belonging to Ferrando and Guglielmo which are in the house. Fiordiligi and her sister will put them on and follow their true loves to fight at their sides in the war like a couple of Polly Olivers, and so leave temptation behind them.

Many people are worried that Da Ponte does not explain how the uniforms come to be hanging up in the young ladies' house. The first and most obvious explanation is perhaps hardly conventional, though doubtless in keeping with the general "immorality" of the opera that so shocked the 19th century. Personally, wanting as far as possible to think the best of everybody, I have always thought the explanation extremely simple, straightforward and commendably respectable: Ferrando and Guglielmo, as army officers, are billeted in the house, a situation not unknown in our own age and an everyday occurrence in 18th-century Europe. How did Count Almaviva first insinuate himself into Dr Bartolo's house in *The Barber of Seville* but by saying that he was a soldier who was to be billeted there?

The casual way in which Fiordiligi is able to lay her hands on the two officers' uniforms certainly appears a little startling on first consideration,

but since Da Ponte did not consider it worthwhile explaining away I think
we can safely presume that there was nothing to explain away to an 18th-
century audience in the first place. Despina goes out, comes back with the
uniforms and accessories muttering audibly that she considers Fiordiligi
is out of her mind, and goes off again.

The next event witnessed by Ferrando, Guglielmo and Don Alfonso
from their point of vantage is the spectacle of Fiordiligi deciding that
Ferrando's uniform will fit her and that Guglielmo's will fit Dorabella.
Fiordiligi puts on helmet and cloak and buckling on the sword proclaims
that she is ready to go in search of her lover and die at his side if need be.
All this naturally delights Guglielmo and when Fiordiligi dramatically
tears off her ornamental headdress he cries "Was there ever a love like
this?"

The long, eventful and extremely amusing sequence of recitative, in
which so much happens and so many personal characteristics are revealed
and developed, comes to an end with Fiordiligi embarking on what we
may pardonably presume is another protestation of rock-like devotion and
eternal fidelity—"Fra gli amplessi in pochi istanti" ("I shall be in the
arms of my true love . . ."):

This, we recognize, is a very subdued and uncertain Fiordiligi indeed.
There is none of the vigorous and spectacular vocal leaping-and-bounding
of the earlier Fiordiligi; instead, with a sudden quickening of the tempo
Mozart has us all in a state of emotional apprehension by the introduction
of a characteristic syncopated accompaniment which might have come
from the more tragic moments of the slow movement of the composer's
great G minor String Quintet:

"How overjoyed he will be to see me," sings Fiordiligi.

Ferrando comes forward out of his hiding place and in the same accents
pours his own heart out with: "And meanwhile I shall die of despair."
The music modulates into C major; Fiordiligi, now severely using the
formal "voi" again, pleads with Ferrando to leave her, but echoing her
phrase in reply he refuses, begging her to pierce his heart with the sword

she holds and if her strength fails her, swearing to guide her hand himself:

The almost note-for-note resemblance between this phrase and the second part of the tune to which Ferrando announces that he plans to spend his winnings on a serenade (see Ex 7, p. 149) is quaint, but probably of no significance. It is remarkable in view of his quite fantastic output that Mozart did not repeat himself more often than he did. Whether or not this present instance was deliberate or subconscious (an aspect of Mozart's creative processes which most scholars show a remarkable reluctance to recognize), it is nevertheless in character, for in a moment Ferrando's ardent "tu" is being answered with similar intimacy by Fiordiligi and we are in the midst of as fine a seduction scene as one could wish for. There is no doubt how it is going to end, for there was surely never a more convincing illustration of an irrevocably broken resistance than Fiordiligi's

Equally, there is a gentle certainty in the promises made immediately afterwards by Ferrando. He tells Fiordiligi that in him she has husband, lover "and more if you wish":

This is the tenderness of the lover who knows he has conquered, and though the clarinets are entirely absent from this whole duet (a curious omission in view of the part they have played all through the opera so far) there is no lack of lyrical feeling in the seductive passage for oboe which leads to the final pages of the scene:

Whether intentionally or not the use of the oboe gives a certain masculinity to the phrase which provides an effective contrast to the simple, extremely feminine and moving words of surrender which Fiordiligi sings in the last of the 3/4 bars in Ex 63—"Fa di me quel che ti par" ("Do with me what you will . . ."):

It is at these last bars that Guglielmo wants to burst in on the happy pair, but Don Alfonso manages to restrain him until Fiordiligi and Ferrando have finished the rest of their duet—a sequence of passages in sixths and tenths, canon and mutual imitation, which shows the newly-awakened lovers to be in harmonic agreement on all aspects of the question. They leave very closely arm in arm, the scene ending, as it began, in A major—the key of the seduction duets of *Figaro* and *Don Giovanni*.

Guglielmo, it is obvious as he emerges angrily from his hiding place with Don Alfonso, has been touched on his most vulnerable spot. The conceited, vain, no-woman-would-be-unfaithful-to-*me* lover has witnessed the seduction of his fiancée by his best friend. He raves and tears his hair as he thinks of his Fiordiligi, "the Penelope, the Artemisia of the century! Nothing but a rascal, an assassin, a cheat, a thief, a bitch!" (Guglielmo is very angry and in fact uses the word "cagna".)

Ferrando returns. "Well?" he says to Guglielmo.

"Where is she?" asks Guglielmo.

"Your Fiordiligi?"

"My Fior—fior di diavolo!"

"You see," says Ferrando quietly and enjoying the irony of a moment of great satisfaction to him, "strictly between friends—one has certain advantages, you know. . . ."

Guglielmo grunts and decides that the women must be punished. But how?

"Marry them," suggests Don Alfonso.

"Marry them?" protest Ferrando and Guglielmo. "As soon marry a volcano or the gates of hell itself."

"Then you will be celibate for life?"

"Do you think men like us will go short of women?"—this, most unexpectedly, from Ferrando.

Don Alfonso agrees that there are plenty of others, but how will *they* behave? And he tells the young men that in their hearts they still love their shattered idols. They do? Then, continues Don Alfonso, they must take them as they are—fickleness and all.

Starting off in a matter-of-fact C major arpeggio suggesting sternness and authority Don Alfonso has what cannot be called an aria but is rather more a musical "incident" in which he tells a cautionary tale, warning

the two lovers that if they are disillusioned they have only their ignorance
to blame—"All men accuse women, but I excuse them" ("Tutti accusan
le donne . . ."):

65. Andante

No 30

Tut - ti ac - cu - san le Don - ne

"Whether they are young, old, pretty, or ugly, they all do it," sings
Don Alfonso. "Repeat it with me: they all do it." Ferrando and Guglielmo
sing the words after him to the motto theme in Ex 1—"Così fan tutte".

Despina enters (though in some productions and recordings she appears
before Don Alfonso's little song) to announce that the ladies have con-
sented to marry the two strangers; a notary will be coming this very
evening and in three days they will be ready to sail away with them.

The three men announce (in close harmony) that they are "con-
tentissimi" and Despina skips off giving herself her usual unsolicited
testimonial to her ingenuity and resourcefulness.

*Scene 4: A brightly lit saloon. An orchestra in the background. A table laid for a
banquet for four people, with silver candelabra. Four richly liveried servants.*

The curtain rises and we are at the Finale, which begins with a bustling
theme in the strings very much in the same temper as the opening of
Act I:

66. Allegro assai

No 31

Despina who is obviously an unsurpassed mistress of improvisation, is
discovered busily ordering the servants about and impressing on them the
importance of this festive hymeneal occasion. The servants promise in
chorus to work fast and willingly—a sentiment vocally endorsed at the
same time by the musicians of the stage orchestra who are clearly only a
"prop" in this scene, for they do not noticeably contribute any musical
honours or diversions.

Don Alfonso comes in to see how things are getting on and promises
handsome tips all round. Don Alfonso and Despina leave by different
doors sharing a *sotto voce* exit line to tell us that the most entertaining
comedy ever seen is now about to be performed.

The sudden sound of trumpets and drums added to the orchestra gives
us less than a bar to prepare for the entrance of a chorus of well-wishers
("Good luck to the happy couples") who sing their greetings to the

accompaniment—according to the stage directions—of the stage band playing a march. It is a somewhat commonplace march in E flat to begin with, but it automatically acquires a little "class" when the chorus hands over to the quartet of lovers and the general "marchiness" is forgotten in a long gentle passage with romantic assistance from clarinets and bassoons. The quartet combines to pay tribute to the assistance they have received from "Despinetta", a thought which is expressed gratefully and formally, with all the trimmings of a rather solemn ensemble which starts in this vein:

The chorus repeat their good-luck message and depart, leaving the two couples proposing that a toast should be drunk. "Let us drown every doubt and banish past memories from our hearts", they sing in a dignified round, a social musical accomplishment enjoyed by many of the gentry in the 18th century. Fiordiligi starts off:

Ferrando and Dorabella follow in turn, but when it comes to Guglielmo's entry there is nothing but a gruff mumbling to be heard as he sits sulkily wishing the toast were poison. Guglielmo's non-participation in the canon is a delicious touch. It is not only very much in character, for the blow to his pride is far more serious to Guglielmo than the loss of his fiancée and he is taking the whole thing very hardly, but because he is a baritone the range of his voice does not permit him to join in the round anyway. The tune includes only one note that is beyond his range, it is true, but Mozart solves what might have proved a tiresome problem superbly.

The round comes to its formal end, the tempo changes and the music modulates to bring in Don Alfonso followed by the Notary, who is ready to perform the ceremony. (Guglielmo has come out of his gloom now and is as anxious to get on with the proceedings as any of them.)

The Notary, of course, is Despina disguised as Avvocato Beccavivi (she seems to specialize in the learned professions), who informs us that the marriage contract is ready and that after a preliminary cough he will read it in a clear voice.

The Notary reads (in a virtual monotone) with the traditionally nasal voice of his profession. I do not know how, when or where this convention of Italian comedy started, but it is a regular characteristic of all notaries in comic opera, persisting from *Così fan tutte* and *Don Pasquale* to *Gianni Schicchi* in our own days.

We learn several interesting things from the reading of the contract, among them that the two strange lovers have names. Ferrando goes by the name of "Sempronio" and Guglielmo by that of "Tizio".* We also learn that the gentlemen who are to marry the "dame ferraresi" are "nobles from Albania". This is the first mention of the foreigners having any specific nationality—at least, the first mention in the libretto as it has come down to us. It may not have been so originally, as I will suggest later.

The marriage contract has just been signed to the applause and congratulations of Don Alfonso and Despina when from outside comes the sound of singing—"Bella vita militar", the military song from Act I (Ex 13).

This off-stage chorus is prefaced by a passage I must quote as, in raising an intriguing question of orchestration, it provides the only example I know in all Mozart of quite remarkably ineffectual scoring. The passage reads:

That run up and the C sharp it ends in are played by a *solo* flute, and in practice it is one of the feeblest noises ever heard in the opera house. Why, when immediately afterwards he uses two flutes in unison, Mozart did not have two flutes to play the scale passage together I cannot imagine. His almost ritualistic adherence to the pattern of his instrumentation prevents him doing what he ought obviously to have done—namely, double the passage either in unison or in octaves with clarinets. The clarinets were last used in the romantic mood of the round; they are not due to be used again until the movement which follows the march, so that clearly rules them out. However, the conductor who today adds a second flute and perhaps even doubles the scale on the two oboes will not, I feel, be guilty of sacrilege. He will merely be nudging Mozart who, for a rare moment in his life, has nodded off. Puristic considerations do not enter into the question: the ear and only the ear is what matters, and even if the feeble little run-up is left as it is the C sharp in the Maestoso bar badly needs reinforcing, for it is the *only* C sharp in a chord scored for two oboes, two bassoons, two trumpets, drums and basses. The competition is unfair; it is also, if we are courageous about it, unnecessary.

The sound of the march throws the wedding party into complete confusion. Don Alfonso, beseeching them all in a typically stern and vigorous descending arpeggio to be calm, goes to the window to report the worst: the ship has returned from the wars, the two officers are disembarking.

Panic sets in; Despina flees and the Albanian bridegrooms are packed

* The legendary trio of "Cajo", "Sempronio" and "Tizio" are the Italian equivalent of "Thingummy", "What's-his-name" and "What-d'ye-call-him".

off into another room, which they leave to slip out through the main door while Don Alfonso is pacifying the distraught sisters whose genuine fear of what will happen to them is expressed in an appropriately tragic cadence in G minor.

Ferrando and Guglielmo appear at the door in their officers' uniforms and sing a delightfully bland and fatuous little duet to say how joyfully they return (by gracious permission of the King) to the loving arms of their sweethearts who have earned "a prize for their fidelity":

Don Alfonso welcomes his friends with surprise and warmth; but the ladies are pale and sad and silent. Don Alfonso explains to the gentlemen (who have carefully remembered to address the particular sister they are supposed to be engaged to) that the shock of their return has rendered the ladies speechless with delight and surprise.

There now occurs a complicated little piece of stage mechanics and "business". Servants enter carrying a large trunk which Guglielmo asks the ladies' permission to have placed in the room into which Despina was seen to escape. This rather elaborate bit of stage-management results in the discovery of Despina, still disguised—except for the wig which she has taken off—as the Notary. She explains quickly who she is and that she just happens to have been to a fancy dress ball (so early in the evening?) dressed as a notary—an explanation which comes as a great relief to the two sisters who note that it apparently satisfies the two lovers.

Meanwhile Don Alfonso draws the officers' attention to the marriage papers he has let fall on the floor. Ferrando and Guglielmo pick them up and register considerable astonishment and indignation which they proceed to give voice to in another passage of close harmony. They are about to go into the room the Albanians were seen to enter, but Fiordiligi and Dorabella restrain them, begging their lovers to pierce their guilty breasts through with their swords in a pathetic phrase:

Before resorting to such extreme measures, however, Ferrando and Guglielmo want to know what it's all about. Fiordiligi and Dorabella point accusingly at Don Alfonso and Despina: the monster and the temptress.

Don Alfonso's reply is to indicate that the answer lies in the other room—and points to the main door through which the lovers returned. Ferrando and Guglielmo stride out purposefully to return a moment later, without helmets, cloaks or moustaches, but with their Albanian clothes ridiculously awry.

With exaggerated, flamboyant gestures Ferrando kneels at the feet of Fiordiligi—"the knight of Albania salutes you, fair lady!"

Guglielmo falls on his knees before Dorabella and echoes his little tune of Ex 50, altering the words to "This little portrait you gave me in exchange for my heart; here it is, Signora," and adding a mocking little flourish in the fourth bar.

Finally, the two men turn to Despina with a united quotation of the final phrase of Ex 40 to congratulate the famous "Doctor" on his prowess.

Lord Harewood, in his admirable chapter on *Così fan tutte*, which he contributed to his edition of *Kobbé's Complete Opera Book* raises an interesting point about this scene. What, he asks in effect, is Ferrando supposed to be quoting? The whole design and symmetry of the libretto make it obvious that if Guglielmo is going to quote what he said to Dorabella, then Ferrando must also quote something which Fiordiligi has heard from the lips of the "Albanian".

Somewhere, it seems clear, an aria of some kind has got lost which, while its inclusion may not have been justified on musical grounds, nevertheless had a certain dramatic significance in that apart from its being needed for quotation and reference in this Finale it gives the only direct indication that Ferrando and Guglielmo are masquerading as Albanians. Without this aria, in fact, it is not until the end of the opera that we are able to infer what manner of exotics the lovers are supposed to be.

Whether or not when he came to this point in the Finale Mozart was setting Da Ponte's words for the first time it is impossible to say for certain. My belief is that Mozart had in fact at least started on a scene of some kind to which these five bars in the Finale are a direct reference. Taken out of their context as they are, it must be said in all conscience that they have no great distinction; which suggests to me more than ever that they must have had some concrete existence at some time during the period of what is known to have been extremely hurried composition, for they have virtually no musical interest as they stand. Indeed, as they stand— since we don't know what Ferrando is talking about—they are virtually meaningless. Despina, as the Notary, has told us he was an Albanian nobleman and we have seen him making love to Fiordiligi; but without our ever having seen him on his knees proclaiming his Albanian nobility nor— which is most important—having seen Fiordiligi falling for it, the joke is a little obscure.

It may be argued that even though the original source of the quotation had been jettisoned *en route* Mozart could still have covered his carelessness and inconsistency by perhaps inserting a near-quotation from some other moment in the Ferrando-Fiordiligi relationship. This seems a reasonable suggestion until we notice that the whole tone of the quotations we hear is one of teasing and gentle mockery. To refer to the duet of Ferrando's seduction of Fiordiligi would, I think, introduce an unnecessarily emotional and even hurtful note into what is, after all, intended to be comedy.

In the end, however, I fear the Case of the Kneeling Albanian Knight must remain an insoluble mystery—fascinatingly intriguing, but one we can unfortunately do absolutely nothing about until the manuscript of an aria comes to light which may well never have been written anyway.

The quotations and misquotations leave Fiordiligi and Dorabella more discomfited than ever, and in their embarrassment they turn, a little unfairly, on Don Alfonso whom they blame for everything. Don Alfonso replies smoothly that everything he has done has been for their own good, and if they will take his advice they will all kiss and be friends, and laugh as he has laughed and will laugh again. In their usual seductive thirds and sixths Fiordiligi and Dorabella turn to their lovers and with richly scored strings (divided violas, of course) in support, promise eternal fidelity:

The two men make a suitable reply which the ladies do not hear as they continue to sing while it is being made.

Personal reflections at an end the six characters turn to us in the audience and advise us to let our actions be guided by reason and to keep a sense of humour in all things.

These anything-but-solemn thoughts are prefaced by a statement of the eight-bar theme by the wood-wind, horns, trumpets and drums of the orchestra only and the final C major movement of the opera is launched on its bright and satisfying course:

We are never told how the lovers finally pair off, for from the moment of reconciliation they sing and are sung to only as couples, and there is no hint of contact between individuals. It is probable that Da Ponte considered the matter scarcely worth mentioning, and indeed on reflection the most likely outcome of *Così fan tutte*—namely, the mutual exchange of marital partners—is not entirely unknown even in our own morally enlightened age. Don Alfonso, after all, was primarily a philosopher, and he may well have engineered the whole thing to prevent two marriages taking place which he regarded as ill-conceived long before the curtain rose.

If the librettist asks us to use our imagination then he gives us a symbolic hint when Fiordiligi puts on Ferrando's uniform and pointedly leaves Guglielmo's for Dorabella. And if that is not convincing then surely operatic convention makes it all as clear as daylight: of course Ferrando and Fiordiligi pair off, for who ever heard of a prima donna marrying a baritone?

On the other hand, there is, of course, just a faint doubt raised by the unique nature of the prima donna's voice. The top part of Fiordiligi's voice obviously gets the tenor; equally, the lower part qualifies her as soul mate for the baritone.

Perhaps there is a more interesting sequel to be written to *Così fan tutte* than one might have thought.

Though we may not always be satisfied by the way *Così fan tutte* is sung in our day, at least I think we may be smug about our insistence that it should be sung in the original text.

It is not very long ago, however, that in Germany Mozart's opera was still being performed in some very strange versions. An edition published in the early 1920's of Charles Annesley's "Standard Opera Glass" presents the plot of *Così fan tutte* with such pleasing divergencies from the book as we know it that I think it merits re-telling in its original quaint language:

Don Fernando and Don Alvar (the synopsis runs) are betrothed to two Andalusian ladies, Rosaura and Isabella.

They loudly praise their ladies' fidelity, when an old bachelor, named Onofrio, pretends that their sweethearts are not better than other women and accessible to temptation. The lovers agree to make the trial and promise to do everything which Onofrio dictates. Thereupon they announce to the ladies, that they are ordered to Havannah with their regiment, and after a tender leavetaking, they depart to appear again in another guise, as officers of a strange regiment. Onofrio has won the ladies-maid, Dolores, to aid in the furtherance of his schemes and the officers enter, beginning at once to make love to Isabella and Rosaura, but each, as was before agreed, to the other's affianced.

Of course the ladies reject them, and the lovers begin to triumph, when Onofrio prompts them to try another temptation. The strangers, mad with love, pretend to drink poison in the young ladies' presence. Of course these tenderhearted maidens are much aggrieved; they call Dolores, who bids her mistresses hold the patients in their arms; then coming disguised as a physician she gives them an antidote. By this clumsy subterfuge they excite the ladies' pity and are nearly successful in their foolish endeavours, when Dolores, pitying the cruelly tested women, reveals the whole plot to them.

Isabella and Rosaura now resolve to enter into the play. They accept the disguised suitors, and even consent to a marriage. Dolores appears in the shape of a notary, without being recognized by the men. The marriage-contract is signed, and the lovers disappear to return in their true characters, full of righteous contempt. Isabella and Rosaura make believe to be conscience-stricken, and for a long while torment and deceive their angry bridegrooms. But at last they grow tired of teasing, they present the disguised Dolores, and they put their lovers to shame by showing that all was a farce. Of course the gentlemen humbly ask their pardon, and old Onofrio is obliged to own himself beaten.

The reason for this remarkable transmogrification is put forward in the author's preface to his synopsis: *Così fan tutte* in its original text, he tells us, "really shows female fickleness, and justifies its title. But the more Mozart's music was admired, the less could one be satisfied with such a libretto. Schneider and Devrient therefore altered it. . . ."
The use of the word "therefore" is masterly.
Of course.
Perhaps it is small wonder, when we consider what could happen to it, that *Così fan tutte* has been in its way the most "difficult" of Mozart's operas. To one generation its irrepressible gaiety was abhorrent, while its serious moments were doubly repellent because they were set in such frivolous surroundings; to another generation the sparkle and vivacity of the comedy obscured the serious moments to the extent of scholars and critics having us believe that everything that was not simple musical comedy was parody. As usual, the truth lies somewhere between the two views, and if we approach it with the broadest-possible open mind we may discover *Così fan tutte* to be perhaps the most sensuously beautiful of all Mozart's operas. Perhaps it is more limited in its variety of characterization than *Figaro*; perhaps it does not cover the huge emotional and dramatic canvas of *Don Giovanni*; but for sheer joy to be derived from richness of colour, beauty of line, unending invention and exquisitely satisfying symmetry of construction, *Così fan tutte* is an unique experience.
Alfred Einstein calls it "iridescent, like a glorious soap-bubble" which is a fine-sounding phrase. But it can be a misleading one, for soap-bubbles suggest something brittle and ephemeral and *Così fan tutte* is anything but that. It has the kaleidoscopic restlessness and unpredictability of a soap-bubble, certainly; and like a soap-bubble, once seen it is never forgotten; but it is not a soap-and-water creation. It is a happily solid, tangible and preservable thing, the careful work of a musical Cellini, not the haphazard result of a child's playing with a clay pipe. It is Mozart's absorption in the pure craftsmanship involved in the composition of *Così fan tutte*, his tremendous technical assurance (always excepting the inexplicable flute in Ex 69) which put this opera in a class by itself.

To me there is nevertheless always something a little sad about *Così fan tutte*; or, more precisely, in the emotions I feel each time I see its final curtain fall. Weber was sure that Mozart could never have written another *Entführung*, for it had the unrepeatable, un-recapturable quality of youth, and Weber was sad about it. To me, the belief that Mozart could have written another *Così fan tutte* if he had lived, because it had the quality of an unparalleled musical maturity, is a saddening thought.
It is saddening because as the final curtain falls on *Così fan tutte* one realizes that it is falling on the last of the great comedies of the greatest of all composers of comic opera.

THE MAGIC FLUTE
(*Die Zauberflöte*)

An opera in two acts by Emanuel Schikaneder. First performed at the Theater auf der Wieden, Vienna, on 30th September, 1791, conducted by the composer.* First performance in England: 6th June, 1811, Haymarket Theatre, London (in Italian). First performance in the United States: 17th April, 1833, Park Theatre, New York.

O F all Mozart's operas perhaps *The Magic Flute* is the one that makes the sternest demands of the listener, for it is only when we approach it in a mood almost of complete unquestioning faith that its ultimate beauty and serenity become apparent. The very simplicity of the music is at once its most charming and its most deceptive quality, a quality which will delight a child while leaving some of his elders unmoved, if not actually bored and irritated.

Above all, perhaps, it is the one work of Mozart's which nobody can expect to enjoy as an automatic matter of course merely because they know *Figaro* and *Don Giovanni* and the others backwards. Whereas *Die Entführung, Figaro, Don Giovanni* and *Così fan tutte* all have certain features in common and to know and love these operas may pardonably be claimed as a pretty comprehensive experience of Mozart, they do not either individually or collectively provide a precedent for *The Magic Flute.*

There is no precedent for *The Magic Flute.* Previous acquaintance with Mozart's operas is not necessary. It may even be a handicap, for the listener will instinctively expect to hear in *The Magic Flute* what he has heard in Mozart's other operas. Certainly, not all the music of *The Magic Flute* will sound strange to him; Mozart's musical voice speaks with the same accent as before. It is just that the composer's thoughts are on a different plane altogether, that his comedy, his drama, his whole musical outlook are somehow permeated by a radiance and a peculiar, incomparable serenity not to be encountered anywhere else in his entire prodigious output.

Perhaps because *The Magic Flute* is so "different" it is the *first* hearing of this opera which can so often be puzzling and disheartening, from which the otherwise whole-hearted and confirmed Mozart enthusiast takes so long to recover. But while I have yet to encounter anybody who has ever written off *The Magic Flute* as a fruitless experience after a second hearing there is always a danger that the disillusioning effect of the first may discourage the listener from risking a return visit.

Once the danger is past, however, the peculiar magic of Mozart's last opera will begin to work, slowly, surely and unendingly as each hearing, in a miraculous and inexplicable way not encountered with any other

* The original billing announced: "Herr Mozart, out of high regard for a gracious and honourable public and friendship for the author of the piece, will himself conduct the orchestra today."

Mozart opera, reveals some new detail or new aspect of the score which one somehow did not notice before.

It is in its infinite richness and variety, its inexhaustible capacity for the provision of new experience that the unique greatness of *The Magic Flute* lies as a work of art. The comparison of a work of art executed in one medium with a work of art executed in another is rarely a satisfactory pastime, for it does little more than express a purely personal reaction. But *The Magic Flute* is in its way the most personal of all operas in the sense that each one of us must approach it in an individual and personal way. For me it has the eternal fascination and moving sublimity of Michelangelo's Sistine Chapel frescoes; it is an artistic experience without parallel which, even at the end of its own immortality, one feels will never entirely give up its final secret.

The legends, facts and theories concerning the genesis of *The Magic Flute* are more numerous and bewilderingly contradictory than in the case of any other of Mozart's operas, and of sufficient complexity to warrant their discussion at considerable length in the course of the four chapters devoted to the opera in the book I would recommend the student to pursue the study in—namely, Edward J. Dent's *Mozart's Operas: A Critical Study* (Oxford University Press, 1947). For present purposes, however, we need not know more than a rough outline of the circumstances relevant to our enjoyment and understanding of the work as we hear it in the theatre, on the radio, or in the somewhat telescoped form of the majority of the versions available on gramophone records.

In May 1791 Mozart was approached with a commission to compose an opera of a kind which was completely strange to him and for a theatre which was no less foreign to his whole life's experience. The commission came from Emanuel Schikaneder, an old friend of Mozart's, actor, singer, proprietor of the Theater auf der Wieden in Vienna, a man of the theatre the foundations of whose immense experience and versatility had been laid in a childhood of abject poverty and struggle as a wandering fiddler. He graduated to actor-manager, touring his own company in *King Lear*, *Macbeth* and *Hamlet* and though he died insane and a pauper he ensured his immortality as the author of the libretto of *The Magic Flute* before he did so.

The four operas by Mozart so far discussed in this volume were all first performed in an atmosphere of royal or near-royal patronage. Shortly after the first performance of *Così fan tutte* in 1790, however, the Emperor Joseph II had died, to be succeeded by Leopold II. The new Emperor had none of the imaginative sympathy of his predecessor; the interest he took in music was purely "official" and to have enjoyed the patronage of Joseph was automatically to earn the disapproval of Leopold, who had little time for the principles and ideals of the man he had succeeded.

Schikaneder's commission, though it was for what was technically a Singspiel,* involved Mozart in what can only be described as a "set-up" vastly different from that in which his last Singspiel—*Die Entführung aus*

* See p. 20.

dem Serail—had been produced. The Theater auf der Wieden was, to put it mildly, a "popular" theatre, its policy to provide a simple-minded public with what it regarded as lavish spectacle, in which great play was made with stage machinery, live animals, and ambitious lighting effects, interspersed with extravagant and vulgar comic "business", songs and general gagging. The most popular form of these unsophisticated entertainments Schikaneder discovered to be what he called "magic" operas, laid in a vaguely Oriental setting with a simple fairy tale plot.

It was just such an opera that Schikaneder originally intended *The Magic Flute* to be. The reasons and theories how and why it came to take the final form we know today are discussed by Professor Dent in the chapters to which I have already referred, where the reader will find much to fascinate him and a convincing case for the support of the claim that Schikaneder had as collaborator a colourful actor whose stage name was Carl Ludwig Giesecke, but who was otherwise Johann Georg Metzler, sometime Professor of Mineralogy and Chemistry at the University of Dublin, where he died in 1833.

Of greater importance than the question whether the number of collaborators concerned with the final version of *The Magic Flute* eventually totalled three or only two, however, is the fact that either way the opera was an all-Masonic product. Schikaneder, Mozart and Giesecke were all Freemasons; indeed, they were all members of the same Viennese lodge from which, one regrets to report, the actor-manager was later ignominiously expelled for reasons totally unconnected with *The Magic Flute*. In some way which has never been conclusively explained there came a moment in the course of the preparation of the opera when the original oriental-fairy-tale-setting of the libretto was forgotten and the whole thing developed instead into a complex allegory glorifying Freemasonry in which contemporary political trends as well as the recent Masonic history of Austria were all worked into a highly moral and heavily symbolized tale of the ultimate triumph of Good over Evil.

This aspect of *The Magic Flute* alone adds to the general confusion likely to afflict the listener hearing the work for the first time, of course. It is bad enough to be confronted with a naïve fairy tale anyway, without getting involved in a Masonic allegory. Whether the listener who is a Freemason derives more in the end from *The Magic Flute* than the listener who is uninitiated it is impossible for a non-Mason to tell. But so far as general contemporary allusions and symbolism are concerned the opera today probably means as much or as little to one class of listener as to the other.

There are, we know (for prominent Masons have told us), essentially and peculiarly Masonic musical characteristics to be found in the score but that does not mean that their *musical* effect is necessarily any less on us who are not Masons. Mozart was far too great and instinctive an operatic craftsman to introduce esoteric little luxuries in the form of musical numbers that could be understood, or at best, fully appreciated, only by one section of the community. What can be considered, if it can be considered at all, as the "Masonic" musical element in *The Magic Flute* makes its effect not because it is underlining or cross-referring to some ritualistic feature of a secret society to which it is possible no member of the audience may belong at all, but because it is the right music for the situation, emotion or dramatic mood which Mozart wants to translate into his own universally understood musical language.

As I have suggested, it is the very simplicity of its music which is the most deceptive feature of *The Magic Flute*. But that does not mean we should spend our lives trying to discover profound hidden meanings or enigmatic allusions. Unlike *Figaro* and *Così fan tutte* and *Don Giovanni*, where one has figuratively to sit forward in one's seat and concentrate intensely for fear of missing anything, *The Magic Flute* is above all others a work which it is essential one should listen to in a mood of complete physical and mental relaxation.

The Irish have a saying that "the Man who made Time made plenty of it." It is a saying that can be paraphrased to apply to Mozart's last opera: "The Man who made *The Magic Flute* made plenty of it." For like Time itself it was born with the breath of Eternity on it.

CHARACTERS IN ORDER OF SINGING:

TAMINO . . . . . . *Tenor*
THREE LADIES, *in attendance on the Queen of
    the Night* . . . . . *Sopranos*
PAPAGENO, *a bird-catcher* . . . . *Baritone*
QUEEN OF THE NIGHT . . . . *Soprano*
MONOSTATOS, *a Moor, in the service of Sarastro* *Tenor*
PAMINA, *daughter of the Queen of the Night* . *Soprano*
THREE BOYS (*the Three Genii*) . . . *Sopranos*
TWO PRIESTS . . . . . . *Baritones*
AN OLD PRIEST . . . . . *Baritone*
SARASTRO, *High Priest of Isis and Osiris* . *Bass*
FIRST PRIEST . . . . . *Tenor*
SECOND PRIEST . . . . . *Bass*
THE SPEAKER . . . . *Speaking part*
AN OLD WOMAN . . . . . *Soprano*
TWO MEN IN ARMOUR . . . *Tenor, Bass*
Priests, Slaves, People.

Scene and Time: Ancient Egypt.

ACT I

Any idea that because *The Magic Flute* has spoken dialogue it is therefore likely to be another Singspiel like *Die Entführung* is loudly dispelled in the very first bars of the Overture. The full force of an orchestra including, and indeed featuring, three trombones announces in a solemn Adagio which must have frightened the original Schikaneder audience out of its wits that this is an opera of profound seriousness and intent. The first three bars—

are often regarded as symbolic of the three knocks made by Masons on the door of their lodge. As we discover later in the Overture, however, the so-called "Dreimalige Akkord" ("the thrice-played chord") which represents this particular Masonic ritual is not only in a different rhythm, but is also scored differently, is written in a different key and is constructed in a different harmonic sequence.

The first passage of 15 slow bars introduces us to an orchestral colouring which is new, for the deep tone of trombones in *The Magic Flute* belongs to a tranquil world which, while it must be considered supernatural, is benevolent and free of the menacing terrors of *Don Giovanni*, though in both works Mozart exploits to the full the dramatic power of careful dynamic changes—particularly the sudden *piano* after the crescendo, and the *sforzato*.

The tempo changes to Allegro and the statement of the subject on which a stupendous fugal Overture is based:

This theme has been shown to have been clearly derived from Clementi's Piano Sonata in B flat (Op. 47, No 2) but there, one might safely say, all resemblance ends. Possession in this case is more than nine points of the law and Mozart's treatment of the theme, its development and the variety of emotional light and shade he extracts from it places this Overture in the class of the finale of the Jupiter Symphony. If there are technical details to be noticed (it is impossible to describe what "happens" in this prodigious display of counterpoint) they are the use made of trombones and trumpets to give rhythmic emphasis to *tutti* passages and the frequent recurrence of drops of major, minor and diminished sevenths found in phrases like

and

The vigorous symphonic development of the theme comes to its formal half-way halt and the tempo reverts to the opening Adagio with the famous "Dreimalige Akkord", now virtually in the form in which it is heard later in the opera, scored for wind, brass and drums:

The Allegro is resumed with further development of the fugue theme and a whole stream of breathtaking contrapuntal ingenuities and inventions are let loose to lead the Overture to its vigorous coda—a passage which presents some surprising *sforzato* effects for horns, trumpets and trombones on unexpected beats of the bar.

Scene 1: A mountainous district with here and there rocks overgrown with trees; at both sides of the stage there are practicable mountains; a round temple in the background.

As the curtain rises Schikaneder's stage direction reads: "Tamino, dressed in a splendid Japanese hunting costume, comes down one of the rocks, carrying a bow, but no arrow; a snake pursues him." The "Japanese hunting costume" is obviously a relic of the opera's early beginnings as a simple oriental fairy story, for now, of course, the setting has become

Ancient Egypt, from which so much Masonic ritual and symbolism is said to derive.

To permit Schikaneder time for his lighting effects and to make the most of his fire-breathing serpent Mozart provides an unusually long orchestral prelude to accompany the action. It is an agitated and impellingly dramatic sequence in which syncopated chords and sudden contrasts of *piano* and *forte* from oboes, bassoons and horns provide a background for music in this vein:

Tamino cries out for help as he tries vainly to escape from the serpent. As he falls unconscious the door of the temple opens and three veiled Ladies appear, each with a silver spear. They make their entry to a commanding phrase supported by an orchestral unison (with trumpets and drums)—"Die, monster!"

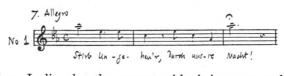

The Three Ladies slay the serpent with their spears and announce triumphantly that the heroic deed is done and the Prince freed by the bravery of their arms (they mean their limbs, not their spears). While the tempo stays the same the music changes now to a more subdued lyrical mood with strings and the warm sounds of flutes and clarinets as each Lady in turn looks at the prostrate form of Tamino and remarks on his beauty:

The Three Ladies unite to assure us that if their hearts were "dedicated to love" then Tamino would be the one for them. They decide to return to the Queen of the Night to give her all the news, hoping that this handsome young man may possibly be able to restore to her the peace of mind she has lost.

"You two go and tell her," says the First Lady, "while I stay here."

Not on her life, answer the other Ladies in effect, and a quarrel develops between them, each insisting that *she* should stay behind and protect the unconscious Tamino. It is a delightful little sequence with an unexpected hint of *opera buffa* suddenly created by the light staccato orchestral accompaniment. This suggestion of comedy is sustained by the change of time and tempo to a 6/8 Allegretto, with an opening orchestral phrase characteristic of the simple effectiveness and charm of the incident:

The Three Ladies continue their soliloquies, separately and in concert, in the vigorous change of time and tempo to Allegro. The theme of their reflections is the same as before—"What wouldn't I give if I could live with this youth! If only I had him alone! But neither of the others is moving an inch!" A somewhat business-like single note from trumpets and drums introduces a practical note of reality to these day-dreams and in their separate ways the Three Ladies, still as charmingly and graciously as ever, resign themselves to the fact that they had better be going.

In a touching little final trio-passage they bid farewell to the still unconscious Tamino, a passage in which, although it is largely sung in three simultaneous parts, the Three Ladies nevertheless continue to express individual as distinct from collective emotions. It is "until *I* see you again" not "until *we* see you again."

To a final flourish of trumpets and drums the Three Ladies go through the temple doors which, according to the stage directions, "open and shut of their own accord."*

The first musical number of the opera ends as the temple doors shut. Like the first scene in *Don Giovanni* this opening scene is also called in the score "Introduction", though perhaps this scene in *The Magic Flute* is not quite so packed with hair-raising incident as its counterpart in the earlier opera. The only casualties at the beginning of *The Magic Flute* apart, one suspects, from the hearts and personal pride of the Three Ladies whose plans have been thwarted, are a dead serpent and a handsome young man in a faint. Nevertheless, for what is technically a Singspiel the evening has so far not been uneventful.

Tamino comes to and still dazed wonders whether he is alive or dead. As he looks around he sees the serpent lying dead at his feet; his bewilderment at the sight is further increased by the distant sound of what the

---

* The stage directions quoted in this chapter are for the most part from Schikaneder's originally published libretto. Those that are not are taken from the full score based on the autograph in the Prussian State Library in Berlin. I shall quote them in full as far as possible, not only to give some idea of the nature of the first *Magic Flute* as it appeared on the stage of the Theater auf der Wieden, but also in the hope that by reminding them of its original character modern producers may get a little nearer the spirit of the opera than recent productions have suggested they know how to.

libretto describes as a "Waldflötchen", a form of "forest-piccolo" ("Wald-" is forest and "Flötchen" is a little flute, after all) which it is difficult to define if, indeed, such an instrument ever existed. The distant sound is "accompanied *piano* by the orchestra; Tamino speaks during the Ritornel". What Tamino says as he speaks is not much, however, for almost immediately he hides himself behind a tree at the approach of a figure we learn to identify from our programmes as Papageno.

Mozart certainly provides "Ritornel" music for Papageno's approach but it is a long time before we hear anything of the forest-piccolo in the long instrumental prelude designed to allow plentiful opportunities for comic "business" by Schikaneder who was the creator of a part which he wrote giving himself all possible scope for the intimate backchat, gags, jokes and anecdotes his public expected of him.

Instead of a forest-piccolo being accompanied *piano* by the orchestra what Tamino hears is an entire orchestral sequence with the first violins playing the tune which begins:

During this prelude, the stage directions tells us, Papageno comes down a footpath carrying on his back a large bird-cage which reaches higher than his head and contains various birds. He also holds in both hands a set of pan-pipes (our *Waldflötchen* has now become *Faunenflötchen* in the script); he plays his pipes and sings. In that order—for before we hear his voice we hear his pipes, a simple little five-note phrase which, embracing the entire compass of the instrument, comes to play an important part in the drama later on:

When Papageno sings he gives us three verses of a little ditty in the vein of a naïve popular song to the tune we have just heard from the orchestra —"Der Vogelfänger bin ich ja" ("I am the bird-catcher . . ."). The simplicity of this little song is as astonishing as its melody, once heard, is unforgettable. And it is perhaps easy to understand that it is one of the principal obstacles in the way of the immediate enjoyment and appreciation of the opera by those hearing *The Magic Flute* for the first time. It is easy to understand, because there can surely be nothing more disconcerting than to have become educated in all the so-called "sophisticated" details of Mozart's other operas, especially the three Italian works, and then to be confronted, in what everybody keeps insisting is his supreme masterpiece, with a trivial jingle that might have been whistled on an 18th-century Viennese street corner (as though that hadn't already happened with "Non più andrai" from *Figaro*).

It is disconcerting, but it is only a matter of patience, perseverance and experience before the newcomer to *The Magic Flute* will forget about being insulted and realize that as with nearly everything Mozart ever did in opera—and certainly everything he ever did in *The Magic Flute*—the whole little episode is completely and unalterably in character. The words of the song by themselves do not matter; they are mere doggerel in which Papageno tells us that if he could catch girls as he catches birds in his net ("by the dozen") he would marry the one he liked best and cradle her in his arms as she slept. Words and music together, however, give us an immediate and comprehensive insight into the character of Papageno—a simple and charming child of nature, perky, quick-witted, good-humoured and immediately likeable.

Tamino emerges from his hiding place and in the long conversation with Papageno that follows each character gets to know something of each other—principally, that Tamino is a Prince and on learning that Papageno's mother had been in the service of the "Queen who flames like a star at night" gets very excited at the possibility that this might be the powerful Queen of the Night herself of whom his father had often told him. Why Tamino should be so curious about the Queen of the Night is not explained, but we learn that Papageno catches birds for the mysterious "star-flaming Queen" and her Three Ladies for which he is rewarded daily with an allowance of "wine, cake and sweet figs."

The dialogue also tells us, which the stage directions do not, that Papageno is dressed in a costume covered with feathers. It seems an odd omission this, in view of the care taken to inform us of Tamino's "splendid Japanese hunting costume", but anyhow it is essential in the dialogue in order to provide Papageno with the opportunity to be insulted by Tamino's suggestion that he is not a human being but a bird of some kind. So far from being a bird, Papageno declares, he has a giant's strength. This leads Tamino to credit Papageno with the destruction of the serpent. The sight of the serpent terrifies Papageno but after making sure that it is dead he pulls himself together and boasts that he strangled the monster with his bare hands, a declaration which earns him Tamino's gratitude and admiration. It also earns him the disapproval of the Three Ladies who enter and as a punishment for his lying boasts pay for his day's catch of birds with a bottle of water instead of wine, a stone instead of cake, and instead of sweet figs a padlock is fastened to his mouth and locked.

The Third Lady turns to Tamino and tells him that she and her colleagues killed the serpent and gives him a portrait sent by their mistress. "It is a portrait of her daughter," says the Third Lady, "and she says if you are not indifferent to her features then happiness, honour and fame await you. Auf Wiedersehen!" With that fair specimen of Schikaneder's dialogue the Three Ladies depart. Tamino, says the stage direction, "has been absorbed from the moment of receiving the picture; his love grows, although he has apparently been deaf to all that was being said."

Gazing at the picture in his hand Tamino sings his only aria of the opera—"Dies Bildnis ist bezaubernd schön" ("This portrait has a magic beauty . . ."):

That rapt opening phrase does not occur again in this aria, and so has a remarkable effect of expressing that unforgettable but unrepeatable moment of love at first sight.

The love song Tamino addresses to the unknown figure in the portrait is the first instance of that peculiar serenity which characterizes the music of *The Magic Flute*. It presents love not as a physical passion but as something eternal and of spiritual sublimity. I don't mean to make this lovely aria sound as forbidding and boring as those words suggest; it is just that as so much of *The Magic Flute* is unlike anything else Mozart ever wrote so the love music also belongs to a different, unfamiliar world. It must not be imagined, however, that the beauty of this aria of Tamino's is "cold" or in any way unemotional. It is just that it doesn't wear its heart on its sleeve, though there is a clear hint of the breathlessness and heartbeating syncopation of Belmonte's aria (see p. 29) when Tamino reflects what he would do if he found the original of the portrait; "I would—I would—"— but as he tells us that he would embrace her and she would be his for life the music subsides once again into the warm and stable mood of the first part of the aria, a warmth to which the tones of clarinets, bassoons and horns contribute, particularly in Tamino's final phrase and the two-bar coda which brings the scene to an end.

As Tamino turns to go he is waylaid by the Three Ladies who speak, not together as they did when menacing Papageno, but one after the other, in such a way that apart from Tamino's interjections, the dialogue is largely a series of sentences each begun by the First Lady, continued by the Second and completed with a full stop by the Third.

From this quaint form of divided labour Tamino learns that the Three Ladies have been talking about him to the Queen of the Night who (they say) on hearing of his fortitude and courage has decided that he is the one to rescue her daughter. The Queen, of course, heard all that Tamino sang as he gazed on the portrait. He is overwhelmed to hear that he has been chosen to rescue what, referring to the beautiful maiden whose picture he still holds in his hand, he calls a little prosaically "Das Original". Tamino is told that the name of *Das Original* is Pamina and that she has been abducted by a wicked magician who lives, the Three Ladies say, "very near to our hills in an agreeable and charming valley—his palace is splendid and heavily guarded."

As Tamino begs the Ladies to lead him to the agreeable and charming valley "a sudden violent and shattering chord with music is heard", a direction by Schikaneder which Mozart proceeds to ignore, regarding off-stage rolls of thunder and such other effects as the producer might consider necessary as quite sufficient to prepare the audience for the scenic transformation which takes place as the Three Ladies, speaking now in unison, announce the approach of their Queen.

The transformation of the scene does not rank as a Change of Scene, for on the verbal cue from the Three Ladies the librettist-producer put all his machinery into action to realize, in the space of a moment or two, the instruction that "the hills divide and the scene is transformed into a magnificent room. The Queen is seated on a throne, which is studded with transparent stars."

Without supplying the "violent and shattering chord with music" (whatever that puzzling pleonasm can mean) which Schikaneder hoped for, Mozart nevertheless provides a dramatic crescendo introduction to the appearance of the Queen of the Night on her throne. In a passage of vigorous accompanied recitative the Queen, in a compelling voice, bids Tamino not to be frightened; a young man such as he is what a mother's deeply wounded heart has greatest need of, and in Mozart's most melancholy key—G minor—she sings of the lot of an unhappy mother whose daughter has been stolen from her:

The Queen then re-creates for Tamino the scene of Pamina's abduction, recalling the girl's terror and struggles, the piteous voice crying for help. "She appealed in vain," sobs the Queen, "for my help was too weak."

It is a moving passage in which Mozart makes much of the elegiac quality of the oboe, the bassoon and the viola, and suggests something of Pamina's desperate struggles by an agitated little figure in the violins.

From recalling the sorrows of the past the Queen of the Night changes the subject to a constructive plan for the future in a determined Allegro Moderato. "You," she says to Tamino, "shall go and rescue her, you shall be my daughter's liberator."—

The Queen's resolute command to Tamino and her promise to reward his success with her daughter's hand are developed in an energetic and fiery episode of coloratura which has at its climax the passage:

The coloratura, which is never overdone for a moment in this aria, has a tremendous dramatic impact. It is not intended as a display of a singer's vocal prowess but of the Queen's character and as we have seen from *Die Entführung*, although to a much lesser degree in that opera, coloratura is often synonymous in Mozart's mind with resolution and anger. Both these qualities are expressed in the part of the Queen of the Night in *The Magic Flute* which at its original performance was sung by Mozart's sister-in-law, Josefa Hofer.

At the end of her aria the Queen of the Night leaves with her Three Ladies and the scene recovers its former appearance. Tamino is alone, and after a sentence or two of spoken reflection on the marvels he has just witnessed sets off to fulfil his destiny. His way is barred, however, by Papageno with his mouth still padlocked and appealing sadly for help in pathetic mumbling phrases as the music starts up again. Two bassoons give an added comic accent as they support in unison Papageno's

Tamino answers Papageno's pleading with regrets that he is powerless to help him, but the situation is resolved by the arrival of the Three Ladies who, on the instructions of the Queen of the Night, remove the padlock from Papageno's mouth. Papageno promises never to tell lies any more and the assembled company unites in a little quintet of moral reflection that if all liars were punished with padlocks there would be no hate, calumny or rancour, only universal love and brotherhood.

Like so much of the music to *The Magic Flute* these passages of the quintet are almost impossible to quote from, for they appear to consist of little but tonic-and-dominant between such arresting unison phrases, when hate, calumny and rancour are mentioned, as:

and the phrase for an unaccompanied oboe which follows it and relaxes the tension to lead to the lines about love and brotherhood:

These details apart, however, we are in the midst of a typical *Magic Flute*

sequence of inspired simplicity which has virtually no meaning on paper at all.

The First Lady now comes forward and presents Tamino with a flute, a magic flute which the Queen of the Night has sent him for his protection and which he has only to play on to ensure his safety in all circumstances. The score bears the instruction that the First Lady gives Tamino "a golden flute"; how this arose originally I do not know, for not only is it shown later in the opera not to have been gold, but the short ensemble which now follows for the five characters is a *sotto voce* dilation on the flute being worth "more than gold or crowns" because its power will enable mankind to enjoy happiness and contentment:

The Three Ladies appoint Papageno (much to his disgust) to accompany the Prince to the castle of Sarastro, the wicked sorcerer. Papageno's disgust springs, as he complains, from the Three Ladies themselves having told him that Sarastro is a tigerish monster who will have him plucked and roasted. He is no less disgruntled when the Ladies tell him that the Prince will look after him. "Damn the Prince!" growls Papageno under his breath, "I value my life."

The First Lady comes forward again with a gift from the Queen, this time for Papageno: a set of silver bells which, like the flute, have magic properties of protection when danger threatens.* There is a short passage of mutual wishes for "Auf Wiedersehen!" and the Three Ladies turn to go. Tamino calls them back, however, and they are asked—by Papageno, which is rather unexpected—the way to Sarastro's castle.

The orchestral colour changes as the Three Ladies turn to answer the question, accompanied by pizzicato strings, clarinets and bassoons, telling Tamino and Papageno that they will be accompanied by the Three Boys, the Three Genii, "young, beautiful, gracious and wise", who will lead them on their journey and whose advice and guidance alone they must follow.

The Ladies announce this to a phrase which has in it a quality we encounter on one or two occasions later in the opera. It is not a *leitmotiv*, or anything like it, but the phrase has a peculiar shape to it making it the *sort* of music which we eventually come to associate not only with the Three Boys but also with the mystic and supernatural element in the story. It is never repeated note-for-note, or even recognizably paraphrased; but in a remarkable way Mozart suggests that we are hearing the same theme each time.

The phrase which prompted these reflections occurs in the course of an

_____

* It seems most likely that the flute became "golden" to give a fairy-tale symmetry to the magic instruments. If Papageno, the commoner, had silver bells, then the royal Tamino's flute had to be golden. Whoever it was first added this little conceit, however, can never have listened very carefully to what Pamina was singing about in a rather important scene in Act II.

eight-bar passage sung by the Three Ladies and shortly afterwards
repeated by Tamino and Papageno:

At the end of their echo of the passage, however, Tamino and Papageno
change the words and bid the Three Ladies farewell and "Auf Wiedersehen"—a thoughtful and courteous gesture which the The Ladies
reciprocate and Mozart deals with in an enchanting dying-away coda.

Scene 2: A gorgeous Egyptian room.

"Two slaves carry beautiful cushions as well as a gorgeous Turkish
table; they spread out carpets." (Schikaneder seemed particularly fond of
the adjective "prächtig"; it occurs both in the stage directions and in the
description of this scene, which is why the word "gorgeous" is used again
so soon.)

The two slaves are joined by a third who is delighted at the possibility
that Monostatos, the Moor whom Sarastro employs to guard Pamina,
may be hanged or impaled in the morning. Pamina has escaped, he
explains; she outwitted Monostatos by loudly calling Sarastro's name
when the Moor (according to habit, we are led to believe) attacked her.
Pamina's assailant was rooted to the spot with terror as she screamed,
whereon she got into a boat and rowed herself across the canal (or
channel? Schikaneder uses the multivocal *Kanal* which can also mean
pipe, drain or sewer) to take refuge in the little spinney of palm trees.

For all their natural curiosity and delight in scandal, however, the
three slaves make a hurried exit when they hear Monostatos calling from
the wings, an exit accompanied by some righteously indignant comments
when they realize that the Moor has recaptured his prisoner. Monostatos,
we gather, is not popular.

This introductory and not entirely dispensable explanatory dialogue
now at an end, Monostatos enters to music with slaves dragging Pamina
after him. He sneers at his captive and tells her that she is as good as dead
(on whose authority he pronounces death-sentences we are not told).
Pamina, whom we now meet for the first time, behaves exactly as we would
expect her to behave—with dignity and a touching regard for what her
death would mean, not to herself, but to her mother. Though the general
mood of the music to all this is one of an agitated Allegro Molto during
which slaves put Pamina in chains, and Monostatos continues his threats
to a captive with a clearly indomitable spirit, Mozart nevertheless manages to introduce a tiny detail of characterization during a sequence of
what might otherwise easily be dismissed as little more than a melo-
dramatic *agitato*.

The detail is superficially so trivial that one hesitates to draw attention
to it lest one be accused of attaching significance to something never

intended to have any. Whether he expected us to notice or not, however, Mozart makes a point of punctuating Monostatos' vehemence with a violin figure which occurs only at these moments:

Monostatos is a distant relation of Osmin in *Die Entführung*—a very black sheep of the same family, in fact. But whereas Osmin's ferocity is lovable as well as comic in its blustering ineffectualness and his bark on the whole is far worse (as well as going much deeper) than his bite, there is an evil quality about Monostatos which is entirely lacking in Osmin. Monostatos, we are left in no doubt at all, represents the Powers of Darkness in the worst sense; he is an unpleasant little man. There is, however, something faintly grotesque and sub-humanly ridiculous about his fussy, atavistic viciousness and it is this characteristic which Mozart frequently underlines in the music associated with Monostatos throughout the opera.

The slaves place Pamina in chains and she falls back unconscious on a couch. Monostatos dismisses the slaves and is left alone with her, his intentions clearly being of the worst and only slightly less than necrophilous.

At this point Papageno appears at the window, not at all sure where he is, but seeing people inside the room he climbs through to the accompaniment of a very Papagenic little tune on the flute:

Papageno gets no further than repeating these four bars—the first phrase of what promised to be a gay little song addressed to the apparently sleeping figure of the beautiful, whiter-than-chalk maiden—when he and Monostatos catch sight of each other. Each is terrified by the appearance of the other, and they run away in different directions asking for mercy of the figure they are sure is the devil himself and shouting "Hoo!"

Pamina comes out of her faint and is joined in a moment by Papageno who tells her in a long stretch of dialogue of all that happened in the previous scene. He persuades her to come away with him and find Tamino; Pamina agrees but hesitates for a moment fearing a trick, but she is reassured by the portrait which Tamino has given Papageno as a means of identifying her. They leave together, though not before they have sung a duet together on the subject of Love which Papageno has raised in the course of bewailing his bachelorhood and despairing of ever finding a Papagena to fill his ample heart with love.

It is a simple duet for we are concerned with two simple people— Papageno the child of nature, and Pamina as yet little more than a child;

it is she, however, who takes the lead in this little scene and using her womanly instinct to console Papageno that "Men who feel love do not lack good hearts"—

The tune undergoes a little decoration in the course of its two strophes but for the most part it has that indefinable simplicity and directness which is the essence of *The Magic Flute*. Even the unexpectedly florid coda in which Pamina might be apeing Fiordiligi (see Ex 43 on p. 169) never loses its naïve quality for all its sudden ranging across nearly two octaves with a jump of a thirteenth thrown in:

Their duet at an end Pamina and Papageno set off in search of Tamino.

Scene 3: A grove. At the back of the stage there is a beautiful temple which bears the words "Temple of Wisdom". This temple is connected by columns with two other temples. The one on the right is inscribed "Temple of Reason"; that on the left "Temple of Nature".

The Three Boys enter, each carrying a silver branch of palm in his hand, and leading in Tamino. We are at the beginning of the Finale (there is no more spoken dialogue in this act) and hear for the first time that *sound* which we come to discover as something peculiar to *The Magic Flute*. It has no precedent in Mozart's works and no posterity, for it remained something which could not be transplanted to any other surroundings or used in any other context. There was only ever one *Magic Flute*. It is not just a matter of the instrumentation, the tune, the harmony, the rhythm, nor even of what we must recognize as the sudden emergence of an entirely new musical style.

It is at this point in the opera, I believe, that we first encounter what can only be called the Mystery of *The Magic Flute*, some of the component parts of which are those elements of instrumentation and so on I have already referred to, together with the unanalysable, indescribable factor which was Mozart's genius.

I have suggested already that *The Magic Flute* is an opera to be listened to and enjoyed only in a state of complete physical and mental relaxation —principally, I am sure, because that is the prevailing mood of the music itself. When the curtain rises (or the lights come up) on this last scene of the first act we enter a world far removed even from the eventful fairy-tale activity of what has gone before. We have our first sensation of having one foot in the half-open door of eternity. And it is a feeling which strikes us long before the Three Boys sing a note. It begins with a single bar of quite astonishingly unexpected orchestral colour created by two bassoons, three trombones, violoncellos, *muted* trumpets, and drums to be played *coperti*—i.e. covered or muffled.

In the space of that one introductory bar Mozart prepares us for the serenity (it is a word one has to keep using with *The Magic Flute*) of the violins in the kind of tune hinted at by the Three Ladies when they first mentioned the Three Boys to Tamino:

This is the tune repeated by the Three Boys as they address Tamino and "brief" him, as it were, in how he must behave on the journey and trials that lie before him. The startling orchestration of the first few bars is not repeated note-for-note, but Mozart punctuates the recitation of the conditional virtues—perseverance, patience and silence—with impressively arresting unison strokes from his trombones and woodwind.

The parts of the Three Boys are unfortunately rarely sung these days by anybody but rather strapping and not necessarily young ladies. Though London County Council regulations proscribe the appearance of small boys on the stage of Covent Garden after tea, or whatever ridiculous time of day it is that the official mentality considers children should be a-bed (the young Mozart who gave concerts when he lived in Ebury Street would certainly have been deemed in need of proper care and attention), there is still no reason why the Three Boys should not be sung by three real boys everywhere else. It is no good producers and operatic managements pleading precedents. The "Three Boys" is not a courtesy title, nor are they *travesti* roles. They are to be taken literally, for Mozart not only conceived these parts in terms of the clear, ethereal tone-colour of boys' voices, but at the original performance of *The Magic Flute* at the Theater auf der Wieden the parts of two of the Boys were taken by Master Tuscher and another lad with the wonderfully Austrian name of Handlgruber, while the third was given—perhaps for nepotistic reasons, perhaps *faute de mieux*—to Mlle Nanette Schikaneder, the eleven-year-old daughter of Schikaneder's elder brother Urban, who took the part of the First Priest.

Tamino asks the Three Boys whether he will be able to rescue Pamina. They reply with almost parliamentary formality that they are unable to give information on that point; then, exhorting him once more to be steadfast, perseverant and silent, they leave.

There now follows what, from the musical point of view, is perhaps the most astonishing scene in the whole opera, for it shows Mozart anticipating what became the aim of composers throughout the 19th century from

Wagner and Verdi to Puccini: to make opera a continuous, uninterrupted piece of music in which plot and conversation are carried on without damaging the continuity of the musical conception or the dramatic structure of the whole.

Though Mozart indicates the scene which now takes place as "recitative" the term cannot be regarded as more than a title of convenience. The scene is certainly superficially based on the traditional elements of orchestrally-accompanied recitative, but it is more than a mere progression from one key to another by means of chords played on and off the beat while the singer declaims in a serious operatic manner. It is a scene which presents drama and action, swift changes of emotion, soliloquy and duologue, reflection and discussion, sometimes by the conventional methods of recitative but more often to the accompaniment and development of little themes and short, expressive musical phrases.

Tamino soliloquizes on the general situation and his plans, warns the wicked sorcerer of his determination to free Pamina and strides to the door of the temple on the right—an action which is accompanied by the unison phrase:

Tamino opens the door and is about to enter when the voice of a priest is heard from inside the temple warning, on the last two notes of the phrase, "Stand back!" It is a dramatic moment as the priest sings in unison with the arresting *forte* of strings and woodwind.

Tamino turns away and goes to the door of the temple on the left. The same phrase accompanies him as before but this time in a different key, and on the last two notes a priest's voice is heard once more warning "Stand back!"

Again Tamino turns away; he goes up to the door of the centre temple and this time he knocks and—as though to suggest that it is better manners to knock before entering than opening temple doors as though they belonged to you—there is no violent cry of "Stand back!" Instead the little door-routine theme subsides quietly into a gentle chord of A flat as an aged priest appears and asks Tamino what he wants.

It has become the habit in recent years not only to refer to the part of this Old Priest in the programme as "the Speaker", or "Orator", but to have the two parts performed by the same actor-singer. I do not know what the precedent for this may be; I suspect its origin to be economic; but there is no suggestion in the score that the Old Priest who sings is the same person as the character so carefully described in the original billing and usual *dramatis personæ* as "Der Sprecher".

The very fact that the Speaker does only speak makes him an impressive and aloof figure as we shall see when we come to the next act. The practice of having the part "doubled" with that of the Priest is not only, as I believe, contrary to the original conception of the opera (the stage direction specifically states, as Tamino stands at the third door: "He knocks, an old priest appears") but if it became universal could deprive us of such a memorable experience as that of seeing an actor with the voice and presence of Carl Ebert, for instance, play the part.

When Tamino learns from the Priest (as I shall continue to call him) that the wicked sorcerer, Sarastro, is to be found in this Temple of Wisdom he turns to leave, crying "Then it is all hypocrisy!" The Priest holds Tamino back and by patient questioning discovers that Tamino's only proof of Sarastro's evil character is what he has been told by a woman.

"Oh, so you were fooled by a woman," remarks the Priest. "A woman does little and talks a lot. You were taken in by the magic of her tongue, were you?"

Tamino does not let this affect his argument that there is no denying Sarastro stole Pamina away from her mother. Calmly and without comment the Priest replies that what Tamino says is true.

"Where is she?" cries Tamino. "Perhaps she has been offered up as a sacrifice."

The Priest replies that he is not yet permitted to tell him. Tamino presses him further but the Priest refuses to say more than that his tongue is tied by oath and duty. "When will you break the silence?" asks Tamino. And the Priest answers: "When the hand of friendship leads you to the temple to join the eternal brotherhood."

The Priest's answer is sung to a superbly impressive phrase in which the vocal line is doubled by the violoncellos:

The effect of this simple couple of bars is tremendous and, I still find, as unexpected to hear suddenly as the passage which it so oddly fore-shadows—the violoncello and double bass accompaniment to the first meeting between Rigoletto and Sparafucile in the second act of Verdi's opera.

The Priest goes back inside the temple and Tamino, left alone, has one of the most expressive phrases in the whole opera to sing, a phrase of intense poignancy and despair as he asks the question: "O eternal night! When will you vanish? When will the Light reach my eyes?"

The answer comes from tenor and bass voices inside the Temple, in short, abrupt words which are accompanied by the violoncellos playing the theme of Ex 28 once more, but this time with trombones giving an added solemnity to an already solemn and eerie sound. "Soon," the answer is intoned, "soon—or never."

"Tell me," Tamino asks the invisible chorus, "does Pamina still live?" The answer comes back to the same solemn orchestral accompaniment, the violoncellos repeating their phrase once more, the trombones adding their sombre accents: "Pamina still lives."

Tamino is overjoyed and the long fantastically varied, moving and dramatic sequence of recitative comes to an end. Tamino takes his flute and begins to play it, in a quaintly touching, rather hesitant way (like the on-stage instruments in *Don Giovanni*, it has no dynamic markings), as a token of thanks to the Almighty:

In the original production of *The Magic Flute* at the Theater auf der Wieden the singer who created the part of Tamino was a certain Benedict Schack, an unusual figure, born in Bohemia, who became an intimate friend of Mozart's and was present, it is said, at the composer's bedside the night before he died. Schack not only sang, however; he was also a composer and had, indeed, written the music for an opera by Schikaneder in 1790, the subtitle of which was "The Magic Island" and in which much was made of a magician who had been initiated into the mysteries of Ancient Egypt.*

For the purpose of *The Magic Flute*, however, after his good tenor voice and general musicianship Benedict Schack's most important asset was the fact that he was an expert flute player—an unusual accomplishment to find on the opera stage, for the most one can usually hope for is a singer who can strum his way through the guitar part of Almaviva's serenade in *The Barber of Seville*. The singing flautist, on the other hand, is so rare that one is tempted to believe that it was only in the original production that one of the magical effects of Mozart's opera was paradoxically rendered doubly magical by the introduction of an unexpected realism.

As Tamino plays we have the characteristic and evocative Schikaneder stage direction: "He plays; at once animals of all kinds come to hear him. He stops and they run away. The birds sing." How much attention was paid by the first *Magic Flute* audiences to Herr Schack's flute playing in

* Schikaneder's original *Magic Flute* company seems to have been unusually talented, for in addition to Schack the original Sarastro, Franz Xaver Gerl (his wife sang the part of the Old Woman), is reported to have collaborated with Schack in the composition of his operas as well as writing one of his own, a comic opera called *Die Maskerade*, produced at the Theater auf der Wieden in 1797 as being "by a former member of this theatre." Why poor Gerl should not have been granted a full credit I do not know.

face of all this opposition from livestock is not reported; nor whether, since Tamino continues to play his flute off and on in the intervals of singing, the animals reappeared at each instrumental reprise and left again immediately Schack the tenor superseded Schack the flautist which, in practice, was fairly often and would have kept stage-management and trainers quite busy.

To very much the same tune as the flute plays in Ex 30, though with obviously necessary simplifications, Tamino sings about the magic tones of his flute and how even the wild beasts of the forest derive pleasure from it—only Pamina, it seems of all living creatures remaining unaffected; and the music switches to a sad C minor for the space of a few bars. Tamino takes up his flute again and plays, hoping that Pamina will hear. There is no reply. Finally Tamino tries a scale of G major over an octave and a half:

The last five notes are the same notes as Papageno's pan-pipes and bring an immediate echo from the distance. Tamino plays the phrase twice more and each time Papageno's pipes answer it. Highly delighted, Tamino rushes off in one direction as Pamina (now rid of her chains) and Papageno enter from the opposite side of the stage looking for Tamino.

The tempo changes with the entrance of Pamina and Papageno to a breathless, anxious little sequence (with effective scoring for divided violas) in which a considerable part is played by a recurrent cadence that first occurs to the words "if we do not find Tamino, they will catch us"—

Papageno takes his pan-pipes and plays; Tamino's flute answers off-stage. Together Pamina and Papageno, delighted to discover Tamino is so near, set off to find him repeating several times, to the tune of the last bar of their rapid little cadence, the words "nur geschwinde" ("we must hurry"). But their way is barred by Monostatos, who with a characteristic sneer mimics their "nur geschwinde". The blackamoor, in typically angular and tuneless phrases, gloats over his captives and calls for slaves to put them in irons. When the slaves appear with chains an idea begins to dawn in Papageno's mind to the accompaniment of pizzicato strings. He takes out his silver bells and plays on them:

This rather polka-like tune, with its simple "chuck-chuck" pizzicato accompaniment has an immediate and magical effect on Monostatos and his slaves. They find the tune entrancing, its rhythm irresistible and in a moment, against their will, they are singing and dancing their way delightedly off the scene. The sheer unexpectedness of the sound of this whole episode is as magical as one could wish.

Pamina and Papageno reflect how wonderful it would be if everybody had magic bells, then enemies would disappear and everything on earth would be happiness and harmony.

The doggerel of Schikaneder's verses at this point is pretty dismal but it cannot destroy the quite extraordinary character of Mozart's music which somehow combines a feeling of immense relief at the passing of a danger (that, at least, is the effect it always has on me) with the expression of the wonderfully simple faith of Pamina and Papageno in the inevitable destruction of evil as they sing together of earthly harmony and the rest:

There is a sudden fanfare of trumpets and drums and a chorus of mixed voices back stage is heard proclaiming "Long live Sarastro!" Papageno trembles with fright at once; Pamina takes things more calmly though nonetheless aware of what may lie ahead. Papageno, panicking and wishing he were a mouse, asks what they should say to Sarastro. In a noble cadence in C major (the only possible key, of course) Pamina replies simply: "The truth, even though it were a crime. . . ."—

The march now gets going, a typical Mozart trumpets-and-drums affair in C major, to bring on to the scene "a procession of people; finally, Sarastro drives on in a triumphal carriage drawn by six lions"— as unconventional and spectacular an entrance as any to be found even in opera.

The march comes to an end (Schikaneder's directions are that the "chorus is sung until Sarastro is out of his carriage") and Pamina kneels before Sarastro and confesses: "Master, I have done wrong; I tried to escape from your power." She sings the words to one of those phrases which become increasingly more frequent in this opera of Mozart's, phrases which are not "tunes" in the sense that phrases in his arias are "tunes", but which are memorable in their own right, as it were, because they have dramatic as well as purely musical significance. It is in just such a phrase that Pamina confesses to Sarastro:

On paper those bars have little distinction; they might be no more than a phrase from a recitative of an *opera seria*. But this little scene is not in recitative, not even in that extraordinarily expressive form of recitative in which the discussion between Tamino and the Priest took place. As Pamina explains how and why she came to escape we encounter that wonderful sense of musical continuity which Mozart develops to its highest pitch in *The Magic Flute*. It is something which cannot be analysed or described; there is nothing formal about it, but every note that is sung or played is in some phenomenal way always "in character". One can only draw attention to the fascinating details which go to make up the whole, to such unexpected "modern" touches, for instance, as the use of violins playing the tune one and two octaves above Sarastro in such phrases as:

The dignity and gentleness of Sarastro is one of Mozart's most inspired conceptions, and we are aware of being in the presence of a figure of divine wisdom and benevolence from the first moment the High Priest sings, bidding Pamina rise to her feet and comforts her with the assurance that her problem is understood. Nevertheless, continues Sarastro, for her own good he is not going to restore Pamina to her mother. The mention of her mother draws from Pamina a phrase which is especially characteristic of this opera and especially, I think, of the music associated with the gentle and sentimental sides of both Pamina and Tamino. We encountered the expressive rising interval of a major sixth in the opening of Tamino's "Dies Bildnis ist bezaubernd schön" (Ex 13); we hear it again when, contrasting with Sarastro's G minor the music proclaims a confident B flat with Pamina's haunting phrase accompanied by flutes, bassoons and tenor clarinets or basset-horns (which we have not heard since *Die Entführung* and now make the first of several appearances in the *Magic Flute* orchestra)—"My mother's name sounds sweet":

Sarastro dismisses the subject of the Queen of the Night and tells Pamina in a characteristically anti-feminist way (a recognizable Masonic aspect of the opera, I am told): "You shall have a man to lead you, for without a man woman is inclined to stray from her natural province." The impressive and gentle tempo of the music changes to Allegro and introduces a busy little figure in the violins:

This intriguing idea is developed and bandied about between one key and the next in the peculiar way Mozart had in his finales. In one form or another it provides the background for a variety of emotions and actions. Its first purpose is to introduce Monostatos who brings in Tamino and places him, as it were, at Sarastro's feet. This action provides Tamino and Pamina with their first sight of each other; it is a rapturous meeting and as they embrace even the chorus, who have been singularly unmoved by events so far, can scarce forbear to ask "What does this mean?" Monostatos takes it on himself to answer by saying that things have gone far enough, and separating the lovers.

The busy little figure of Ex 39 continues on its restless course as Monostatos kneels before Sarastro and in a typically obsequious way suggests how clever he has been to catch such a slippery customer—"You know me," he says, "—my vigilance——"

"We should strew laurels," says Sarastro, and turning to his followers adds, "give the good fellow——"

"Your grace is reward enough," says Monostatos, modestly.

"—give the good fellow," Sarastro continues, "only seventy-seven strokes on the soles of his feet."

"But Master," cries Monostatos, "I didn't expect to be rewarded like that!"

"Don't thank me," says Sarastro with grim humour, "it is only my duty."

The wretched Monostatos is led away, his ears ringing to the sound of the chorus's almost epigrammatic praise of Sarastro, the divinely wise, who rewards and punishes impartially.

Solemnly Sarastro orders the two strangers, Tamino and Papageno, to be led to the temple for their initiation. Two Priests come forward and (according to the stage directions) "bring a kind of sack to cover the heads of the two strangers."

As Tamino and Papageno are led towards the temple the chorus sings what can best be described as a hymn on the theme of Virtue and Justice, which in a loud and festive C major with prominent passages for the trombones, brings down the curtain on the first act.

ACT II

Scene 1 : A palm grove; all the trees are of silver with leaves of gold. There are eighteen thrones of leaves; on each throne is a pyramid and a large black horn bound with gold. In the centre , the largest pyramid and the largest trees.

Schikaneder's first stage direction reads: "Sarastro enters with the other priests in a solemn procession, each carrying a branch of a palm tree. A march with wind-instruments accompanies the procession."

Mozart in fact took the liberty of adding strings to the "march with wind-instruments" but this did not detract for a moment from the almost supernatural solemnity of this March of the Priests. (Dr Alfred Einstein, in a particularly happy phrase, describes this element in the music of *The Magic Flute* as "a kind of secular awe" which is "far removed from churchliness.")

The March, which is in two sections, both of which are repeated, is almost devoid of any expression marks. It is indicated to be played simply "sotto voce" throughout except for three instances of *sfp* mutually affecting the flute, first basset-horn and first violins.

The opening phrase shows in its last two bars that characteristic rhythm which we first heard associated with the Three Boys (Ex 21):

On reflection perhaps those two final bars may be found to be typical of Mozart marches in general, for almost the same cadence occurs in the march in the third act of *Figaro*, for instance. On the other hand, the sheer physical sound of this March of the Priests could not be further removed from the whole tonal world of *Figaro* or, so far as I know, of anything else in all Mozart's music for the theatre. Here indeed is the orchestral colour of "secular awe" created by a single flute, which shines out like a star in its octave above the strings, two basset-horns, two bassoons, two horns and the three trombones.

When the priests have assembled the march ends and there follows a scene of spoken dialogue in which Sarastro, the Speaker and priests discuss the admission of Tamino as a candidate for initiation. Sarastro, in answer to questions by the priests, assures the gathering that Tamino is Virtuous, Silent and Charitable. The priests show acceptance of Sarastro's words by blowing on the black horns the "Threefold Chord"—the "Dreimalige Akkord"—heard in the Overture (Ex. 5), but scored slightly differently this time with basset-horns in place of clarinets, different notes for 2nd trumpet and 2nd trombone, and a complete absence of kettle-drums. The omission of the drums, I imagine, is intended to preserve the illusion that the three chords are played by the priests who have not been issued with drums.

Sarastro continues his case in support of Tamino, explaining that it was because Pamina had been chosen by the gods for Tamino that she had been taken from her proud mother—"that woman who hopes to deceive mankind by trickery and superstition and to destroy our firm and solid temple. That," Sarastro emphasizes, referring to the threat to the temple, "is the one thing she shall not do." Tamino, as an initiate, shall help them defend the temple and punish wickedness. Once more the priests sound the three chords.

The Speaker now rises and questions Sarastro, asking forgiveness that he should have any doubts, but is Sarastro sure that Tamino will have strength to come through the ordeals he will have to face? "He is a Prince, remember," adds the Speaker.

"He is more than that," replies Sarastro. "He is a man."

"And if he should die young in his attempts?"

"Then he is given up to Osiris and Isis and will enjoy the favour of the gods before we shall." And the threefold chord is blown for a third time. The Speaker and a priest leave the scene to instruct Tamino and his companion, Papageno, in the duty of mankind and the power of the gods.

There now follows what the score calls a little prosaically "Aria with Chorus", but which is in practice Sarastro's superb invocation to Isis and Osiris, his prayer that they should grant wisdom and patience and give guidance to the new pair about to undergo the tests of initiation:

41. Adagio

No 10

O I - sis und O - si - ris schenket der Weisheit Geist dem neu-en Paar

If ever Mozart brought a new sound to music it was in the accompaniment to this magnificent bass aria. The whole colour—instrumental and vocal—is deliberately "dark"; the voice spends most of its time in the lower part of its register—as a matter of simple statistics half the notes of the melody lie in the range

42.

—while the orchestral accompaniment is allocated to the most sombre-toned instruments at Mozart's disposal. The orchestra is made up of the two basset-horns, two bassoons, three trombones, violas in two parts and violoncellos unsupported by double basses. This accompaniment is without doubt one of the most astonishing musical sounds ever created by man, unequalled in its warmth and sense of infinite expanse and depth. And yet, paradoxically, for all that it ought to sound "dark" and in consequence gloomy, the effect is anything but dark in that sense; it has a peculiar radiance which, according to the way it looks on paper, by rights ought not to be there at all. It is a scene which can be one of the unforgettable experiences of all music, for every epithet that has ever been inspired by *The Magic Flute* applies to it.

The two verses of Sarastro's "O Isis und Osiris" are punctuated and finally rounded off by the chorus of priests—two tenor, two bass parts, which add yet another tone-colour to the rich ensemble.

Slowly, when the aria is finished, Sarastro leaves the stage followed by the others.

Scene 2 : A small forecourt in the Temple where the ruins of fallen columns and pyramids may be seen among some thorny bushes. On either side of the stage there are high practicable Egyptian gates, through which adjoining buildings are visible.

Schikaneder's stage directions are for some reason a little out of sequence at the beginning of this scene, for it is only after he has described the entrance of the characters that he remembers to mention that it is "Night; thunder in the distance."

Into this dark and menacing scene Tamino and Papageno are led, their heads still enveloped in sacks, by the Speaker and another Priest. The two candidates have the sacks removed from their heads, but the gesture is a somewhat empty one, for the Speaker and the Priest depart leaving Tamino and Papageno in pitch darkness. The dialogue which follows was for the most part clearly intended as a vehicle for the comedy and antics of Emanuel Schikaneder, and even when the Speaker and the Priest return carrying torches and instruct the candidates in the nature of their final tests, a good deal of the time is taken up by funny lines for Papageno. (I have a suspicion that these "delaying tactics" were deliberately introduced to obscure, or at least postpone the impact of the Masonic allegory and the undercurrent of political satire.)

The Speaker concentrates on Tamino while the other Priest, described in the libretto as "Second Priest", acts largely as Papageno's "feed" as he instructs him in the trials he will have to face.

The first test is to be that of Silence. Tamino must not speak a word to Pamina when he sees her, and Papageno must keep absolutely silent when he eventually meets his Papagena for the first time. The candidates and their mentors shake hands.

A duet now follows sung by two priests (tenor and bass), a simple unpolyphonic sequence in which Tamino and Papageno are warned against the wiles of women. This, it is explained, is the first rule of their fraternity and the priests repeat a short cautionary tale to an oddly cheerful tune:

43. Andante

No 11

Bewahret euch vor Weiber- tücken: dies ist des Bun-des er-ste Pflicht!

The unfortunate subject of this story, who so far forgot himself as to fall into a woman's power, wrung his hands in vain. The moral pay-off comes in a four-bar cadence which has always delighted me inordinately by its entrancing incongruity—"Death and despair were his fate," the Priests sing, accompanied by the sombre tones of two bassoons, three trombones, basses and divided violas. And the words are sung *sotto voce* to the almost flippant strains of

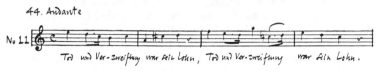

The two singers take their leave of us with a reprise of the phrase played by the full orchestra—trumpets, drums and all in a deliciously effective point-making *piano*.

I have never been able to sort out these final enchanting bars. I can only suppose that the Priests are deliberately "throwing away" the topic of death and destruction to impress Tamino and Papageno with the idea that this sort of thing happens every day in those parts.

The Priests not only go out to that remarkable coda, but they take their torches with them and Tamino and Papageno are left in darkness again.

They do not have to wait long for temptation to come their way and their trial to begin, for barely a moment elapses before the Three Ladies rise up through the trap-door and immediately start singing with comic indignation—"What's all this? You in this terrible place? You'll never get out of here alive!"—

The Three Ladies do their best to make the men talk and undermine their morale by baiting them with alarming predictions. Papageno shows unmistakable signs of weakening, but Tamino controls him and the quintet proceeds as a test of endurance for all concerned. The Three Ladies warn the men against believing the Priests, quoting the Queen of the Night as authority that "he who joins their band will go straight to hell." The women's voices chatter and cajole and they very nearly succeed in breaking down Papageno's resistance, for they know—as he himself admits—that he is a natural chatter-box and it can only be a matter of time before he capitulates. Papageno, who is admirably characterized in this movement, is particularly perturbed by all the business of being sent to hell, especially as the Queen of the Night said it.

"She is a woman," Tamino tells him, "and she has a woman's mentality,"—a judgment which Tamino delivers contemptuously to show that he is learning the brotherhood's attitude to women rapidly and with aptitude. At length, rather hurt at their treatment, the Three Ladies reluctantly and ashamedly agree to leave the two men; two such strong minded personalities will clearly never talk. These sentiments are also expressed by Tamino and Papageno who are thus provided with words for their musical share of the closing stages of the quintet.

As the Three Ladies turn to go, the voices of the Priests are heard coming from inside the Temple; a menacing unison phrase for male voices and orchestra warns the Ladies that the threshold of the Temple is sacred: "The women must go down to hell!"

Schikaneder pulls out a couple of extra special effects for this: "A terrifying chord with all instruments; thunder, lightning and thunderclaps together with two loud rumbles of thunder". Mozart obliges with the "terrifying chord" played "with all instruments", reinforcing the two diminished sevenths with trumpets, trombones and drums, to send the Three Ladies plunging through the trap-door. The music envelops and follows them in a descending diminuendo arpeggio while Papageno is so overcome by the experience that he cries "Woe!" three times and falls senseless to the ground as the music ends, a little surprisingly, on the chord of G minor.

According to the libretto the "Dreimalige Akkord" is now heard again to herald the return to the scene of the Speaker and the Second Priest.

The Speaker congratulates Tamino on having successfully passed his first test, the trial of Steadfastness, and placing the sack over the Prince's head once more leads him away for further examination.

The Second Priest, having revived Papageno, pays his charge no compliments, but after a comic line or two from the bird-catcher, puts the sack over his head and leads him off.

Scene 3: A pleasant garden with trees planted in the form of a horseshoe; in the centre there is a bower of flowers and roses in which Pamina is sleeping. The moon shines on her face. In the foreground is a grassy bank.

Monostatos enters and after a short pause sits down to nurse his sore feet, and in a spoken soliloquy, to reflect on the harsh treatment he has received and to gaze on the sleeping form of Pamina. He wonders whether he dare steal a kiss—"a little kiss might be forgiven, surely" and he creeps grotesquely backwards and forwards as he sings "Alles fühlt der Liebe Freuden"—a number which (already marked *sempre pianissimo*) either Mozart or Schikaneder has prefaced in the score with the instruction that it "must all be sung and played as quietly as though the music were in the far distance":

46. Allegro

No 13

sempre pianissimo

The words of this little strophic song are surprisingly bitter, for Mono-statos bewails in them his "hated black skin" and the black man's lot that denies him the pleasures of love enjoyed by the rest of mankind—"Am I not flesh and blood?" he cries.

We are prevented from feeling too much sympathy for the Moor and the chip he has on his shoulder, or considering at all seriously the colour problem which the scene raises, by the emphasis Mozart lays on the grotesqueness of the character. We have no time to take in all the implications of what Monostatos tells us from the depths of his black heart, for we are too busy laughing—and not kindly either—at his presumption and the ridiculous figure he cuts when he begs the moon to hide its face so that it will be dark when he kisses the white figure of Pamina.

The relationship between Monostatos and Osmin is particularly apparent in this number; not only does Mozart give us one of his typical "wrong-footed" tunes which added "Turkish" colour to the music of *Die Entführung* (Monostatos' first phrase consists of five bars, his second of seven), but he also gives a prominent, and indeed almost incessant, part in the orchestra to the piccolo—a first and last appearance of the instrument in this opera which at once adds a piquant and exotic touch to the quick-silver brilliance of the aria.

When he has finished his song Monostatos approaches Pamina. There is a roll of thunder and the Queen of the Night "appears through the centre trap-door in such a way that she stands in front of Pamina".

"Back!" cries the Queen. Pamina awakes and Monostatos scuttles off as fast as he can to watch events from a hiding place at a safer distance.

In a short scene of dialogue between mother and daughter we learn a little more of the background of the story. Pamina tells her mother that Tamino has "withdrawn from the world and from mankind" and is dedicated to the Initiated.

"Then I have lost you for ever," says the Queen; and she explains that with the death of Pamina's father her own power has gone. He voluntarily gave into Sarastro's keeping (for he, too, had been one of the Initiated) the all-powerful "sevenfold shield of the sun", which the High Priest carries on his breast. The Queen had pleaded with her husband before his death not to give the shield away, only to be rebuked in an uncom-promisingly anti-feminist way and told not to concern herself with men's affairs.

"Then I have lost my lover for ever?" asks Pamina.

"He is lost," replies the Queen, "if you cannot persuade him to escape with you through the underground chambers of the temple before the first rays of the sun light up the earth."

"But mother," continues Pamina, "why shouldn't I still love the youth, even when he is initiated? After all, my father was a member of the brotherhood and he spoke highly of their goodness and reason and virtue. Sarastro is no less virtuous."

At this the Queen of the Night exclaims violently: "What do I hear? You, my own daughter, could defend this monster, and love a man who is in league with my mortal enemy?" The Queen gives Pamina a dagger;

she tells her to kill Sarastro with it and bring back the "sevenfold shield of the sun".

Pamina begins to protest but is overruled by her mother who breaks into a fine and furious aria of vengeance in Mozart's "demonic" key of D minor—the vengeance of hell that boils in her heart: "Der Hölle Rache kocht in meinem Herzen":

In this aria there is none of the wheedling and melancholy of the Queen's first number in Act I. This is a scene of fire, fury, and an obsessed hatred. The coloratura begins comparatively early on in the aria this time and the music develops like a tremendous *concertante* movement in which the drama is emphasized by the fierce hammer strokes of trumpets and drums which send the high notes, the C's and D's and F's *in alt*, streaking across the scene like sparks struck from a white-hot iron.

In a forceful second section the coloratura itself is more restrained; but there is still vigour in the singer's determined, defiantly proclaimed octaves in such phrases as

At the bar before the coda of this aria, a pause is indicated which may just possibly have been the cue for a cadenza in the original production. If this ever was so it is a convention which has fortunately become obsolete, for the climax of the aria depends above all things on the relentless drive towards the great coda, the terrific invocation by the Queen of the Night before she sinks through the trap-door: "Hear me, ye gods of vengeance—hear a mother's oath!"

In the silence which follows the Queen's descent Pamina is left alone, gazing in a stunned manner at the dagger in her hand. Monostatos comes out of his hiding place and reveals yet another charming facet of his character: he proceeds to blackmail Pamina, and grabbing the dagger threatens that unless she surrenders to his advances he will tell Sarastro of the plot to kill him. Pamina is terrified, but resolutely refuses to yield; which, of course, immediately brings up the chip on Monostatos' shoulder. Why won't she love him? Because he is black, he supposes. The blackamoor is beginning to turn really nasty and threatening to kill Pamina when Sarastro appears. Monostatos protests that he has saved his Master's life; he has exposed the plot to kill him.

Sarastro replies that he knows all about that and sends the Moor away, unpunished, the victim of an evil woman's plans. Monostatos leaves, telling us in an aside that he is going to enlist the help of the Queen of the Night.

Pamina turns to Sarastro and begs him not to punish her mother. He replies that revenge of any kind is contrary to all the teaching of the Temple of Wisdom. "You will see how I shall revenge myself on your mother," Sarastro explains. "Heaven give your Tamino courage and fortitude in his trial, then you will be happy with him and your mother, her pride laid low, will go back ashamed to her castle. . . ."

Sarastro expresses his whole philosophy and that of the teaching he represents in an aria of almost overpoweringly noble simplicity. It is a slow, dignified strophic song consisting of two verses in which Sarastro tells Pamina that within the sacred halls of the Temple vengeance is unknown—"In diesen heil'gen Hallen kennt man die Rache nicht":

If anything this is a finer, more moving aria even that "Isis und Osiris". It makes its tremendous effect without resort to unusual tone-colour in the orchestra, without the impact, emotional, dramatic and sensuous, of the chorus of Priests to provide interlude and coda, or the atmosphere of an impressive ritualistic setting.

The aria is indeed so elemental in its whole conception that in the entire course of its inevitable diatonic progress there are no more than three accidentals. The first is a B sharp in the vocal line which is a purely decorative variant of the opening phrase; the second is an A sharp in the second violin part which enables the same opening phrase to modulate eventually to the dominant B major; while the third accidental is merely the same A sharp echoed an octave higher as the orchestra repeats the modulating cadence immediately afterwards.

My purpose in drawing attention to such apparently trivial details as the introduction of three accidentals in the key of E major (only one of which is indispensably relevant) is to show Mozart's genius for using what may be called the "primary colours" of music. This aria for Sarastro has been described as a "divine utterance"; it is certainly one of the most profoundly moving ever conceived by man, for it is one of the simplest. This same simplicity and adherence to diatonic "primary colours" is a particular feature of the tune of one of the other great humanist utterances of music: the theme of the Finale of Beethoven's Ninth Symphony. It is as though both Mozart and Beethoven in their search for universal truth found it in the fundamental simplicity of the diatonic scale.

If there is any "colour" to be found in the orchestral accompaniment to Sarastro's aria it is the result of a quite uncanny restraint and economy of means. Here we have none of the huge breadth and depth of the wind instruments and violas of Sarastro's earlier aria, but in its place the normal string complement playing throughout with occasional help from one, sometimes two flutes, two bassoons and two horns. The solo flute's contributions are perhaps what gives the movement its real indescribable magic, for there is surely no other instrument which so unmistakably and with such certainty creates an atmosphere of other-worldly serenity. The instrument's function is simplicity itself; it consists of little more than echoing a couple of Sarastro's phrases in each of the two verses which form the total content of the aria—two verses sung to identical accompaniments and without even a special "first-time-bar" or coda to take Sarastro and Pamino off at the end.

Scene 4: A Hall large enough for a flying machine to move in. The flying machine is decorated with roses and flowers [I like Schikaneder's constant distinction between "roses" and "flowers"] *and has a practicable door. Right in the foreground are two grassy banks.*

We have to wait a moment or two for the appearance of Schikaneder's *pièce de résistance*, the Flying Machine, because first Tamino and Papageno are led in by the Speaker and the Second Priest, who abandon the candidates to face the trial of silence; a special warning is given to Papageno who is told that the gods punish the breaking of silence with thunder and lightning.

Tamino maintains silence, but Papageno is soon tempted to talk when an ugly old woman, appearing through the trap-door in answer to his complaint that the Priests haven't left a drop of water, let alone anything else to drink, brings him a jug of water. She scares him by announcing that he is her lover, and she is on the point of telling him her name when there is a loud roll of thunder and she hobbles away. Papageno swears he will not speak another word.

Schikaneder's famous Flying Machine now comes down out of the flies (how often do we see *that* in our proud mechanical age?), decorated with roses and bearing, in addition to the Three Boys, a table laden with food and drink. One of the boys carries Tamino's flute and another the casket containing Papageno's bells; the instruments, it seems, had been taken away by the Priests at an earlier unspecified stage in the story.

Apart from bringing welcome refreshment the Three Boys bid Tamino and Papageno welcome for the second time to Sarastro's kingdom; the third time, they promise, will be a joyful occasion rewarding Tamino's courage and Papageno's silence. A feature of the Boys' trio, which has none of the solemn Masonic air of their earlier music, is a series of will-o'-the-wispish, almost flippant little figures for the violins with occasional trills reinforced by flutes and bassoons. While the voices sing in this vein—

the violins flutter away—perhaps to suggest the lightness of Schikaneder's airborne Flying Machine—with phrases never played above *piano* such as the entrancing coda:

The Three Boys, having "set out the table in the middle during the trio, fly away." Papageno starts eating and drinking almost at once; Tamino, more seriously inclined, insures against the temptation to talk by playing his flute (as there is no indication exactly what he should play it is usually the practice to repeat the tune in Ex 30).

Pamina enters, overjoyed to find her lover again, but both Tamino and Papageno refuse to speak to her, first one and then the other making signs to her to leave them. "At least tell me the reason for your silence!" pleads Pamina. But no answer comes. She can only believe that Tamino no longer loves her—"Ach, ich fühl's, es ist verschwunden . . ." ("I feel it—the joy of love has vanished for ever . . ."):

This aria, with its inspired orchestral reticence (one flute, one oboe, one bassoon, strings—the same as for "Deh vieni" in *Figaro*, but in Mozart's tragic key of G minor), is an almost unbearable outpouring of grief in which the final expression of Pamina's suicidal despair reaches its climax, not in the voice, but in an orchestral postlude of barely three bars all told. Suddenly, it seems, Mozart feels there are emotions too deep for words, too harrowing for the human voice, and he crystallizes Pamina's grief and hopelessness in a heart-breaking phrase which he suddenly draws out of thin air, for it has not been even hinted at before:

Purist as I am in many respects I am pleased to report that I have never had to sit through the sequence of dialogue which Schikaneder wrote to follow Pamina's heart-rending exit. For sheer hideous, not even unconsciously comic, anti-climax there is little in the history of opera to compete with Papageno's opening line as he sits down and "eats hastily"—"See, Tamino? I can keep quiet when I have to. . . ."

The superfluous character of the whole episode may be gathered from the stage events which occur in the course of eight short speeches by Papageno: (1) the Three Chords are played (now called the "Threefold Trombone Sound"); (2) Tamino leaves, trying vainly to take Papageno with him; (3) Sarastro's six lions come on and frighten Papageno; (4)

Tamino blows on his flute, returns quickly and the lions troop off again; (5) the Three Chords; (6) the Three Chords; (7) Tamino drags Papageno away against his will; (8) Papageno has an exit line about there being no need to hurry, there is plenty of time to be roasted in hell; (9) merciful transformation.

Scene 5: The vaults of the pyramids.

Mozart's infallible sense of the theatre obviously did not let Schikaneder's anxiety to get an easy laugh and some applause for the performing lions divert him from the over-all design of the opera's music. Though the dialogue scene following Pamina's exit may have been a monumental anti-climax the composer's unerring instinct led him to open the next scene with the only possible musical sequel: a chorus of Priests whose undisturbed and peaceful world of wisdom and ritual provided the strongest possible contrast to the intensely human, emotional experience of the preceding scene.

The three trombones are heard in the orchestra again, restoring a mood of tranquillity and impressiveness as the Priests sing a hymn extolling to the gods the virtues of Tamino, the new candidate who will shortly be proved worthy of initiation:

The procession of Priests which this chorus accompanies includes Sarastro and the Speaker. Among the others two priests carry an illuminated pyramid on their shoulders; the rest all carry transparent pyramids, the larger of which contain a lantern. At the end of the Chorus the scene continues in dialogue.

Tamino is led before the assembly of Priests for the first time. Sarastro then calls for Pamina, who is brought in, her head covered by the same kind of sack earlier worn by Tamino and Papageno. Sarastro removes the covering from her head and bids the lovers take farewell of each other. As Pamina approaches her lover Tamino cries "Stand back!" In the trio which follows on this cue Pamina's first natural reaction is to cry "Shall I see you no more, my dearest?", but Sarastro reassures her that she and Tamino will see each other again and be happy:

In this trio, which has an accompaniment featuring busy arpeggios by bassoon, violas and violoncellos, the two men tend to pair off and leave Pamina on her own. The psychological effect of this is remarkable, for we get the impression, which we are meant to get, of Pamina's complete isolation where affairs of initiation and other purely masculine prerogatives are concerned. Her doubts and questions and natural apprehension are answered and countered by the men in duet, so that even when Pamina understandably reproaches Tamino with "If you loved me as I love you, you would not be so calm about things . . ." in a characteristic and melancholy G minor phrase (she has still not recovered all her confidence and composure after her last aria)—

—both Sarastro and Tamino answer simultaneously in the resolute, calm, almost cheerful tones which Pamina finds so disconcerting.

When they come to discuss the actual emotion of parting Pamina is joined by Tamino in a passage of conventional harmonic agreement, but when Sarastro interrupts with "Tamino must leave again", Tamino echoes his superior's phrase in identical terms, while Pamina's comment, to virtually the same words, is appreciably different. Pamina retains her individuality throughout this trio in a remarkable way; it is as though in the course of the shattering emotional experience of her great G minor aria in the previous scene she had suddenly grown up from an adolescent into a mature woman whose earlier childlike faith has given way to an understandable scepticism. There is more than just a suggestion of a woman's instinctive fear and concern for her lover's safe return in the apprehensive way Pamina answers the determined, almost brusquely hearty tones of Sarastro and Tamino and their "now he/I must go":

As the time for parting approaches, however, the two lovers come closer together in their singing and their farewell has a dignity which we come to recognize as typical of a love which is basically "different" from what we know of operatic love generally. Its path is not altogether smooth, but it is clear from the beginning that it is not going to be a tragic love; there is no jealousy, scarcely a suggestion of passion even, and in the passages of farewell that end the trio Mozart introduces a note of optimism and reassurance which seem to dispel even Pamina's misgivings. Certainly one can imagine no more solid basis for confidence, as the lovers say farewell for the last time, than Sarastro's final deep-toned "We shall meet again" ("Wir sehen uns wieder!").

Pamina, Tamino and Sarastro leave and Papageno, who is in trouble again, enters looking for Tamino. He tries the door Tamino has just gone through but is greeted by a voice crying "Stand back!", a thunderclap, flames bursting out from the door and a loud chord. The loud chord was not supplied by Mozart either on this occasion or the next when Papageno goes through the same routine with the door he just came in and voice, thunder and fire greet him as before. Papageno, finding that he can go neither forward nor back, sits down and weeps.

The Speaker enters to tell Papageno that by rights he deserves to be condemned to wander in eternal darkness, but the gods have relented, though of course there can be no question of his becoming one of the Initiated.

Papageno is not greatly disconcerted by the news, remarking that there must be lots of people like him around, and what he really wants is a glass of wine.

"Otherwise you have no wish in the world?" asks the Speaker. Papageno replies: "Not so far." The Speaker, observing that nothing could be simpler than the granting of such a wish, leaves the scene and a large jug of red wine immediately pops out of the ground. Papageno drinks, feels much better, and reflects that perhaps he does want something else after all. He takes out his bells and plays them as he sings "Ein Mädchen oder Weibchen" ("A girl or a wife is what Papageno wishes for . . ."):

This is the beginning of the tune of what we might call the refrain of Papageno's song. He sings it three times and after each refrain follows it with a verse in which the time changes to a 6/8 Allegro very typical of Mozart's "peasant" music in *Figaro* and *Don Giovanni*:

The aria is punctuated, accompanied and generally decorated by variations on the glockenspiel—a different obbligato for each of the three refrains and verses increasing in difficulty and charm as the number proceeds.*

This little song was obviously something for which Mozart had a particular affection; we find it providing him with an excuse to have some typically professional fun at one of the performances following the première at the Theatre auf der Wieden. Mozart tells in one of his letters to his wife of an evening he spent, having delegated the direction of the orchestra to somebody else, listening to *The Magic Flute* as a kind of busman's holiday:

"During Papageno's aria with the glockenspiel I went behind the scenes as I felt a sort of urge today to play it myself. Just for fun, at the point where Schikaneder has a pause, I played an arpeggio. He was startled, looked into the wings and saw me. When he came to his next pause I played no arpeggio. This time he stopped and refused to go on. I guessed what he was thinking and played another chord. He then hit the glockenspiel and shouted 'Shut up!' Whereupon everybody laughed. I rather think this joke taught many people in the audience for the first time that Papageno doesn't play the instrument himself."

If ever there was an instance of the sense of fun which pervades so much of Mozart's music, and which is so necessary to its satisfactory performance, it is surely shown in that thoroughly professional and human incident. One can hardly imagine Wagner, for instance, going backstage to improvise on Beckmesser's lute in his *Meistersinger*.

In answer to the wish which Papageno keeps repeating in his song the old and ugly little woman comes on the scene again, "dancing with the help of her stick." The comedy routine between the two characters is very much the same as at their first meeting, with the difference that this time the little old woman, having extracted Papageno's oath to be true to her (though only by threatening him with an eternal diet of bread and water), does not immediately sink through the floor; she changes into Papageno's young and beautiful counterpart, Papagena, who is dressed in identically the same feathered costume.

But before Papageno can do more than stammer "Pa-Pa-Papagena!" the Speaker intervenes and rather gruffly sends Papagena packing, telling her that Papageno is not yet worthy of her. Papageno tries to follow her, but the Speaker commands him to stand back. Papageno, in a moment of unexpected defiance, retorts: "The earth can swallow me up before I stand back!"

On which the earth immediately opens, Papageno is swallowed up and the scene changes.

Scene 6: A small garden.

With this scene the Finale to *The Magic Flute* begins, a long, dramatically eventful sequence of music which, without benefit of any more spoken

* The "glockenspiel" of Mozart's day was a keyboard instrument with hammers which struck steel strips. Owing to the ridiculous limitations of its modern, keyboard-less descendant on which it is impossible to play any of the "glockenspiel" music of *The Magic Flute*, a celeste is usually used to take the place of what Mozart called in his score *istrumento d'acciaio*, or "steel instrument".

dialogue, takes the story from the complicated, unresolved state in which we find it at the beginning of this scene to its final curtain more than a hundred pages of full score later on.

No sooner do the lights go up on this scene in the garden than the Three Boys are directed to "come down" on to the stage. It seems that this time they do not descend from the flies by Schikaneder's precious Flying Machine, for there is no suggestion of the airborne music which accompanied their last spectacular entrance. Instead, they are heralded by the solemn sounds played by wind instruments we associated with them on their first appearance as the voices which—coincidentally—began the Finale to Act I as they now begin the Finale to Act II.

This time, however, they arrive on an empty stage to sing us a moral little song about the sun's rays and the ideal world in which the earth will be as heaven, and mortals the equals of the gods. The solemn (one supposes Masonic) atmosphere is created immediately by the first statement of the tune in an introduction by clarinets, bassoons and horns:

At the end of the trio, which is accompanied sometimes by strings, sometimes by wind instruments only, a sudden change of rhythm and key (not of tempo) introduces an uneasy note. The Three Boys are appalled to see Pamina approaching, on the verge of madness in her belief that Tamino has left her; and the placid E flat of the opening sequence is transformed into a grim and foreboding C minor. The Three Boys stand to one side as Pamina enters, the better to watch over her.

Pamina comes in, "half demented", in her hand a dagger which she addresses in disjointed poignant phrases as her lover—"So you are my bridegroom who will end my sorrow?"—

The Three Boys, who have watched Pamina with increasing anxiety, now come forward to reason with her. Pamina begs them to leave her to die rather than live with a broken heart, and her despair deepens in a long and agitated passage in G minor, a passage filled with astonishing little chromatic twists in the harmony and a restless syncopated accompaniment which reaches its climax as Pamina, raising the dagger to stab herself, is held back by the Three Boys.

The tempo changes to Allegro and the key to a more optimistic, almost cheerful E flat as the Three Boys assure Pamina that Tamino still loves her, and indeed is willing to brave death for her sake; and though they cannot explain why Tamino would not speak to her they convince her that all will be well. When the Three Boys offer to take Pamina to see her lover the four voices unite for the first time in a joyful final passage proclaiming that true loving hearts are protected by the gods:

Scene 7: The stage is transformed into two huge mountains; in one is a waterfall, from which the rushing and roaring of water can be heard; the other spits forth fire; each mountain has a wrought-iron gate through which fire and water are visible. When the fire burns the backcloth must glow a bright red, while where the water flows there is a black mist. The front wings represent rocks, each wing incorporating an iron door.

Tamino, "lightly clad and without sandals", is led in by two men in black armour. "Fire burns in their helmets", the stage directions run, "they read out the transparent writing which is inscribed on a pyramid. This pyramid stands high up in the centre, near the gates."

The Two Men in Armour read the inscription to music which is one of the most remarkable sounding movements in an opera already liberally supplied with such movements. The music is in the form of a *fugato* for strings which follows a solemn trombone-coloured introduction and is based on the phrase

As the *fugato* proceeds in its steady relentless tempo the Men in Armour read the inscription on the pyramid and they do so singing to the tune—the tenor an octave higher than the bass throughout—of the chorale "Ach Gott, von Himmel sieh' darein."

The already sinister effect of the tonal colour created by the tenor and bass voices in octaves is increased still further by the doubling of the voice part by flute, oboe, bassoon, and trombones across three bare octaves. It is an uncanny sound unlike anything else in Mozart's music, for in spite of the comparatively encouraging words of the inscription—"Who walks this road burdened with cares shall be purified by fire, water, air and earth, and overcoming the fear of death shall rise to heaven from

earth and so enlightened be worthy of initiation in the mysteries of Isis"—
there is in its whole mood an undercurrent of darkness and mystery which
might well be unnerving even to such a steadfast and courageous a figure
as Tamino.

Tamino does not weaken, however, and he announces that he is ready
to face his ordeals. As he moves towards the iron gate Pamina's voice is
heard off stage calling: "Tamino, stop! I must see you . . ."

The tempo changes as Tamino excitedly asks the Men in Armour if
that was Pamina's voice he heard. The Men in Armour reply that it was
and tell him so in as cheerful and unchorale-like a manner of tune as
the one in which Tamino asked the question; they also tell him that he is
now absolved from the oath of silence and that Pamina, who will go hand
in hand with him through the Temple, has shown herself by her courage
and lack of fear of darkness and of death itself worthy to be initiated
with him. The doors open; Pamina enters and the lovers embrace.

It is Pamina who sings first in a phrase completed by Tamino, which is
almost unbearably moving in its calm understatement and suggestion of
a heart too full for words:

Those bars, with that characteristic opening interval of a major sixth,
somehow express in an astonishing, unequalled way all the inexpressible
relief and relaxed happiness which only those who have experienced a
long enforced parting and a final happy reunion can fully understand.
In the restraint and dignity of this meeting we see more clearly than ever
the whole nature of the love of Tamino and Pamina, its firm, unhysterical
stability and lack of sensuality.

It is in this scene particularly that we notice markedly how Pamina
has grown up since the start of the story. She is now on an equal footing
with Tamino and indeed takes the opportunity to tell her lover one or two
things he didn't know before—such as, for instance, the origin of the magic
flute which her father fashioned from a thousand-year-old oak. (So much
for the "golden" flute of some over-imaginative 19th-century producer.)
It is entirely due to Pamina, in fact, who first raises the question of the
flute, that Tamino is reminded of its powers at all; otherwise, it seems,
he was prepared to go through the trials of fire and water without any
form of protection.

As the lovers resolve to face their ordeal they are joined by the Men in
Armour to make up a short passage for vocal quartet, in which the First
Man, the tenor, is given every opportunity to celebrate his release from
the sinister austerity of the chorale by a florid vocal part of high G's and
A's entirely appropriate to a *primo uomo* whether *armato* or not.

"The doors close behind them," read the stage directions, and as they set out on their trials, "Tamino and Pamina can be seen walking onwards; the roar of fire and the howling of wind are heard; at times also the dull rumble of thunder and the rushing of water. Tamino plays his flute; he is accompanied from time to time by muffled drums."

The slow march which takes Tamino and Pamina through the fire is a moment of incredible tenseness, having about it an air of strain and isolation which is somehow thrown more sharply into relief by the supreme ethereal simplicity of the solo flute as it goes its solitary, confident way accompanied by the remote syncopated beats of the muffled drums and the soft chords of horns, trumpets and trombones:

Perhaps Professor Dent came nearest to describing the effect of this scene when he wrote that it "forces upon the listener a tense feeling of self-concentration, and gives us exactly the sensation of going through some difficult and dangerous experience."

The relief which Tamino and Pamina feel as they come successfully through their first ordeal and the confidence they feel as they face the next is expressed in a characteristically calm passage for the two voices in tenths and sixths:

Tamino takes up his flute again as the lovers, facing the ordeal by water, "are seen to descend and after a little while to emerge again; a door opens directly and the entrance to a brightly lit temple is visible. A solemn silence. This sight should convey the most consummate splendour."

The music Tamino plays on his flute during the second ordeal is identical with that which takes him and Pamina safely through the first. In a brief phrase of two bars the lovers give thanks to the gods, and a mixed-voice chorus acclaims their triumph with trumpets and drums to the fore, bidding Tamino and Pamina enter the Temple as worthy Initiates.

Scene 8: The garden as in Scene 6.

Papageno comes in searching for Papagena and playing his pan-pipes, full of contrition that his inability to stop chattering has clearly lost him an enchanting wife, although he admits it serves him right.

On the face of things it must be said that Papageno does not appear to be unduly melancholy and there is considerable optimism, at least, in the phrase which occurs frequently both in the orchestra and the voice part:

After a time, however, melancholy sets in with a sequence in G minor and Papageno decides to hang himself. A last desperate return to the major has no effect and he ties a rope to a tree, announcing that he will blow his pan-pipes three times and if there is no answer after the third then he will say his farewell to the cruel black world. This scene is traditionally filled with a great deal of comic "business" and considerable play is always made of Papageno's unwillingness to blow his pan-pipes for the third and final time.

Papageno—usually with an endless *ritardando*—at last plays the fifth and final note for the fatal third time and there is no sign of any Papagena. Sadly, in an exaggeratedly tragic G minor again, he bids goodnight to the false world. Just as he is about to hang himself the Three Boys appear from above and save him and, after scolding him for not making the most of his one time on earth, remind him that he has only to play his bells to produce his Papagena immediately.

Papageno takes out the bells and plays them, punctuating his performance by singing a little tune which is wonderfully characteristic of the disarming innocence and naïvety of so much of this score:

While Papageno continues to be absorbed in his bells the Three Boys go to their Flying Machine (this is the first mention of it in this scene, it may be said), bring out Papagena and leave the almost speechless couple together.

The duet which follows is something virtually impossible to describe or analyse, or suggest how it builds up after the instrumental passage for strings (the background, Schikaneder indicates, for "comic play") which enables the two ecstatically delighted bird-like lovers to get their breath and make sure that they are really real:

Here, as a last wistful reminder, we have concentrated all the charm of the Mozart who was the unsurpassed composer of *opera buffa*, giving an enchantment and brilliance to a love duet which is no less a love duet for developing into a remarkably virtuoso tongue-twisting patter-song of a kind only Rossini ever approached and he never equalled. The unrestrained gaiety and sheer happiness of this duet, with its little discussion of family planning, is something which I have always found intensely moving; the very everyday ordinariness of Papageno, with his lack of heroic virtues and noble qualities, and his liberal share of human failings and cravings, is the most attractive feature of a nature which is not only warmly sympathetic, but in whose destiny and happiness one takes a strangely personal interest. So it is that I never fail to hear this entrancing duet without feeling a great personal satisfaction that everything has turned out so well for Papageno and his Papagena at last. Heaven knows their troubles haven't been spectacular, but they have been frustrating and tiresome enough one way and another.

Papageno and Papagena end their duet and a bubbling little instrumental coda helps them on their way to live happily ever after. We do not see them again.

Scene 9: Before the Temple.

The cheerful, carefree G major of the duet is now supplanted by a hushed, sinister figure in octaves in the strings, which Mozart keeps going through the episode which follows:

Through both trap-doors there appear Monostatos, the Queen of the Night and the Three Ladies carrying black torches. Their intention, they tell us in a *sotto voce* conspiratorial way, is to break into the Temple and destroy its occupants. Monostatos, making sure before he goes any further that the reward for his treacherous defection is still "on", confirms with the Queen that he is to have Pamina as his wife. The Queen reassures him and is seconded in this by her Three Ladies.

From the distance there comes the sound of muffled thunder and rushing water, a sound which disconcerts the Queen and her Three Ladies as well as the Moor. In a final resolute phrase in C minor the Queen's followers declare their allegiance. But the "loudest chord" interrupts them and there is "thunder, lightning and storm." The Queen and her retinue, taking with them two long descending phrases in which they bewail the utter destruction of their power, sink into "eternal night".

Scene 10: The stage is now transformed for the final scene into a vast sun.

"Sarastro stands aloft, Tamino and Pamina are both dressed in priestly robes. Near them on both sides stand the Egyptian Priests. The Three Boys carry flowers."

In a short phrase describing how the sun has driven away the night and destroyed the dark powers of hypocrisy and evil Sarastro guides the music to its final E flat movement. The chorus of followers hail the Initiates and give thanks to Isis and Osiris, and they do so to noble phrases:

A moment later we come to what may be considered the coda to the whole opera. The tempo changes to Allegro, the time to 2/4; the unpredictable Mozart bids us take leave of his masterpiece with light hearts and in the space of a bar we are back in the simple unsophisticated world of the Singspiel as the final chorus is introduced by the orchestral phrase which eventually brings down the curtain in the composer's most characteristically unfussy, unpompous way:

While I hope that by this study of *The Magic Flute* I shall have done a little to disturb the sceptic and encourage the novice not yet fully initiated in the mysteries and delights of this opera, there is no doubt that of all Mozart's operas it is the one to which every listener reacts differently and individually.

To some the magic element of this opera written for a lower-class 18th-century Viennese audience is comparable to that now vulgar and degraded entertainment, the English Christmas pantomime; to me the magic has always been so wholly convincing that it has never entered my head to consider whether what I see and hear is "real" or not. *The Magic Flute* to me has a reality surpassing that of the first fairy tale one is told as a child, and like a fairy tale it must be taken completely seriously; *The Magic Flute*, like any religion, can offer nothing to the sceptic. It must be believed in wholeheartedly, or it has no existence at all.

So it is that the charges of inconsistency which may be levelled at the libretto and the elaborate political satire so thinly disguised in a Masonic allegory are in the end irrelevant. It is interesting to note, perhaps, how Schikaneder suddenly goes off on a different tack half way through the story of the opera and changes the Queen of the Night from the wronged and heart-broken mother that she was at the beginning of the story into an evil figure, at the same time promoting Sarastro from wicked sorcerer to High Priest; but none of this makes the *music* any less consistent. The Queen's first aria is nonetheless a fierce and determined statement of her point of view and it convinces—as it is meant to convince—Tamino.

The only glaring "inconsistency" resulting from all this is the purely ironic one of the magic flute itself, which is given to Tamino as an instrument with which to perform evil, but which is ultimately used in the cause of good.

The allegorical significance of the action has, of course, little more than an academic interest to us today. But at the time of its first production it is obvious that *The Magic Flute* said a number of things which contemporary Freemasons considered needed saying, and though the Empress Maria Theresa had been dead for eleven years her suppression of Freemasonry in 1764 still rankled enough in some Viennese minds in 1791 to make the significance of the Queen of the Night instantly apparent, and to see in Tamino the personification of Maria Theresa's son, Joseph II, who openly protected the Order when he came to the throne. Of the other characters Pamina was said to represent the Austrian people, Sarastro was modelled on Ignaz von Born, a prominent Freemason and eminent scientist, and Monostatos represented the clergy in general and the Jesuits in particular.*

In the end, however, none of this really matters very much, nor does knowledge or ignorance of the original allegorical intentions of the libretto affect one way or the other the impact and significance of Mozart's music. Whether the Queen of the Night, for instance, is meant to represent Maria Theresa or Lizzie Borden makes no difference in the end to the fact that on the evidence of Mozart's music she remains primarily neither more nor less than an angry and frustrated woman, and it is as such that she comes compellingly to life. She may have been conceived as a symbol; she survives as an intensely vital and human figure.

As I come to the end of this book and look back on the months I have spent with Mozart's scores beside me, I find myself reviewing an unique and unforgettable experience. In the pages of those scores—in the freshness of *Die Entführung*, the wit and warmth of *Figaro*, in the panoramic variety of musical expression and contrast in *Don Giovanni*, the charm and gaiety of *Così fan tutte*, in the unsurpassed wisdom and serenity of *The Magic Flute*—there is in some miraculous way contained the whole illogical, contradictory, unclassifiable collection of mankind's strength and failings which are the basis of all human behaviour.

"Illogical, contradictory, unclassifiable." Are these not perhaps almost the real, fundamental peculiarities of Mozart's genius? Is there not something magnificently illogical, contradictory and unclassifiable—and consequently so overwhelmingly convincing—in the grief to be found in *Die Entführung*, in the sadness and depth of *Figaro*, in the comedy-with-murder, and the tragic overtones of the "dramma giocoso" of *Don Giovanni*, in the unexpected seriousness which rises through the laughter of *Così fan tutte*, in the tremendous conception of *The Magic Flute* which has all these qualities and so much more besides?

Mozart, we are too often told, was a "classic", and in that carelessly, sometimes criminally, applied label there lies the root of most of the misunderstanding of Mozart's genius. Rightly or wrongly, a "classic"

---

* For the reader interested in what might be called the "behind-the-scenes" aspect of Schikaneder's libretto I would recommend once again the fascinating chapters on *The Magic Flute* in Dent's *Mozart's Operas*.

suggests something, if not dead, at least over-formal and bearing little relation to what is known smugly as "contemporary thought." Shakespeare, whom Mozart so closely resembles in so many ways, is also a "classic", and his reputation among so many of the compulsorily educated young of this country is in consequence utterly deplorable.

The truth is, of course, that Mozart and Shakespeare are "classics" only in so far as their arts are seen by much later generations to have conformed to the formal conventions of their day which we now consider "classic". In practice—that is, in the opera house and the theatre—there were never two more thoroughly professional, adaptable and unpretentious craftsmen whose genius was almost incidental to their constant preoccupation with the fulfilment of commissions and the entertainment of the public. Their characters expressed their thoughts in sonata form and blank verse not because their creators were "classics", but because those were the most readily available forms of operatic and dramatic expression and the public was familiar with them.

The greatness of Mozart, like the greatness of Shakespeare, lies in his power to affect us today as he affected our ancestors hearing his operas for the first time, and as he will affect our descendants when their turn comes; it lies, above all, in his unique insight and sympathy and accurate observation of human nature which made of his characters creatures whom we can recognize as living and loving, laughing and dying like the rest of us.

Like the rest of us? Perhaps not quite; for they share with their creator, Wolfgang Amadeus Mozart, the gift of immortality.

APPENDIX

An "Index of Contexts" by which the reader may refer to the dramatic situation in which the more familiar individual items occur in Mozart's operas.

DIE ENTFÜHRUNG AUS DEM SERAIL

THE MARRIAGE OF FIGARO

DON GIOVANNI

COSÌ FAN TUTTE

THE MAGIC FLUTE

GENERAL INDEX
MOZART'S ORCHESTRATION

GENERAL INDEX

INDEX OF MOZART'S ORCHESTRATION

A CATALOG OF SELECTED
DOVER BOOKS
IN ALL FIELDS OF INTEREST

A CATALOG OF SELECTED DOVER
BOOKS IN ALL FIELDS OF INTEREST

DRAWINGS OF REMBRANDT, edited by Seymour Slive. Updated Lippmann, Hofstede de Groot edition, with definitive scholarly apparatus. All portraits, biblical sketches, landscapes, nudes. Oriental figures, classical studies, together with selection of work by followers. 550 illustrations. Total of 630pp. 9⅛ × 12¼.
21485-0, 21486-9 Pa., Two-vol. set $29.90

GHOST AND HORROR STORIES OF AMBROSE BIERCE, Ambrose Bierce. 24 tales vividly imagined, strangely prophetic, and decades ahead of their time in technical skill: "The Damned Thing," "An Inhabitant of Carcosa," "The Eyes of the Panther," "Moxon's Master," and 20 more. 199pp. 5⅜ × 8½. 20767-6 Pa. $3.95

ETHICAL WRITINGS OF MAIMONIDES, Maimonides. Most significant ethical works of great medieval sage, newly translated for utmost precision, readability. Laws Concerning Character Traits, Eight Chapters, more. 192pp. 5⅜ × 8½.
24522-5 Pa. $4.50

THE EXPLORATION OF THE COLORADO RIVER AND ITS CANYONS, J. W. Powell. Full text of Powell's 1,000-mile expedition down the fabled Colorado in 1869. Superb account of terrain, geology, vegetation, Indians, famine, mutiny, treacherous rapids, mighty canyons, during exploration of last unknown part of continental U.S. 400pp. 5⅜ × 8½. 20094-9 Pa. $7.95

HISTORY OF PHILOSOPHY, Julián Marías. Clearest one-volume history on the market. Every major philosopher and dozens of others, to Existentialism and later. 505pp. 5⅜ × 8½. 21739-6 Pa. $9.95

ALL ABOUT LIGHTNING, Martin A. Uman. Highly readable non-technical survey of nature and causes of lightning, thunderstorms, ball lightning, St. Elmo's Fire, much more. Illustrated. 192pp. 5⅜ × 8½. 25237-X Pa. $5.95

SAILING ALONE AROUND THE WORLD, Captain Joshua Slocum. First man to sail around the world, alone, in small boat. One of great feats of seamanship told in delightful manner. 67 illustrations. 294pp. 5⅜ × 8½. 20326-3 Pa. $4.95

LETTERS AND NOTES ON THE MANNERS, CUSTOMS AND CONDITIONS OF THE NORTH AMERICAN INDIANS, George Catlin. Classic account of life among Plains Indians: ceremonies, hunt, warfare, etc. 312 plates. 572pp. of text. 6⅛ × 9¼. 22118-0, 22119-9, Pa. Two-vol. set $17.90

ALASKA: The Harriman Expedition, 1899, John Burroughs, John Muir, et al. Informative, engrossing accounts of two-month, 9,000-mile expedition. Native peoples, wildlife, forests, geography, salmon industry, glaciers, more. Profusely illustrated. 240 black-and-white line drawings. 124 black-and-white photographs. 3 maps. Index. 576pp. 5⅜ × 8½. 25109-8 Pa. $11.95

CATALOG OF DOVER BOOKS

THE BOOK OF BEASTS: Being a Translation from a Latin Bestiary of the Twelfth Century, T. H. White. Wonderful catalog real and fanciful beasts: manticore, griffin, phoenix, amphivius, jaculus, many more. White's witty erudite commentary on scientific, historical aspects. Fascinating glimpse of medieval mind. Illustrated. 296pp. 5⅜ × 8¼. (Available in U.S. only)   24609-4 Pa. $6.95

FRANK LLOYD WRIGHT: ARCHITECTURE AND NATURE With 160 Illustrations, Donald Hoffmann. Profusely illustrated study of influence of nature—especially prairie—on Wright's designs for Fallingwater, Robie House, Guggenheim Museum, other masterpieces. 96pp. 9¼ × 10¾.   25098-9 Pa. $7.95

FRANK LLOYD WRIGHT'S FALLINGWATER, Donald Hoffmann. Wright's famous waterfall house: planning and construction of organic idea. History of site, owners, Wright's personal involvement. Photographs of various stages of building. Preface by Edgar Kaufmann, Jr. 100 illustrations. 112pp. 9¼ × 10.
23671-4 Pa. $8.95

YEARS WITH FRANK LLOYD WRIGHT: Apprentice to Genius, Edgar Tafel. Insightful memoir by a former apprentice presents a revealing portrait of Wright the man, the inspired teacher, the greatest American architect. 372 black-and-white illustrations. Preface. Index. vi + 228pp. 8¼ × 11.   24801-1 Pa. $10.95

THE STORY OF KING ARTHUR AND HIS KNIGHTS, Howard Pyle. Enchanting version of King Arthur fable has delighted generations with imaginative narratives of exciting adventures and unforgettable illustrations by the author. 41 illustrations. xviii + 313pp. 6⅛ × 9¼.   21445-1 Pa. $6.95

THE GODS OF THE EGYPTIANS, E. A. Wallis Budge. Thorough coverage of numerous gods of ancient Egypt by foremost Egyptologist. Information on evolution of cults, rites and gods; the cult of Osiris; the Book of the Dead and its rites; the sacred animals and birds; Heaven and Hell; and more. 956pp. 6⅛ × 9¼.
22055-9, 22056-7 Pa., Two-vol. set $21.90

A THEOLOGICO-POLITICAL TREATISE, Benedict Spinoza. Also contains unfinished *Political Treatise*. Great classic on religious liberty, theory of government on common consent. R. Elwes translation. Total of 421pp. 5⅜ × 8½.
20249-6 Pa. $6.95

INCIDENTS OF TRAVEL IN CENTRAL AMERICA, CHIAPAS, AND YUCATAN, John L. Stephens. Almost single-handed discovery of Maya culture; exploration of ruined cities, monuments, temples; customs of Indians. 115 drawings. 892pp. 5⅜ × 8½.   22404-X, 22405-8 Pa., Two-vol. set $15.90

LOS CAPRICHOS, Francisco Goya. 80 plates of wild, grotesque monsters and caricatures. Prado manuscript included. 183pp. 6⅛ × 9⅜.   22384-1 Pa. $5.95

AUTOBIOGRAPHY: The Story of My Experiments with Truth, Mohandas K. Gandhi. Not hagiography, but Gandhi in his own words. Boyhood, legal studies, purification, the growth of the Satyagraha (nonviolent protest) movement. Critical, inspiring work of the man who freed India. 480pp. 5⅜ × 8½. (Available in U.S. only)
24593-4 Pa. $6.95

ILLUSTRATED DICTIONARY OF HISTORIC ARCHITECTURE, edited by Cyril M. Harris. Extraordinary compendium of clear, concise definitions for over 5,000 important architectural terms complemented by over 2,000 line drawings. Covers full spectrum of architecture from ancient ruins to 20th-century Modernism. Preface. 592pp. 7½ × 9⅝. 24444-X Pa. $15.95

THE NIGHT BEFORE CHRISTMAS, Clement Moore. Full text, and woodcuts from original 1848 book. Also critical, historical material. 19 illustrations. 40pp. 4⅝ × 6. 22797-9 Pa. $2.50

THE LESSON OF JAPANESE ARCHITECTURE: 165 Photographs, Jiro Harada. Memorable gallery of 165 photographs taken in the 1930's of exquisite Japanese homes of the well-to-do and historic buildings. 13 line diagrams. 192pp. 8⅜ × 11¼. 24778-3 Pa. $10.95

THE AUTOBIOGRAPHY OF CHARLES DARWIN AND SELECTED LETTERS, edited by Francis Darwin. The fascinating life of eccentric genius composed of an intimate memoir by Darwin (intended for his children); commentary by his son, Francis; hundreds of fragments from notebooks, journals, papers; and letters to and from Lyell, Hooker, Huxley, Wallace and Henslow. xi + 365pp. 5⅜ × 8. 20479-0 Pa. $6.95

WONDERS OF THE SKY: Observing Rainbows, Comets, Eclipses, the Stars and Other Phenomena, Fred Schaaf. Charming, easy-to-read poetic guide to all manner of celestial events visible to the naked eye. Mock suns, glories, Belt of Venus, more. Illustrated. 299pp. 5¼ × 8¼. 24402-4 Pa. $7.95

BURNHAM'S CELESTIAL HANDBOOK, Robert Burnham, Jr. Thorough guide to the stars beyond our solar system. Exhaustive treatment. Alphabetical by constellation: Andromeda to Cetus in Vol. 1; Chamaeleon to Orion in Vol. 2; and Pavo to Vulpecula in Vol. 3. Hundreds of illustrations. Index in Vol. 3. 2,000pp. 6⅛ × 9¼. 23567-X, 23568-8, 23673-0 Pa., Three-vol. set $41.85

STAR NAMES: Their Lore and Meaning, Richard Hinckley Allen. Fascinating history of names various cultures have given to constellations and literary and folkloristic uses that have been made of stars. Indexes to subjects. Arabic and Greek names. Biblical references. Bibliography. 563pp. 5⅜ × 8½. 21079-0 Pa. $8.95

THIRTY YEARS THAT SHOOK PHYSICS: The Story of Quantum Theory, George Gamow. Lucid, accessible introduction to influential theory of energy and matter. Careful explanations of Dirac's anti-particles, Bohr's model of the atom, much more. 12 plates. Numerous drawings. 240pp. 5⅜ × 8½. 24895-X Pa. $5.95

CHINESE DOMESTIC FURNITURE IN PHOTOGRAPHS AND MEASURED DRAWINGS, Gustav Ecke. A rare volume, now affordably priced for antique collectors, furniture buffs and art historians. Detailed review of styles ranging from early Shang to late Ming. Unabridged republication. 161 black-and-white drawings, photos. Total of 224pp. 8⅜ × 11¼. (Available in U.S. only) 25171-3 Pa. $13.95

VINCENT VAN GOGH: A Biography, Julius Meier-Graefe. Dynamic, penetrating study of artist's life, relationship with brother, Theo, painting techniques, travels, more. Readable, engrossing. 160pp. 5⅜ × 8½. (Available in U.S. only) 25253-1 Pa. $4.95

SUNDIALS, Albert Waugh. Far and away the best, most thorough coverage of ideas, mathematics concerned, types, construction, adjusting anywhere. Over 100 illustrations. 230pp. 5⅜ × 8½. 22947-5 Pa. $4.95

PICTURE HISTORY OF THE NORMANDIE: With 190 Illustrations, Frank O. Braynard. Full story of legendary French ocean liner: Art Deco interiors, design innovations, furnishings, celebrities, maiden voyage, tragic fire, much more. Extensive text. 144pp. 8⅜ × 11¾. 25257-4 Pa. $10.95

THE FIRST AMERICAN COOKBOOK: A Facsimile of "American Cookery," 1796, Amelia Simmons. Facsimile of the first American-written cookbook published in the United States contains authentic recipes for colonial favorites—pumpkin pudding, winter squash pudding, spruce beer, Indian slapjacks, and more. Introductory Essay and Glossary of colonial cooking terms. 80pp. 5⅜ × 8½. 24710-4 Pa. $3.50

101 PUZZLES IN THOUGHT AND LOGIC, C. R. Wylie, Jr. Solve murders and robberies, find out which fishermen are liars, how a blind man could possibly identify a color—purely by your own reasoning! 107pp. 5⅜ × 8½. 20367-0 Pa. $2.50

THE BOOK OF WORLD-FAMOUS MUSIC—CLASSICAL, POPULAR AND FOLK, James J. Fuld. Revised and enlarged republication of landmark work in musico-bibliography. Full information about nearly 1,000 songs and compositions including first lines of music and lyrics. New supplement. Index. 800pp. 5⅜ × 8¼. 24857-7 Pa. $15.95

ANTHROPOLOGY AND MODERN LIFE, Franz Boas. Great anthropologist's classic treatise on race and culture. Introduction by Ruth Bunzel. Only inexpensive paperback edition. 255pp. 5⅜ × 8½. 25245-0 Pa. $6.95

THE TALE OF PETER RABBIT, Beatrix Potter. The inimitable Peter's terrifying adventure in Mr. McGregor's garden, with all 27 wonderful, full-color Potter illustrations. 55pp. 4¼ × 5½. (Available in U.S. only) 22827-4 Pa. $1.75

THREE PROPHETIC SCIENCE FICTION NOVELS, H. G. Wells. *When the Sleeper Wakes, A Story of the Days to Come* and *The Time Machine* (full version). 335pp. 5⅜ × 8½. (Available in U.S. only) 20605-X Pa. $6.95

APICIUS COOKERY AND DINING IN IMPERIAL ROME, edited and translated by Joseph Dommers Vehling. Oldest known cookbook in existence offers readers a clear picture of what foods Romans ate, how they prepared them, etc. 49 illustrations. 301pp. 6⅛ × 9¼. 23563-7 Pa. $7.95

SHAKESPEARE LEXICON AND QUOTATION DICTIONARY, Alexander Schmidt. Full definitions, locations, shades of meaning of every word in plays and poems. More than 50,000 exact quotations. 1,485pp. 6½ × 9¼. 22726-X, 22727-8 Pa., Two-vol. set $29.9

THE WORLD'S GREAT SPEECHES, edited by Lewis Copeland and Lawrence W. Lamm. Vast collection of 278 speeches from Greeks to 1970. Powerful and effective models; unique look at history. 842pp. 5⅜ × 8½. 20468-5 Pa. $11.95

HOW TO WRITE, Gertrude Stein. Gertrude Stein claimed anyone could understand her unconventional writing—here are clues to help. Fascinating improvisations, language experiments, explanations illuminate Stein's craft and the art of writing. Total of 414pp. 4⅜ × 6⅜. 23144-5 Pa. $6.95

ADVENTURES AT SEA IN THE GREAT AGE OF SAIL: Five Firsthand Narratives, edited by Elliot Snow. Rare true accounts of exploration, whaling, shipwreck, fierce natives, trade, shipboard life, more. 33 illustrations. Introduction. 353pp. 5⅜ × 8½. 25177-2 Pa. $8.95

THE HERBAL OR GENERAL HISTORY OF PLANTS, John Gerard. Classic descriptions of about 2,850 plants—with over 2,700 illustrations—includes Latin and English names, physical descriptions, varieties, time and place of growth, more. 2,706 illustrations. xlv + 1,678pp. 8½ × 12¼. 23147-X Cloth. $75.00

DOROTHY AND THE WIZARD IN OZ, L. Frank Baum. Dorothy and the Wizard visit the center of the Earth, where people are vegetables, glass houses grow and Oz characters reappear. Classic sequel to *Wizard of Oz.* 256pp. 5⅜ × 8. 24714-7 Pa. $5.95

SONGS OF EXPERIENCE: Facsimile Reproduction with 26 Plates in Full Color, William Blake. This facsimile of Blake's original "Illuminated Book" reproduces 26 full-color plates from a rare 1826 edition. Includes "The Tyger," "London," "Holy Thursday," and other immortal poems. 26 color plates. Printed text of poems. 48pp. 5¼ × 7. 24636-1 Pa. $3.50

SONGS OF INNOCENCE, William Blake. The first and most popular of Blake's famous "Illuminated Books," in a facsimile edition reproducing all 31 brightly colored plates. Additional printed text of each poem. 64pp. 5¼ × 7. 22764-2 Pa. $3.50

PRECIOUS STONES, Max Bauer. Classic, thorough study of diamonds, rubies, emeralds, garnets, etc.: physical character, occurrence, properties, use, similar topics. 20 plates, 8 in color. 94 figures. 659pp. 6⅛ × 9¼. 21910-0, 21911-9 Pa., Two-vol. set $15.90

ENCYCLOPEDIA OF VICTORIAN NEEDLEWORK, S. F. A. Caulfeild and Blanche Saward. Full, precise descriptions of stitches, techniques for dozens of needlecrafts—most exhaustive reference of its kind. Over 800 figures. Total of 679pp. 8½ × 11. Two volumes. Vol. 1 22800-2 Pa. $11.95
Vol. 2 22801-0 Pa. $11.95

THE MARVELOUS LAND OF OZ, L. Frank Baum. Second Oz book, the Scarecrow and Tin Woodman are back with hero named Tip, Oz magic. 136 illustrations. 287pp. 5⅜ × 8½. 20692-0 Pa. $5.95

WILD FOWL DECOYS, Joel Barber. Basic book on the subject, by foremost authority and collector. Reveals history of decoy making and rigging, place in American culture, different kinds of decoys, how to make them, and how to use them. 140 plates. 156pp. 7⅞ × 10¾. 20011-6 Pa. $8.95

HISTORY OF LACE, Mrs. Bury Palliser. Definitive, profusely illustrated chronicle of lace from earliest times to late 19th century. Laces of Italy, Greece, England, France, Belgium, etc. Landmark of needlework scholarship. 266 illustrations. 672pp. 6⅛ × 9¼. 24742-2 Pa. $14.95